W9-CSY-103

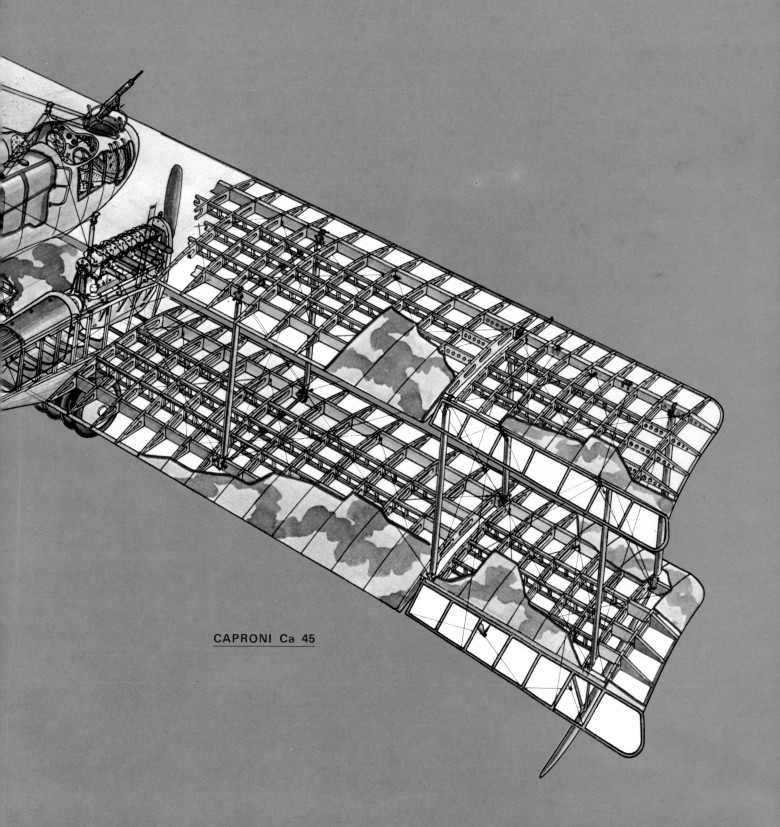

CAPRONI Ca 45

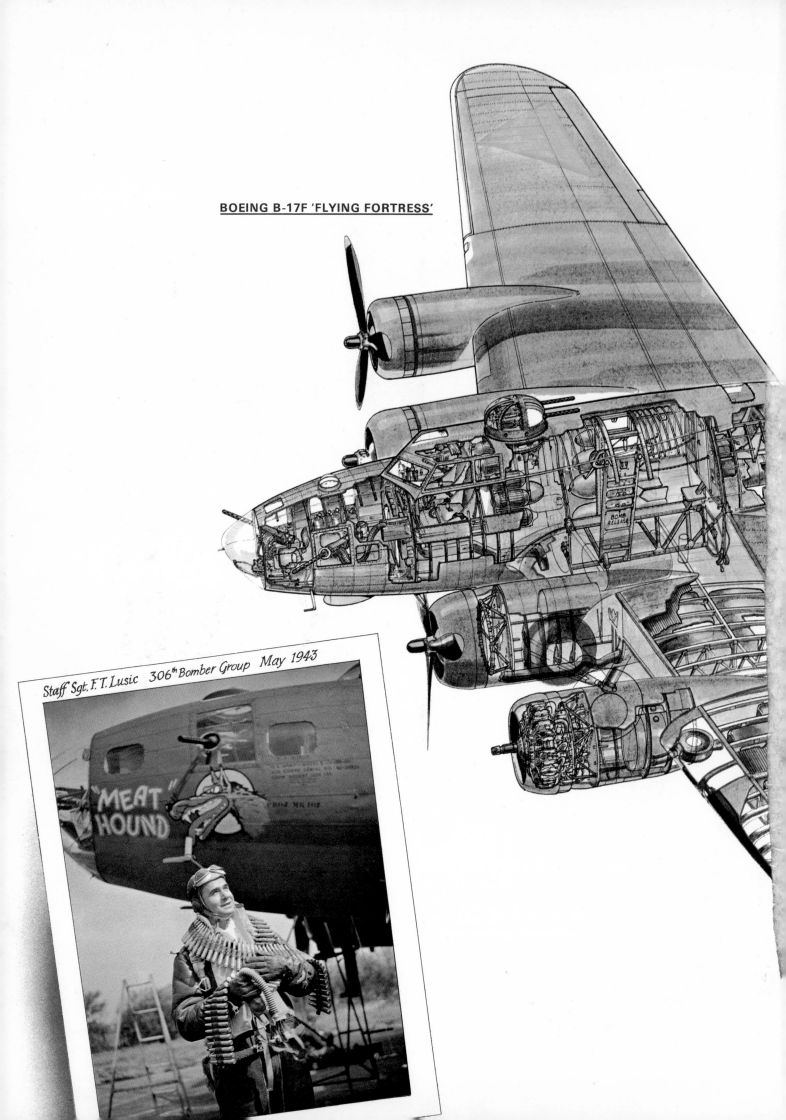

BOEING B-17F 'FLYING FORTRESS'

Staff Sgt. F.T. Lusic 306ᵗʰ Bomber Group May 1943

"MEAT HOUND"

The Story of
THE BOMBER
1914-1945

Bryan Cooper
Illustrated by
John Batchelor

octopus

CONTENTS

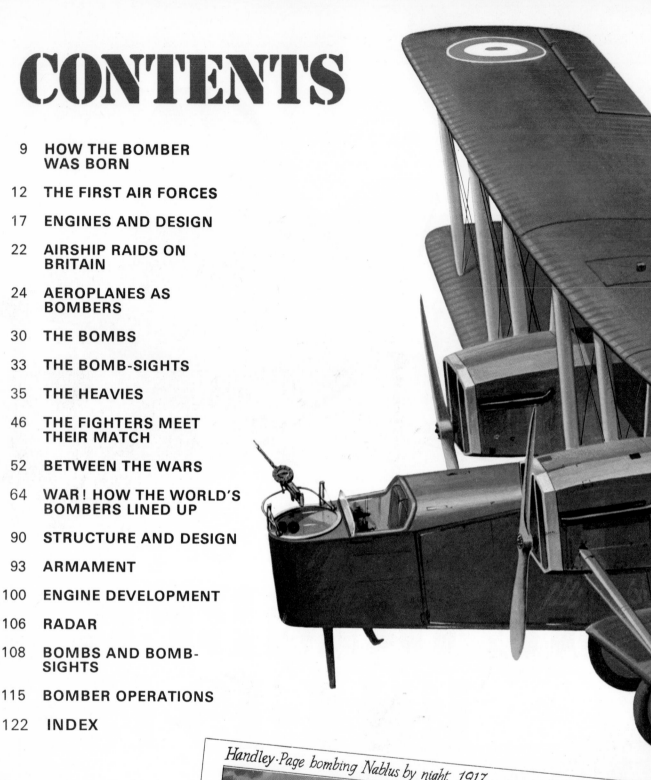

First published 1974 by
Octopus Books Limited
59 Grosvenor Street, London W1

ISBN 0 7064 0410 6

© 1974 Phoebus Publishing Company

Produced by
Mandarin Publishers Limited
14 Westlands Road, Quarry Bay,
Hong Kong
Printed in Hong Kong

Photographs on jacket and title page courtesy of Popperfoto; painting (right) by Stuart Reid courtesy of Imperial War Museum (Robert Hunt Library)

Handley-Page bombing Nablus by night 1917

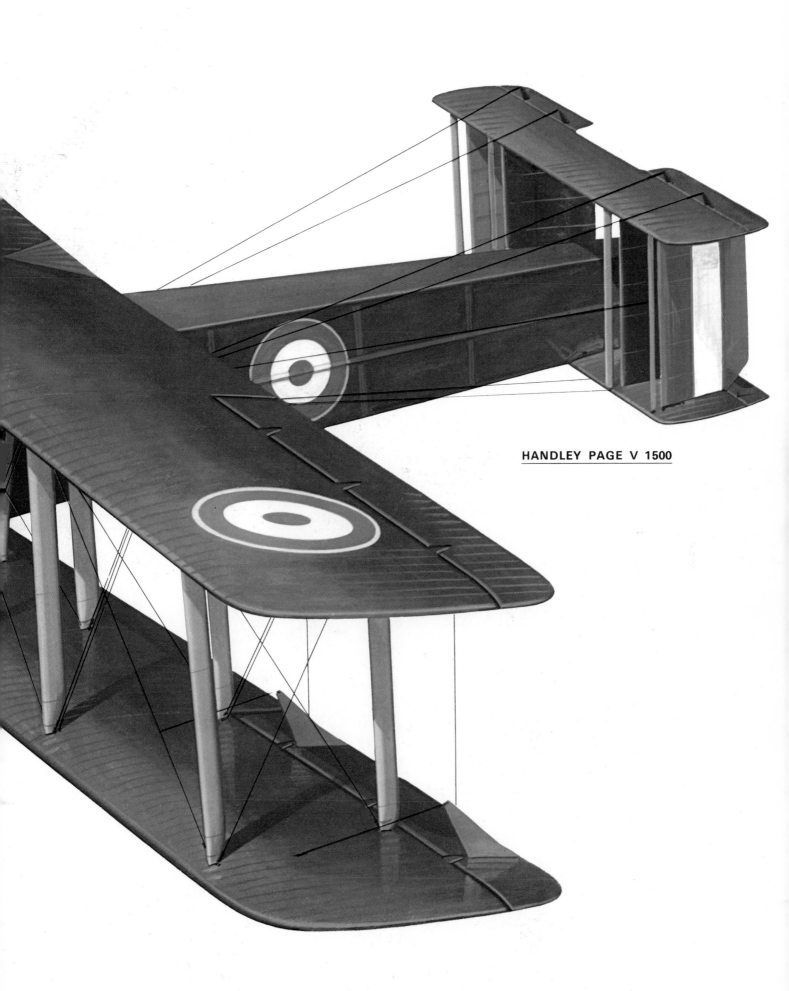

HANDLEY PAGE V 1500

Imperial War Museum

CAPRONI Ca 42

Gross weight: 16,535 lb **Span:** 98 ft
1 in **Length:** 49 ft 6 in **Engine:** 3×270 hp
Fiat, Isotta-Fraschini, or American Liberty
Armament: 4 machine-guns **Crew:** 5
Speed: 87 mph at ground level **Ceiling:**
9,840 ft **Range:** 7 hr **Bomb load:**
3,910 lb

HOW THE BOMBER WAS BORN

'Aviation is good sport, but for the army it is useless.' This comment, attributed to General Foch, one of the more enlightened of military leaders, typified the prevailing attitude to an innovation which was to play an increasingly important role in warfare . . .

Like so many concepts of modern warfare, aerial bombing on a large scale was first developed during the First World War. The two main ingredients – bombs and a means of delivering them – were already in existence. The bombs were simple metal shells containing explosives and a detonator, which could be set off by a time fuse, and with fins to give more stable and accurately predictable flight. Such weapons had been conceived of since the earliest days of flight, but use of aeroplanes for bombing came about only when it was found how vulnerable airships were to defensive fire from the ground, and to attacks in the air.

Although several types of aeroplane were available in 1914, and experimental bombing from aeroplanes had been carried out before the war, their military potential was not generally appreciated by the strategists of the combatant nations. Consider-

Above left: German ground crew member loading a 25-kg bomb

ing the flimsy nature of these craft, mostly two seaters, it was understandable. Most were unable to fly higher than a few thousand feet and their average speed of about 60 miles per hour could be reduced to a crawl by strong headwinds. They were not only vulnerable to ground fire but their performance was also seriously affected by carrying the added weight of bombs or machine-guns.

For the most part, the military leaders of all the major powers saw the main function of aircraft as reconnoitring for the infantry and spotting the fall of shot for the artillery – merely an extension of the observation balloon. It was the pilots and observers who showed the fighting potential of their machines by taking pot-shots at enemy planes with hand-guns. This eventually led to the development of specifically designed single-seat fighters armed with fixed forward-firing machine-guns.

In a similar way, the use of early reconnaissance aircraft for dropping bombs led to the evolution of the true bomber – that is, an aeroplane designed to carry and deliver bombs in level flight, against a specific target, over medium or long range distances.

The true beginning

At the start, just as reconnaissance aircraft were armed only with pistols, many of the first bombs dropped were simply grenades or canisters filled with gasoline, dropped over the sides of open cockpits. The French even threw down steel darts (*fléchettes*) in the hope of disrupting German infantry and cavalry formations.

The first aircraft used for both fighting and bombing were the general purpose types which were already in existence when war broke out. In fact, a Voisin III, the type most widely used for bombing by the French in the early days of the war, was also the first to shoot down an enemy aircraft in aerial combat. And it was with an Avro 504, the first British bomber, and the type to make the first organised raid in history, that some of the earliest experiments were made in fitting a machine-gun, leading to the development of the true fighter.

Two basic configurations were predominant at that time: the tractor aeroplane, with the engine and propeller in front, and the pusher type, like the Voisin, in which the engine and propeller were mounted behind a tub-like nacelle seating the pilot

The main production model of Caproni's Ca 4 series of huge triplanes was brought into service in 1918. It was used by the British RNAS and air units of the Italian army and navy

and observer, the tail being carried on booms. Both were made in biplane and monoplane form, biplanes being the more common. The pusher type soon became obsolete, but it was the most successful in the early days since the observer in front had a much better field of vision. (In two-seater tractor aircraft the second crew member invariably sat in front but since his view and ability to fire were restricted by the propeller and wing struts, the positions were later reversed.)

Using the experience with these general purpose types, different classes of aircraft were developed to meet specific requirements. An account of bombers might well be limited to the type defined as 'an aircraft designed to drop bombs in level flight'. These have been built in great variety up to the present day and indeed are the ones mainly dealt with here. But there have been others such as dive-bombers, torpedo-bombers and fighter-bombers combining a dual role. These, with aircraft designed primarily for a ground attack role in support of infantry, might be grouped separately as strike aircraft. However, the most important examples are included in this book. In fact, as we have implied, almost every basic tactical and strategic use of bombers was first tried out during the First World War.

Combined role

The fighter-bomber is a particular case in point. Like the Voisin, the earliest bombers combined both roles, but thereafter, the development of bombers took a separate course from that of the fighters designed to intercept them. Except for a period in the 1930s when a few notable bombers actually flew faster than the fighters of the day, they generally had to make up for their lack of speed by carrying heavier armament. This, together with the need to carry the largest possible bomb load, necessitated a continual compromise in design between weight, size and range on the one hand, and speed and altitude on the other. Although some remarkable engineering advances were made by bomber designers, such as the geodetic form of construction, for the most part they had to make use of the materials currently available. And most of the pioneering effort, in terms of speed at any rate, went into fighter design. For example, a number of exceptional engines were specifically designed for fighters whereas bombers usually had to make use of the same type of engines.

In more recent times however, with the development of small but powerful atomic missiles – as well as the atom bomb itself – there has not been the same need to consider weight of bomb load as the measure of a bomber's capability. The development of sophisticated defence systems, including supersonic fighters, has meant that bombers must be able to compete on an equal footing in both armament and speed. Largely because of the enormous costs involved the future of the true bomber was at one time in some doubt. This has been partly resolved by the American decision to go ahead with the B-1 strategic bomber, capable of three times the speed of sound. However, for reasons of cost and modern strategic planning, the fighter-bomber is one of the most common types now in service with the air forces of the world. The wheel has turned full circle back to the kind of aeroplane first used offensively sixty years ago.

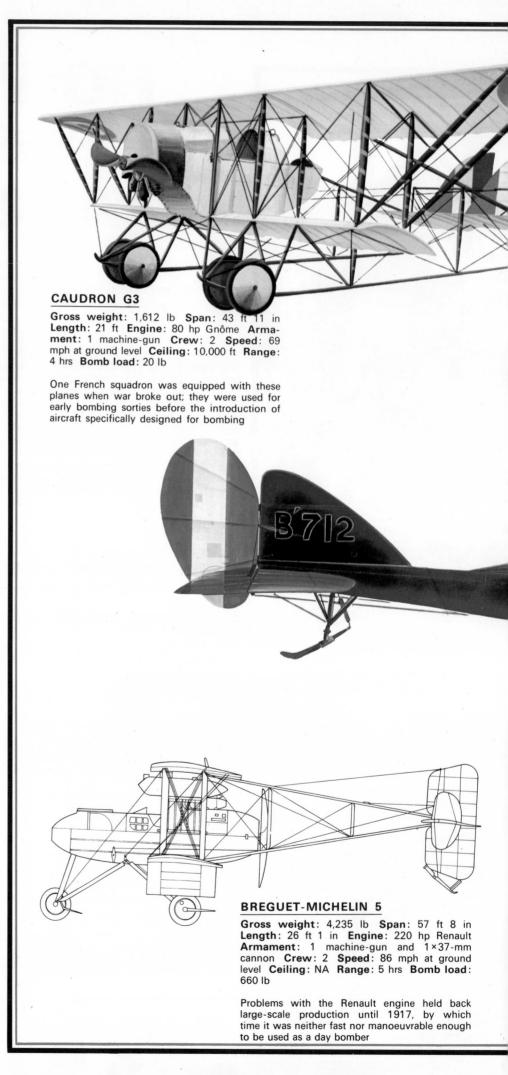

CAUDRON G3
Gross weight: 1,612 lb **Span:** 43 ft 11 in **Length:** 21 ft **Engine:** 80 hp Gnôme **Armament:** 1 machine-gun **Crew:** 2 **Speed:** 69 mph at ground level **Ceiling:** 10,000 ft **Range:** 4 hrs **Bomb load:** 20 lb

One French squadron was equipped with these planes when war broke out; they were used for early bombing sorties before the introduction of aircraft specifically designed for bombing

BREGUET-MICHELIN 5
Gross weight: 4,235 lb **Span:** 57 ft 8 in **Length:** 26 ft 1 in **Engine:** 220 hp Renault **Armament:** 1 machine-gun and 1×37-mm cannon **Crew:** 2 **Speed:** 86 mph at ground level **Ceiling:** NA **Range:** 5 hrs **Bomb load:** 660 lb

Problems with the Renault engine held back large-scale production until 1917, by which time it was neither fast nor manoeuvrable enough to be used as a day bomber

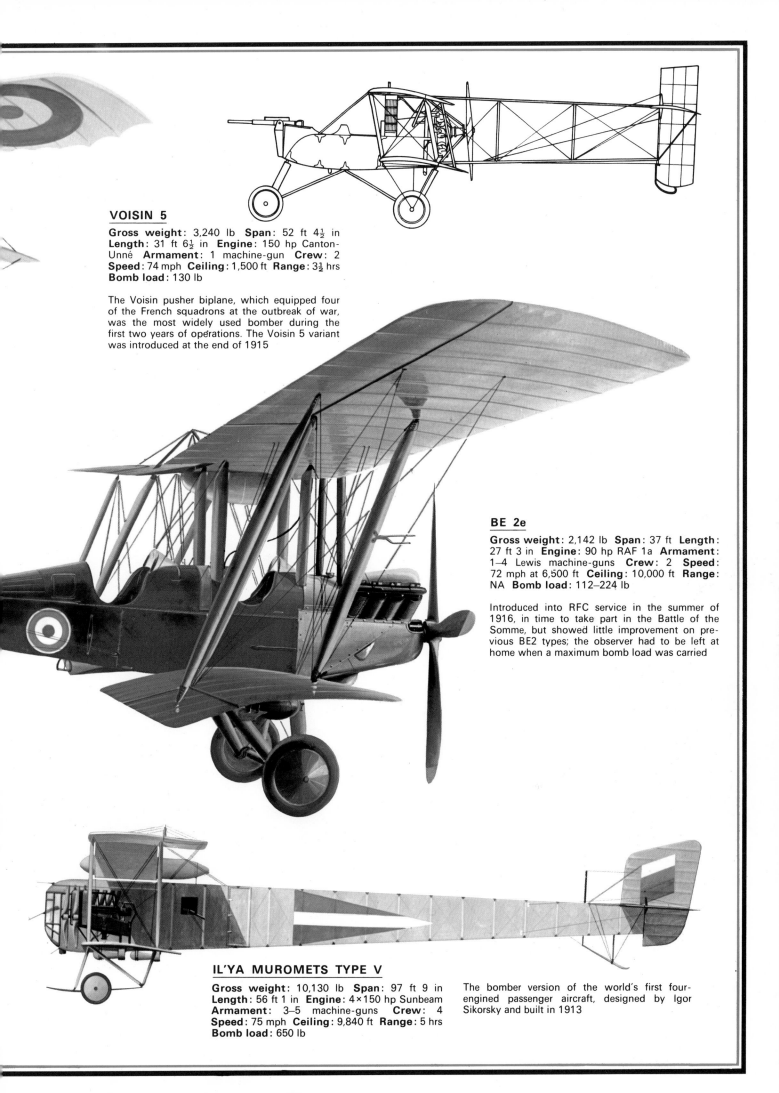

VOISIN 5

Gross weight: 3,240 lb **Span:** 52 ft 4½ in
Length: 31 ft 6½ in **Engine:** 150 hp Canton-
Unné **Armament:** 1 machine-gun **Crew:** 2
Speed: 74 mph **Ceiling:** 1,500 ft **Range:** 3½ hrs
Bomb load: 130 lb

The Voisin pusher biplane, which equipped four
of the French squadrons at the outbreak of war,
was the most widely used bomber during the
first two years of operations. The Voisin 5 variant
was introduced at the end of 1915

BE 2e

Gross weight: 2,142 lb **Span:** 37 ft **Length:**
27 ft 3 in **Engine:** 90 hp RAF 1a **Armament:**
1–4 Lewis machine-guns **Crew:** 2 **Speed:**
72 mph at 6,500 ft **Ceiling:** 10,000 ft **Range:**
NA **Bomb load:** 112–224 lb

Introduced into RFC service in the summer of
1916, in time to take part in the Battle of the
Somme, but showed little improvement on previous BE2 types; the observer had to be left at
home when a maximum bomb load was carried

IL'YA MUROMETS TYPE V

Gross weight: 10,130 lb **Span:** 97 ft 9 in
Length: 56 ft 1 in **Engine:** 4×150 hp Sunbeam
Armament: 3–5 machine-guns **Crew:** 4
Speed: 75 mph **Ceiling:** 9,840 ft **Range:** 5 hrs
Bomb load: 650 lb

The bomber version of the world's first four-
engined passenger aircraft, designed by Igor
Sikorsky and built in 1913

THE FIRST AIR FORCES

Though several countries had shown interest in military aviation in the years before the war, this quickly lapsed, and most of the early experiments in bombing were carried out through individual enterprise rather than official policy. Many of these early experiments were to prove of value as the war progressed

Even though bomber aircraft as such did not exist at the beginning of the First World War, the threat of bombing was well recognised. Visionaries like H. G. Wells had foreseen the destruction that might some day rain from the skies. As early as 1670 a Jesuit monk, Francesco de Lana, produced the first known design for a lighter-than-air craft. It did not work, but from his writings, it is clear that de Lana saw the possibilities of airborne invasion and bombing, and indeed referred to the destruction of cities and ships by fireballs hurled down from the sky.

The difficulties of bombing from balloons were self-evident for they could only travel where the wind took them. Nevertheless, such attempts were frequently made in the latter half of the 19th century, one of the first being by the Austrians in 1849 when unmanned hot air balloons carrying 30-lb time-fused bombs were launched against Venice.

It was the invention of the dirigible (steerable) airship at the turn of the century that made bombing a practical and a frightening possibility. Although such craft were also developed in Britain, France, the United States and Italy, it was in Germany, with the pioneering work of Count Ferdinand von Zeppelin, that the rigid airship made its greatest strides. At the beginning of the war the Germans possessed more and better airships than any other nation. These, rather than planes, were intended to provide Germany's primary means of bombing.

Until a few years before the war Britain

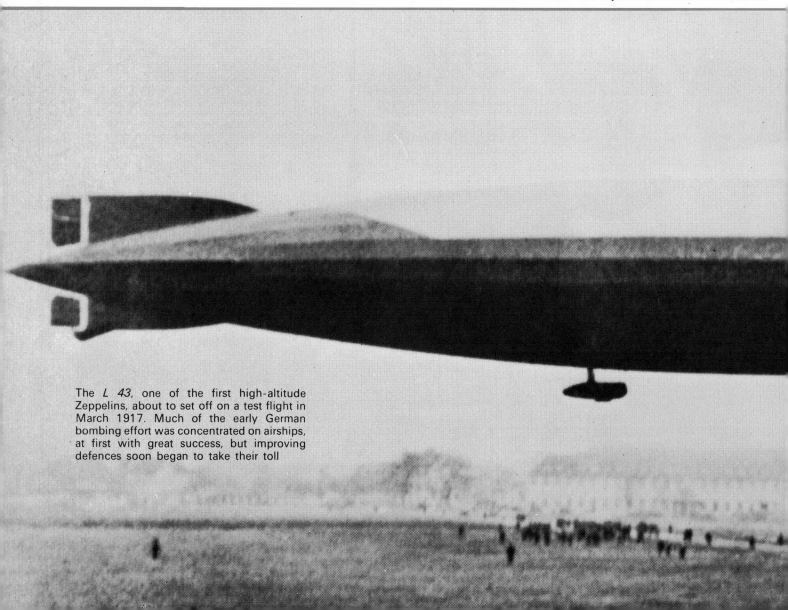

The *L 43*, one of the first high-altitude Zeppelins, about to set off on a test flight in March 1917. Much of the early German bombing effort was concentrated on airships, at first with great success, but improving defences soon began to take their toll

had largely neglected aviation development, but government indifference and indecision between lighter– and heavier-than-air machines gave way under the threat of Zeppelin attack to a belated attempt to develop defensive aeroplanes.

Meanwhile, the first experiments at dropping bombs from aircraft were carried out in the United States, by the great pioneering designer/constructor Glenn Curtiss in 1910, using dummy bombs. The following year, live bombs were dropped during a military exercise by Lt M. S. Crissy from a Wright biplane. Both the US Army and the US Navy showed some initial interest. In fact, in 1908 the US Army had been the first combat service in the world to buy an aeroplane for evaluation. But the authorities lost enthusiasm for military aviation and although the US Army and Navy both established aeronautical divisions, the US Army Air Arm had only 20 planes on its strength when war broke out in Europe, all of them obsolete, and the Naval Air Arm was almost non-existent. While the Americans later built thousands of French and British aircraft under licence, no aeroplane of American design fought in France during the First World War. The only American aircraft used in combat were Curtiss flying-boats, employed by the British Royal Naval Air Service for anti-submarine patrols.

However, one result of those early bombing experiments was the evident necessity for some kind of aiming device to enable bombs to be dropped accurately. This led Lt Riley Scott to invent the first bomb-sight in 1912. It was installed in a Wright biplane of the US Army, and was a simple device of wires and nails. Of particular interest was the fact that the bomb-aimer lay in a prone position in the nose of the aircraft and viewed the ground through a mica window, anticipating the bombing method of many years later. Also, the bombs were carried horizontally underneath the aeroplane, also common practice years later, instead of being dropped over the side or carried vertically in racks.

Italy in the lead

Italy was the first country in the field of military aeronautics, having established an Army Aeronautical Section equipped with balloons as early as 1884, and it was also the first country to drop bombs on an enemy during war. This was on 1 November 1911, during the Italo-Turkish war, when Lt Gavotti dropped four grenades of 4.4 lb each on Turkish troops in Libya. Further raids followed, causing more consternation than damage. Then the Turks protested that an Italian aircraft had bombed a military hospital at Ain Zara and an immediate controversy arose in the Italian, Turkish and neutral Press. There was no independent way at that time of establishing whether a hospital had actually been bombed and the Italians reasonably pointed out that no similar protest had been made when their warships shelled Ain Zara a few days earlier. But many felt there was something particularly inhuman about aerial bombs, and the controversy about the subject has continued ever since.

When Italy entered the war in May 1915 against Austria and Hungary, her Army Air Service was perhaps more highly trained than any other and in an excellent state of readiness. This was offset to some extent by the fact that most of her 150 aircraft were French types such as Nieuport and Blériot monoplanes and Maurice-Farman pusher biplanes, already out-dated. An exception, however, was the Caproni Ca 30/33 series which, together with the Russian Il'ya Muromets, were the first very large planes built. These certainly gave Italy the lead in heavy bombing during the early part of the war.

The series began in 1913 with the Ca 30 powered by three Gnôme rotary engines, one of which was mounted as a pusher in the central nacelle while the other two drove, indirectly, two tractor propellers in twin fuselage booms. The indirect drive was not successful and was abandoned in the Ca 31, the outer pair of engines being re-located at the front of the booms. This became the standard configuration for the series. The first bomber to be built in quantity for the Italian Army Air Service was the Ca 32, in which the rotary engines were replaced by three Fiat inline water-cooled engines of 100 hp each. Deliveries began within three months of Italy's declaration of war and went into action almost immediately. They were easy to handle, had an excellent range, and could carry up to 200 lb of bombs.

AVRO 504

Gross weight: 1,574 lb **Span:** 36 ft
Length: 29 ft 5 in **Engine:** 80 hp Gnôme
Armament: Optional Lewis **Crew:** 2
Speed: 62 mph at 6,500 ft **Ceiling:**
13,000 ft **Range:** 4½ hrs **Bomb load:**
4×20 lb

Britain's first effective light day bomber,
notable for RNAS raids on Zeppelin sheds
in Germany. Also used for bombing airships
in flight

CAPRONI Ca 32

Gross weight: 7,280 lb **Span:** 72 ft 10 in **Length:** 35 ft 9 in **Engine:** 3×100 hp Fiat A10 **Armament:** 2 machine-guns **Crew:** 3–4 **Speed:** 72 mph at ground level **Ceiling:** NA **Range:** 340 miles **Bomb load:** 200 lb

The first production version of the Caproni to enter service with the Italian Army Air Force, in August 1915, and the basis of Italy's strategic bomber arm. An excellent plane to handle with greater range than most aircraft of that time

The Ca 33 version was put into production the following year. It had a multi-wheel landing gear for operations from rough ground and included, for the first time, two gun positions – one in the front cockpit, ahead of the two pilots who sat side by side, and another at the rear. This type was so successful that it was also built under licence in France.

France moves in

France had made greater headway in aviation than any other country before the war, with the result that the French Army possessed the widest range of flying machines – about 138 in all. An Army Air Arm had been established by 1914 and with the approval of General Joffre, one of the few military leaders to see a potential for aircraft in the war beyond mere reconnaissance, this force began to explore various offensive possibilities. The smaller single-seat tractor scouts like the Nieuport biplane and Morane-Saulnier monoplane were formed into fighter squadrons (*escadrilles de chasse*) which were attached to each army for the purpose of harrying German reconnaissance craft. And within weeks of the outbreak of war, the larger two-seater pusher biplanes were formed into a bomber group (*l'ère Groupe de Bombardement*) consisting of three six-machine squadrons, under Commandant Göys.

The French bomber group, quickly joined by another two, was equipped with various Henri and Maurice Farman types, the twin-engined Caudron, the Bréguet-Michelin and the Voisin 13.50 (so named from its 13.50 metre wingspan). These pusher biplanes were completely blind from the rear, and as the idea of aerial combat did not exist before the war and since the bomb-aimer/gunner in front enjoyed a wide range of vision, they had things very much their own way to begin with, being sturdy and dependable. The Voisin was the most widely used for bombing in the early days. It could carry a bomb load of about 200 lb for three hours at a maximum speed of 55 mph and could take off and land on the roughest ground. More than 2,000 IIIs were built and supplied not only to France but also to Britain, Belgium, Italy and Russia.

The Zeppelins

In Germany, both the army and navy had established aviation corps before the war in which the pride of place was given to Zeppelins. Compared to the planes of that period, the dirigible airship was a formidable weapon. It had a speed of about 50 mph, barely less than that of most aircraft, and a much greater ceiling and range. It could cruise far behind the front lines and carry bomb loads of around 1,000 lb – impossible with aircraft until the development of multi-engined types like the Caproni. The Military Aviation Service, formed in 1912, had a fleet of six large airships and three smaller ones, to which were added three airships from a commercial airline service. The German Naval Air Service was primarily committed to the airship for the task of reconnaissance over the North Sea. But as a result of two airship disasters in 1913, it had only one Zeppelin actually in operation at the outbreak of war.

As well as airships, the Military Aviation Service was equipped with a mixed collection of 246 aircraft comprising single and two-seater Type A monoplanes like the Rumpler and Etrich Taube, and Type B biplanes of which the Albatros, Aviatik and LVG were the most common.

These were all tractor types, since Germany did not then possess any pusher planes, and none of them was armed. In fact, the development of faster aircraft had been restricted in case speed should interfere with careful observation. The Service was completely subservient to the Army with its squadrons disposed between Army HQ and Army Corps.

Within two months of the outbreak of war, however, some of the Type Bs were equipped as bombers and formed into a bomber force known as the *Fliegerkorps des Obersten Heeresleitung* (Air Corps of GHQ) comprising thirty-six aircraft divided into two wings which were given the code-name 'carrier-pigeon units'. This force was led by Major Wilhelm Siegert, a pilot himself and an aviation enthusiast, who was to play a vital part in the development of the German Army Air Service.

Britain – a late starter

The air units of all the nations mentioned came under the control of the army, the navy, or both. Britain was late in the field and it was not until 1911 that the Air Battalion of the Royal Engineers was formed, comprising a miscellany of planes, small airships, man-lifting kites and balloons. A year later the Royal Flying Corps was formed as a joint service with naval and military wings. Although the objective of military aviation in Britain was limited to reconnaissance over land and water, the RFC had one great advantage: it was a single organisation and not split up into army and navy groups as in most other countries. However, six weeks before war broke out, when Britain had 113 aircraft operational, the Admiralty decided to form its own Royal Naval Air Service. This became largely responsible for the defence of Britain, especially against the threatened Zeppelin raids. The RFC was relegated to the status of a corps attached to the army; in August 1914, the four RFC squadrons operational at the time were sent to France to join the British Expeditionary Force.

As far as equipment was concerned, a major difference in policy marked Britain's two services. The War Office had decided in 1911 that it would be more economical to build its own planes. Accordingly, it established the Army (later Royal) Aircraft Factory at Farnborough, employing Geoffrey de Havilland as chief designer and test pilot. The research effort at Farnborough concentrated on producing an aeroplane of inherent stability which would fly straight and level with little effort required on the part of the pilot so that he could devote most of his attention to observation. This was achieved with the BE2, which was given military trials in 1912. It was the first of a series of two-seater tractor biplanes, which reached its peak with the BE2c version. Well over 1,000 of this model were delivered during the first years of the war, making it the RFC's standard observation machine. However, very few were available at the outbreak of war and the War Office had to continue buying French aircraft to make up the deficiency. The result was that the RFC squadrons consisted of a mixed bag of Farman pusher biplanes, Blériot and Morane-Saulnier monoplanes alongside a few BE2s and BE8 'Bloaters'. This last, named from its fish-like appearance, in the

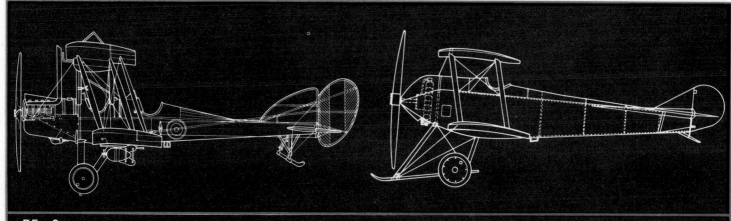

BE 2

Gross weight: 2,352 lb **Span:** 37 ft **Length:** 27 ft 3 in **Engine:** 150 hp RAF 4a **Armament:** 1–2 Lewis machine-guns **Crew:** 1 **Speed:** 102 mph at ground level **Ceiling:** 12,500 ft **Range:** NA **Bomb load:** 2×20 lb

A more powerful version of the BE 2c, introduced in an attempt to combat the menace of the Fokker monoplane in 1916

SOPWITH TABLOID

Gross weight: 1,120 lb **Span:** 25 ft 6 in **Length:** 20 ft 4 in **Engine:** 80 hp Gnôme **Armament:** 1 Lewis **Crew:** 1 **Speed:** 92 mph **Ceiling:** NA **Range:** 3½ hrs **Bomb load:** 20–40 lb

The fastest biplane in the world when it first appeared in 1913. Capable of climbing to 1,200 ft in one minute

early days was used as one of the RFC's first bombers.

The Royal Navy, on the other hand, had preferred to buy the products of the embryonic British aircraft industry and thus supported the development of some of the best aircraft used during the war. In addition to some French types, the RNAS was equipped with the single-seat Sopwith Tabloid, Bristol Scout, and Martinsyde SI, the two-seater Avro 504 – the first British bomber – and seaplanes like the two-seater Short Folder and the single-seat Sopwith Schneider. It was with a Folder, in July 1914, that the RNAS began to drop torpedoes, although the first torpedo launch from a plane had been made by the Italians several months earlier.

The Russian version

Most of the 224 aircraft in service with the Russian Army at the outbreak of war were of French and German design, built under licence in Russia, and as the war progressed, further aircraft were imported from France, Britain and the United States. Only in one field did the Russians lead the way with planes of their own design, and that was with the heavy bomber. The *Grand* biplane, designed by Igor Sikorsky (who was later to achieve fame as the pioneer of helicopters) was built in 1913. This was the world's first four-engined aeroplane, intended to carry passengers in great comfort. From it, Sikorsky developed a production series, the Il'ya Muromets, but with the threatened outbreak of hostilities ten of these were purchased by the Russian Army for military trials.

After experiments with various types of armament and bomb racks it was found that the huge planes with their roomy cabins had too low a speed and limited an altitude for offensive purposes. Accordingly, Sikorsky designed a lighter version, the Il'ya Muromets Type V, and deliveries of these began early in 1915 to the special 'Squadron of Flying Ships' formed the previous December. This was both the first specialised bomber to be built and also the first to be powered by four engines – initially British Sunbeams of 150 hp each. The name Il'ya Muromets became a class name for a variety of wartime types, some of them mounting machine-guns. These could fire from the sides of the fuselage through doors and windows, upwards from a crow's-nest position in the centre of the top wing, downwards from a platform under the fuselage and rearwards from an installation in the extreme tail, thus anticipating the heavily armed large bombers of the Second World War.

Over seventy of these remarkable aircraft were produced, and in some 400 raids over East Prussia only one was lost in air combat. The need for long-range and consequently big aircraft was obvious in a country as large as Russia, but the success of the Il'ya Muromets was also responsible for the Russians' preference for the heavy bomber as a weapon, which has lasted to the present day.

The needs of the other combatant nations were supplied primarily by the major powers, the Belgian Army for instance being equipped with French planes, while the even smaller Turkish air units used German types, most of them passed on after they had become out-dated on the Western Front. The more extensive squadrons of Austria-Hungary were equipped at the start with a variety of Etrich Taube monoplanes and Lohner arrow-wing (*Pfeil*) biplanes, together with Albatros B Is which had been designed in Germany by Ernst Heinkel and were made under licence in Austria by the Phoenix company.

Throughout the war Austria continued to rely on aircraft supplied by Germany or built under licence, but in its own right Austria was an important supplier of engines, especially the Austro-Daimler and the Hiero, on which Dr Ferdinand Porsche worked. Since engines were of such vital importance in aircraft design, it is worth considering their development before describing the first use of bombers in the First World War.

Caproni Ca 41 triplanes used by the Royal Naval Air Service in Italy for a short period towards the end of the war

Caproni, Milan

ENGINES AND DESIGN

The major — and often insurmountable — problem confronting early bomber designers, was getting the machines to fly at all. The major choices open to them — air-cooled or water-cooled engines; monoplane, biplane or triplane construction; of wood, metal or a combination — were often made on the basis of availability rather than sound reasoning. Nevertheless, tremendous strides had been made by the end of the war

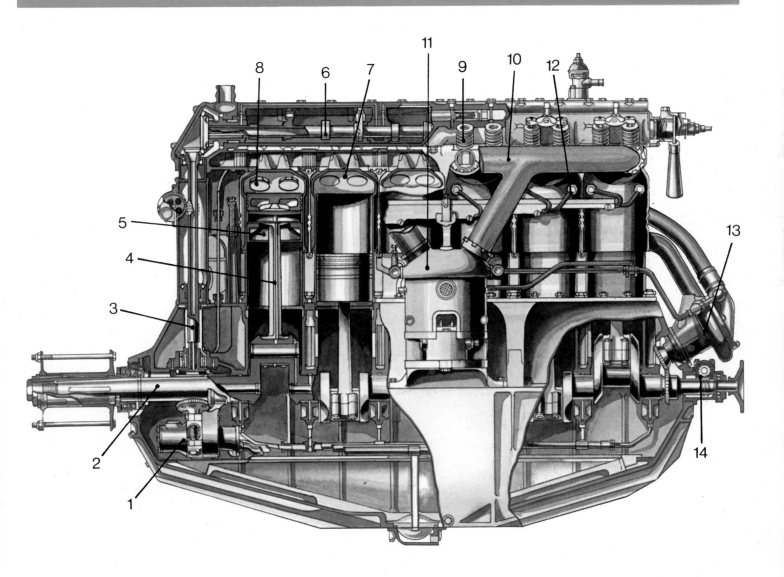

1 RECIPROCATING PLUNGER OIL PUMP

2 CRANK SHAFT

3 CAM SHAFT DRIVE SHAFT

4 CONNECTING RODS

5 ALUMINIUM PISTON (SECTIONED)

6 OVERHEAD CAM SHAFT

7 CYLINDER HEAD

8 VALVES

9 VALVE SPRINGS

10 INDUCTION MANIFOLD

11 DUPLEX CARBURETTOR

12 SPARK PLUGS

13 CENTRIFUGAL WATER PUMP

14 INTERRUPTER GEAR CAM

AUSTRO-DAIMLER ENGINE
Power: 200 hp at 1,400 rpm **Cylinders:** 6
Weight/power ratio: 3.64 lb per BHP

By August 1914 the designers of aircraft engines had already established the main families that were to last until the general introduction of the gas turbine more than thirty years later. Many of the earliest engines were based on those used in motorcars and thus had cylinders cooled by water jackets and disposed in rows, driving on a multi-throw crankshaft. But there was one outstanding engine, the Gnôme rotary, invented by Laurent Séguin in France in 1907, that established a totally new configuration.

Although the American Farrand Car had tried a cruder version of the same idea, the Gnôme set a new standard in engineering design, and by weighing only about two-and-a-half pounds for each horsepower it roughly doubled the ratio of power to weight generally available at that time. The first Gnôme had seven cylinders arranged radially, like the spokes of a wheel. A mixture of petrol and castor oil (lubricant) was admitted to the crankcase and then, via flap-valves in the pistons, to the combustion spaces in the cylinders. The crankshaft was fitted to the aircraft so that when the engine was running, the cylinders and the crankcase rotated, taking the propeller with them. The spinning cylinders had high gyroscopic inertia which damped out vibration and made for sweet running, but they tended to impart gyroscopic forces to single-engined aircraft. It was this factor that gave the fighting scouts much of their manoeuvrability – and also made them difficult to handle. The only drawback was that although they could turn very smartly in one direction, they were very sluggish in turning to the other and enemy aircraft could usually guess what they would do in combat. For this reason some engines were adapted to reverse the propeller's normal direction. The gyroscopic characteristic was less marked with multi-engined bombers that used the rotary engine, such as the twin-engined French Caudron G4, G6 and the Italian Ca 30 and 31 Capronis, but it was certainly evident in the RFC's single-engined BE8 'Bloater', especially when carrying a 100-lb bomb.

New techniques
Unlike almost every other petrol engine of the time, the Gnôme was machined from high-tensile steel. This was costly even in mass-production, but it established a trend of fine precision engineering which gradually eliminated the crop of engines put together from cruder pieces of steel, cast iron, brass and copper. The spinning cylinders were easy to cool by the slipstream but introduced problems of carburisation and mixture distribution which were only partly overcome by the development of the *Monosoupape* Gnôme, with only one valve in each piston serving for both inlet and exhaust. Though the original 50 hp engine was developed to give 80, 150, and finally, in two-row form, over 200 hp, it was obsolescent by 1916. So too was the only other important family of engines with radially disposed cylinders in the First World War. These were the Swiss/British/French Canton-Unné or Salmson engines – static radials with fixed liquid-cooled cylinders and propellers mounted on the rotating crankshaft. They gave good service, especially in the Voisin pusher biplanes and the Short bomber seaplanes, but the experimental French SM I bomber of 1916 could hardly expect to be successful as its

Salmson engine, arranged sideways in the fuselage, drove two propellers on the wing struts by means of long shafts and bevel gears.

By 1916 almost all the engines pouring off the assembly lines in ever increasing numbers were of the in-line or Vee type. A few had air-cooled cylinders (the cooling scoop of the British RE8 reconnaissance biplane could be seen a mile away) but the vast majority had water cooling, even though this was clumsy, heavy and vulnerable. Practically every aircraft on the side of the Central Powers used a six-in-line water-cooled engine, the most common makes being Mercedes, Maybach (based on an early airship engine) and Austro-Daimler. The French developed advanced and powerful models of Renault and Hispano-Suiza engines, first used in the Letord series and the Spad S XI respectively. And the winning Mercedes Grand Prix racing car of 1914 served as a starting point for the British Rolls Royce aero engines. By 1917 Rolls Royce had produced versions of the Vee-12 Eagle giving 360–375 hp, with outstanding efficiency and reliability, for the giant Handley Pages and Vickers Vimy bombers.

Though by this time the air-cooled radial was suddenly coming into favour, the powerful and efficient Vee-12 was dominant at the end of the war. This was also the arrangement adopted in the United States for the Liberty engine, created in a matter of days by a committee of engineers (mainly from automobile companies) and swiftly pushed through a troublesome development into production on an unprecedented scale. The Liberty, ultimately rated at well over 400 hp, served the US Army for fifteen years, beginning with the DH4, built under licence in America.

The greatest scope for variation in design lay in choosing the location of the radiator made necessary by the water-cooled engine. One of the simplest and least vulnerable schemes was the frontal car-type arrangement with the radiator forming a bluff face immediately behind the propeller as in the Handley Pages and DH9a (or, in the case of a pusher, such as the Gotha, at the front of the nacelle). Other bombers had radiators in a box flush with the top wing (LVG and Halberstadt); inclined on each side of the engine cowl (Voisin and Bréguet); disposed vertically on the struts above the engine (Caproni Ca 40); arranged vertically up the sides of the fuselage and then slanting in to meet above the engine (Armstrong Whitworth FK8); or in a box in front of the upper centre-section (Lloyds and Lohners). Many bombers of the Central Powers such as Aviatiks and DFWs had Hazlet radiators, looking just like those used for domestic heating, fixed on the side of the fuselage in sections so that they could be shortened in cold weather and enlarged in summer.

Wire and plywood
A major factor in design was the materials available at any given time. Early aircraft made use of obvious proven materials, the preferred choice being carefully selected hardwood. For example the widely used Rumpler C-1 had ash for the top (compression) booms of the wing spars and spruce for the lower (tension) booms. Ribs were generally built up from pieces of hardwood and plywood, glued and pinned. Only at major joints and places bearing especially heavy loads were metals used – the most common material being steel. On the other hand, a large number of aircraft were built up from thin-walled steel tube,

GOTHA GV
Gross weight: 8,745 lb **Span:** 77 ft 9 in **Length:** 40 ft 7 in **Engine:** 2×260 hp Mercedes D IVa **Armament:** 3–4 machine-guns **Crew:** 3 **Speed:** 87 mph at ground level **Ceiling:** 21,320 ft **Range:** 520 miles **Bomb load:** 1,300 lb

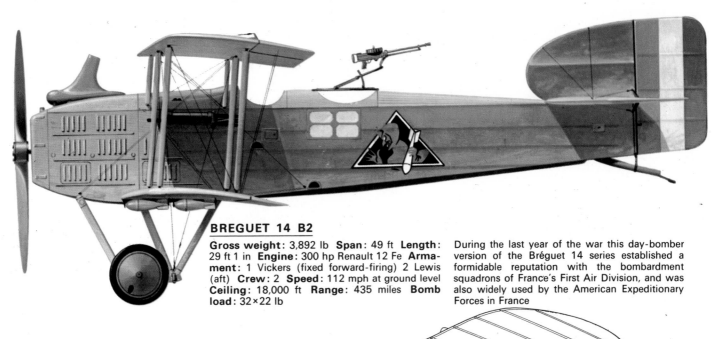

BREGUET 14 B2

Gross weight: 3,892 lb **Span:** 49 ft **Length:** 29 ft 1 in **Engine:** 300 hp Renault 12 Fe **Armament:** 1 Vickers (fixed forward-firing) 2 Lewis (aft) **Crew:** 2 **Speed:** 112 mph at ground level **Ceiling:** 18,000 ft **Range:** 435 miles **Bomb load:** 32×22 lb

During the last year of the war this day-bomber version of the Bréguet 14 series established a formidable reputation with the bombardment squadrons of France's First Air Division, and was also widely used by the American Expeditionary Forces in France

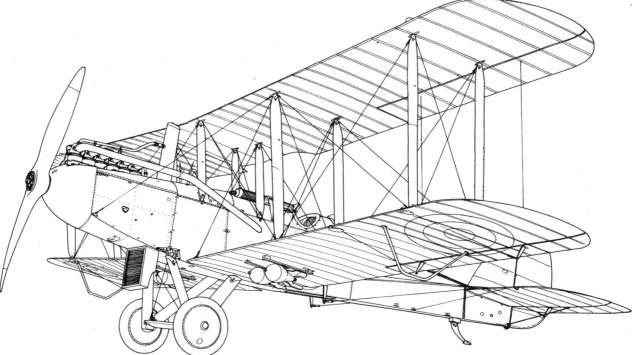

DH 9

Gross weight: 3,669 lb **Span:** 42 ft 5 in **Length:** 30 ft 6 in **Engine:** 230 hp BHP **Armament:** 1 Vickers; 1–2 Lewis machine-guns **Crew:** 2 **Speed:** 118 mph at 10,000 ft **Ceiling:** 17,500 ft **Range:** NA **Bombs:** 2×230 lb or 4×100 lb

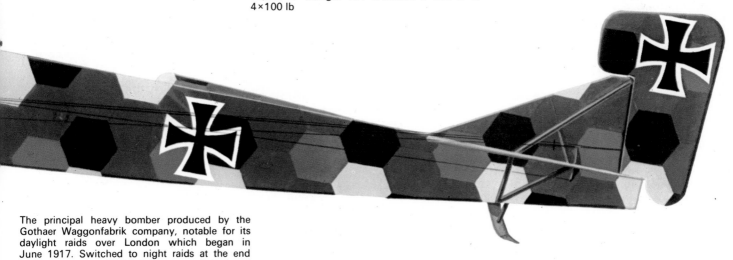

The principal heavy bomber produced by the Gothaer Waggonfabrik company, notable for its daylight raids over London which began in June 1917. Switched to night raids at the end of that year, when British fighters were introduced with the speed and operational altitude necessary for successful interception

Flight International

Lamblin radiators on the DH 9

either welded, or held by bolted or riveted joints. This was simple and quick to make and the weight factor was competitive. Even wooden aircraft often had steel-tube tails. Covering was invariably of doped fabric, though often the front fuselage was skinned in plywood. Undercarriage and wing struts were nearly always of steel tube, sometimes with light wood fairings to change the round tube to a streamline form. Wheels were thin steel rims held by multiple wire spokes, often faired by a disc of fabric. Very often there was no trailing-edge member in the wing except for a single wire, which was bent by the tension of the doped fabric to give a scalloped outline.

Such were the difficulties of making a strong, rigid biplane cellule (wing assembly) that the Paul Schmitt bombers had no fewer than twelve structural bays, with six pairs of interplane struts on each side of the fuselage. On such machines, streamlined rigging wire was a great advantage, especially the British Rafwire with a cross-section like that of a raindrop. Some of the fastest bombers, the Ansaldo SVA family for example, had no bracing wires at all. The Voisin bombers, though of primitive design and low performance, were of all-steel construction and could be left out in any weather in the certainty that they would not deteriorate or warp.

Deliberate warping of the wings was the common way of providing lateral control in 1914, but by 1915 nearly all new bombers had ailerons, often on all wings. Another change was that, whereas many 1914 bombers had rudders and elevators only, by 1915 it was usual to hinge these surfaces to fixed fins and tailplanes. Wheel brakes were never fitted but some aircraft, especially German ones, had a claw arrangement which would plough a furrow across the airfield to bring the machine more quickly to rest.

In November 1916 Bréguet produced the Type Br 14 in which extensive use was made of aluminium. This light metal was used for most of the wing structure and under-carriage, and even in sheet form for the fuselage decking around the cockpits. Though use was still made of wood, steel and fabric, aluminium helped to keep many thousands of Br 14 bombers in worldwide use until after 1930. In 1917, German Professor Hugo Junkers produced his J-1 in which almost the whole airframe was duralumin (aluminium/copper alloy), the unbraced wings and tail having a robust skin of corrugated dural.

Design errors

In the earliest bombers the first objective was to design a machine that would fly at all, because many failed to achieve even that. Next came reliability, while such considerations as flight performance and bomb load were to some degree bonuses. Aircraft design at that time was anything but an exact science. It was not uncommon for a design team to follow a winner with a distinctly inferior machine. For example, the early Caproni Ca 30 bombers were followed late in 1917 by the giant triplane Ca 40 family. These, though robust and well engineered, had such a 'built-in head-wind' that they were easy meat for defending scouts and AA artillery in the daytime and had to be used at night. This made bombing even more random than before. These impressive-looking aircraft illustrated the fact that adding more power did not necessarily give better performance. In contrast the small Italian SVA series, with only 220 hp, carried a useful bomb load and were possibly the fastest machines used in the First World War.

Before 1920, aircraft design was very much a matter of opinion, often vehemently expressed yet backed by the slenderest of evidence. Some designers contended that the structural integrity of the triplane more than made up for its other shortcomings; most favoured the biplane, and a very small number (none was a designer of large bombers) considered the monoplane in-

herently superior. In the same way there was no evidence to suggest that four 100 hp engines might be superior to two 200 hp, beyond the obvious fact that, first, the aircraft would fly better with one engine failed, and second, the chances of engine failure were twice as great.

With most multi-engined bombers it was possible for a courageous crew member to reach a faulty engine in flight and attempt to rectify the trouble. In some designs, notably the German Siemens-Schuckert R-types, the engines were installed in the fuselage purposely to render the whole propulsion system and cooling radiators readily accessible during a mission. The usual fate of such designs was a short period on operations, followed by a much longer period as a trainer in an environment where poor performance was less likely to prove lethal.

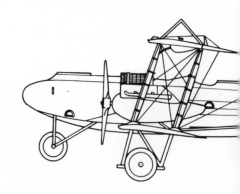

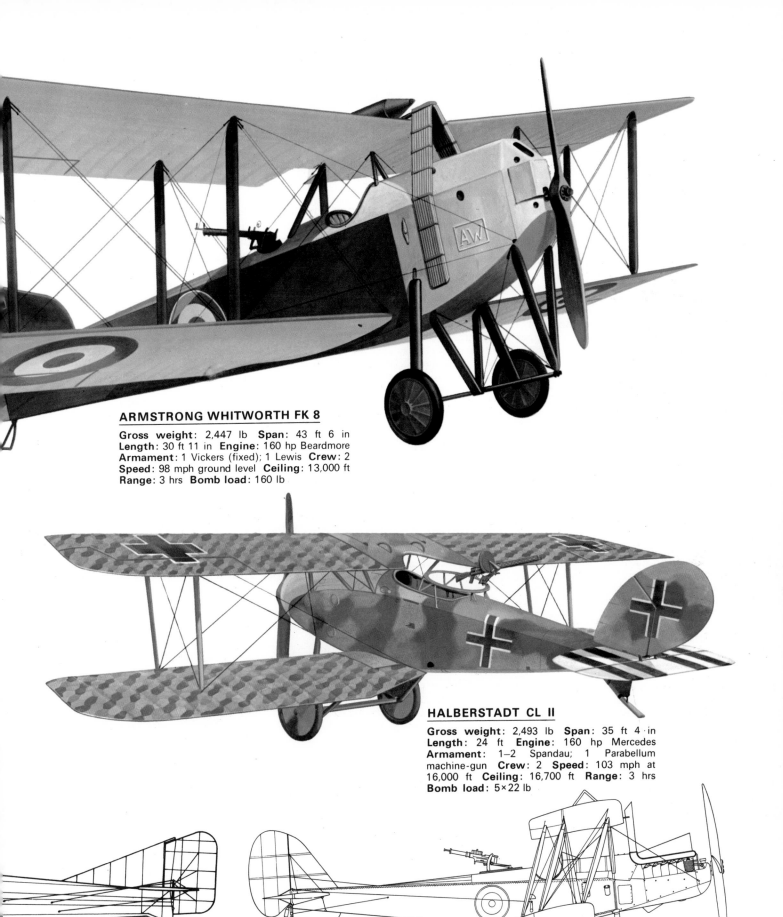

ARMSTRONG WHITWORTH FK 8
Gross weight: 2,447 lb Span: 43 ft 6 in
Length: 30 ft 11 in Engine: 160 hp Beardmore
Armament: 1 Vickers (fixed); 1 Lewis Crew: 2
Speed: 98 mph ground level Ceiling: 13,000 ft
Range: 3 hrs Bomb load: 160 lb

HALBERSTADT CL II
Gross weight: 2,493 lb Span: 35 ft 4 in
Length: 24 ft Engine: 160 hp Mercedes
Armament: 1–2 Spandau; 1 Parabellum
machine-gun Crew: 2 Speed: 103 mph at
16,000 ft Ceiling: 16,700 ft Range: 3 hrs
Bomb load: 5×22 lb

LETORD 4
Gross weight: 4,818 lb Span: 58 ft Length:
37 ft 1 in Engine: 2×160 hp Lorraine-Dietrich
Armament: 3–4 machine guns Crew: 2–3
Speed: 82 mph at 6,500 ft Ceiling: 14,000 ft
Range: 3 hrs Bomb load: 300 lb

RE 8
Gross weight: 2,869 lb Span: 42 ft 7 in
Length: 27 ft 10 in Engine: 150 hp RAF 4a
Armament: 2–3 machine-guns Crew: 2
Speed: 98 mph at 6,500 ft Ceiling: 11,000 ft
Range: NA Bomb load: 260 lb

AIRSHIP RAIDS ON BRITAIN

The advantages of airships as bombers were enormous in the early days of the war. Almost as fast as the planes then in existence, their range and bomb-load were far superior. But their days were numbered: more effective defences and better fighters made their vulnerability painfully clear. By the end of their short career, however, the Zeppelins had firmly established the concept of strategic bombing

German airships were the first craft to be used for bombing in the First World War. Only two days after Germany's invasion of Belgium, the Zeppelin Z 6 was sent to attack Liège. It was damaged by gunfire from the ground however, and was wrecked during a forced landing near Cologne. Before the month of August was out, two more Zeppelins had been shot down while on their first operational missions. One of them was captured by the French. It was at such an early stage of the war that the Germans learned the bitter lesson of just how vulnerable were the mighty Zeppelins on which they had pinned such faith.

Their basic mistake had been to direct them over strongly defended battle areas during the hours of daylight when they made such large, slow-moving targets. Nevertheless the disasters shattered the enthusiasm of the German High Command for the airship as a weapon. Although a small number of army airships were later used on bombing raids over Britain, it was the German Naval Air Service which exploited the Zeppelin to its fullest extent, not only in strategic raids over Britain, but even more so in the reconnaissance over the North Sea which was its main task. Much of the success of the German navy against Allied shipping was due to the observation maintained by airship patrols, which during the course of the war, made 971 scouting flights over the North Sea, and 220 over the Baltic.

Meanwhile, the army learned to limit tactical Zeppelin raids over the front line to the hours of darkness, thus anticipating the dark-painted night bomber.

The first attack

Without the more sophisticated bombing devices developed later, bombs dropped at night were even more inaccurate than those dropped by day. So the Military Aviation Service turned its main attention to aircraft which were beginning to show they had uses other than mere reconnaissance. As early as 13 August 1914 a Taube flown by Lt Franz von Hiddeson dropped two light bombs on the outskirts of Paris. Urgent orders were put through for some of the large bomber aircraft which German designers had on their drawing boards but which had previously aroused little interest. At the same time a special bomber force of existing aeroplanes, unsuitable though they were, was set up under GHQ command.

In taking over the main responsibility for Zeppelin bombing raids on Britain, the German Naval Air Service pioneered some of the techniques used later by aircraft. In

the same way, their efforts led to the development of anti-aircraft defences which stood Britain in good stead at the end of 1916 when the first German heavy bombers came into service. It was early in the January of 1915 that the Kaiser sanctioned airship raids on Britain but limited them to military establishments such as shipyards and arsenals. However, since the raids were made at night and the airships often drifted far off course, the commanders had little idea where their bombs might fall. Many fell on undefended villages in East Anglia, particularly after the black-out became widespread, making it even more difficult to differentiate between military and civilian targets.

The first airship raid took place on the night of 19 January 1915 when two Zeppelins dropped bombs on Kings Lynn, Yarmouth, and several villages in the area. The bombs themselves were not large, mostly 110-lb high explosives and 6½-lb incendiaries with a limited destructive capability. Less than

half-a-dozen people were killed, but this was the first time that a civilian population had ever been subjected to systematic bombing, and the terror and sense of outrage that it produced was out of all proportion to the weight of bombs dropped.

Reprisals were called for, leading eventually to raids on Berlin by British bombers. Meanwhile, the Zeppelin raids continued: in twenty raids during 1915, thirty-seven tons of bombs killed 181 people and injured 455. So there seemed little point in pretending *not* to bomb London when the airship crews had little idea where their bombs were falling anyway. In fact the capital was bombed by mistake on 31 May, when seven civilians were killed and thirty-five injured. Two months later, the Kaiser lifted his ban on bombing London, and raids on that city, as well as others such as Liverpool and the Tyneside area, began in earnest.

The Zeppelin crews, though, didn't have everything their own way. They had to contend with storms and gales that often

forced them to crash land, usually with fatal results. This was the fate, only one month later, of the two airships which had made the January raid. And the organisation of the British defences improved as time went on. To begin with, the Royal Navy was responsible for the defence of London and the major cities while the Army took care of ports and military installations. Guns such as 3 and 4-in quick firers and 1-pounder pom poms were converted for anti-aircraft use and even machine-guns were placed on high-angle mountings and fitted to motorcars for mobility. Searchlights were introduced, manned first by special constables.

Counter measures

Until the crews gained experience, there were many false alarms when illuminated clouds were mistaken for Zeppelins. Nevertheless, just as the bombing brought a new terror not exactly justified by the damage to property and loss of life actually caused, so the airship crews learned what it was like to be in a huge, slow-moving target, flying at no more than 6,000 feet, held in the beam of a searchlight and being fired at from the ground. Such was the fear this aroused that when five Zeppelins tried to raid London in August, only one got within thirty miles and the returning crews told dramatic stories of searchlights and anti-aircraft fire which did not actually exist. They bombed the wrong targets and the firing was only from rifles.

The new series of giant Zeppelins which came into service in 1916 were able to fly as high as 12,300 ft, and a novel device was introduced to reduce their chance of being caught in searchlight beams. While the airship cruised safely above the clouds, a streamlined car with an observer inside was lowered nearly 3,000 feet on a steel cable so

that the observer could direct the bombing by telephone. In the spring and summer of that year, the Zeppelin raids reached their peak, with a dozen or more craft taking part in a single attack. But the height at which they flew, although making it easier to elude the defences, imposed even greater strains on the crews who were often airborne for twenty-four hours or more at temperatures of 30° below zero in winter. And the ground defences were also improving. In February the Army took over the entire responsibility for home defences and several months later, the RFC's BE2c aircraft were fitted with fixed forward-firing machine-guns for the first time, following the 1915 invention by the French and Germans of interrupter gear which enabled these guns to be synchronised to fire through the propellers. It was this invention that turned the early reconnaissance aircraft into lethal fighters.

Aircraft had brought down Zeppelins before but by the unorthodox method of flying above and dropping bombs on them. The first to be destroyed in this way – and the first to be destroyed in aerial combat – was brought down on 7 June 1915 by Flt Sub-Lt R. A. J. Warneford, of the RNAS, flying a French Morane Parasol Type L. He set fire to the airship LZ 37 over Ghent by dropping six 20-lb bombs on it and was awarded the Victoria Cross. But by mid-1916, the British aircraft were armed with machine-guns which could not only be aimed more accurately but could fire incendiary bullets. These, along with phosphor shells from anti-aircraft guns spelled doom for the hydrogen-filled airships.

The first victory by a defending fighter at night came on 2 September 1916 when Lt William Leefe Robinson of 39 Squadron RFC shot down one of twelve naval and four military airships which had set out to

raid London. Flames from the burning Schutte-Lanz airship SL 11 could be seen fifty miles away. Robinson too, was awarded the Victoria Cross for his success, which marked the beginning of the end of the airship menace.

The new class of airship which was coming into service could fly at 18,000 ft in an attempt to avoid the fighters, but at that height the crew suffered even more severely from the cold and had to use oxygen, while the craft themselves were subject to greater hazards from treacherous wind changes. When eleven airships set out to bomb London at the beginning of October, they became so scattered that only one person was killed in the city, while one of the Zeppelins was lost with its entire crew – shot down by a BE2c over Potters Bar. In the last raid of 1916, eight weeks later, two out of ten Zeppelins were lost. The total number of raids during the year was twenty-three, during which 125 tons of bombs were dropped, killing 293 people and wounding 691.

End of the airship

The Germans were reluctant to admit defeat but the short day of the airship as a bomber was over. Only eleven more raids were made against England, seven in 1917 and four in 1918. The last was on 5 August 1918 when five Zeppelins launched a surprise attack which resulted in the loss of their latest and best airship, the L 70, together with *Fregattenkapitän* Peter Strasser, the officer who had led the naval airship force so courageously since the very beginning of the war. It was not an end to bombing, of course, as towards the end of 1916 aircraft were beginning to take over that role with growing effectiveness. But the Zeppelins had played their part, albeit at a tremendous cost. Of the eighty-eight airships built during the war (seventy-two for the German navy), over sixty were lost; thirty-four due to accidents and forced landings caused by bad weather and the remainder shot down by Allied aircraft and ground fire. In fifty-one raids on Britain they dropped 5,806 bombs (a total of 196½ tons), killing 557 people, injuring a further 1,358, and causing an estimated £1½ million damage. This was not too highly significant in itself, considering the thousands who were dying in the trenches in France every day, but the raids were of considerable military value as they hampered war production and diverted men and equipment from more vital theatres of war.

It is estimated that the airship and aircraft raids together reduced the total munitions output by one sixth. And by the end of 1916, the British home-based air defences included twelve RFC squadrons and a large force of anti-aircraft guns and searchlights, requiring 12,000 men.

The airship raids were the first ever attempt to defeat a country by the bombing of military and civilian targets in the homeland rather than attacks on military targets in the battle zone – strategic and psychological bombing as distinct from tactical bombing. Its success gave rise to a whole new school of military thought which was put into effect with far greater destruction during the Second World War. Much of the initial success was due to the fact that bombing was an unknown factor before the First War and its effect on an unprepared civilian population was therefore considerably greater.

The wreckage of Zeppelin *L 10* in the shallows off Cuxhaven. Returning from a scouting flight on 3 September 1915, she was struck by lightning and fell in flames, killing all on board

Imperial War Museum

AEROPLANES AS BOMBERS

Early aeroplane bombing raids were limited to the battle-zone and its vicinity. The German Zeppelins had the range to attack more distant targets, but the first strategic raid by plane was carried out by the British – not by the RFC but by the navy

One of the great advantages which the Zeppelin of 1914 had over the aeroplane was, of course, its range – more than 2,000 miles at a time when most planes were hard pressed to fly 150 miles without having to land to refuel. It was range that made it possible for the Germans to pioneer the bombing of an enemy's homeland and in particular his capital city. Military leaders believed that the capture of an enemy's capital city somehow marked his defeat. London was chosen by the Germans because it could be reached by flying across the North Sea and thus avoiding the battle zones of the Western Front, whereas Paris could only be reached by battling through the Allied air patrols over France. Only two airship raids were made on the French capital throughout the war and one of two Zeppelins making one attempt was destroyed. But apart from the need to avoid the Western Front, range gave a wide choice in the selection of targets. In fact, airship range was always greater than that of aircraft. In 1918, the Germans were even able to contemplate raids on New York with their newest Zeppelins which had a range of 7,500 miles. Strasser, head of the German Naval Air Service, was planning such a raid when he was killed with the destruction of the L 70.

Meanwhile, during the early stages of the war when planes were first used for bombing, their missions generally had to be confined to the battle-zone or targets in the near vicinity. The French Voisin and Farman bombers were particularly effective in tactical missions against military targets, proving themselves to be virtually an extension of artillery, for which the French had been enthusiasts since the days of Napoleon. The earliest French bombs were

actually converted Canton-Unné 90-mm and 155-mm artillery shells with the addition of fins and impact fuses. The French might well have undertaken the first strategic aeroplane bombing raid of the war – a mass attack on the Kaiser's personal headquarters at Mézières in September 1914 – but for some reason the planned raid was cancelled.

The German 'carrier-pigeon' bomber units were also used during the first months of the war, although to a lesser extent because of the emphasis placed on airships. They might have been used for strategic raids as early as February 1915, when plans were made for them to bomb England. An experimental night bombing raid was carried out on Dunkirk at the end of January, but before the raid itself could be carried out, the force was transferred to the Eastern Front where it gave considerable assistance at the battle of Gorlice-Tarnow in March. As it was, the first ever strategic raid by a plane was carried out by the British – not by the RFC, as might have been expected, but by the RNAS.

'Samson's boys'
In August 1914, while the four RFC squadrons were sent to France to operate under army command from a base at Maubeuge, an RNAS squadron under Cdr Samson was despatched to Ostend to assist an attempted naval diversion by a brigade of marines.

Among the aircraft were two Sopwith Tabloids, tiny single-seat tractor biplanes, which before the war had been a favourite sporting machine. The diversion was planned by Winston Churchill, then First Lord of the Admiralty, but it did not materialise and within three days the marines were

FRIEDRICHSHAVEN G III

Gross weight: 8,700 lb **Span:** 78 ft **Length:** 42 ft 2 in **Engine:** 2×260 hp Mercedes D IVa **Armament:** 4×7·92-mm machine guns **Crew:** 3 **Speed:** 88 mph at 3,280 ft **Ceiling:** 14,800 ft **Range:** 5 hrs **Bomb load:** 2,200 lb

The main production model of the Friedrichshaven G series which, together with the Gotha bombers, formed the mainstay of the German heavy bomber units during the last two years of the war

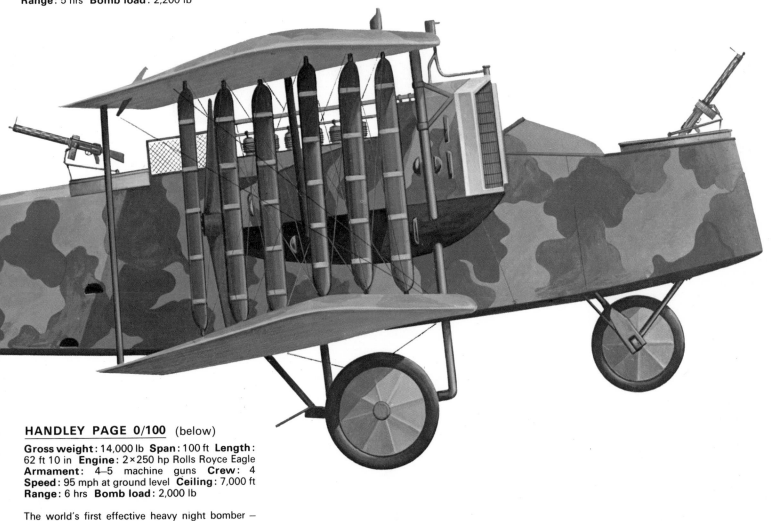

HANDLEY PAGE 0/100 (below)

Gross weight: 14,000 lb **Span:** 100 ft **Length:** 62 ft 10 in **Engine:** 2×250 hp Rolls Royce Eagle **Armament:** 4–5 machine guns **Crew:** 4 **Speed:** 95 mph at ground level **Ceiling:** 7,000 ft **Range:** 6 hrs **Bomb load:** 2,000 lb

The world's first effective heavy night bomber — the biggest British warplane of the war

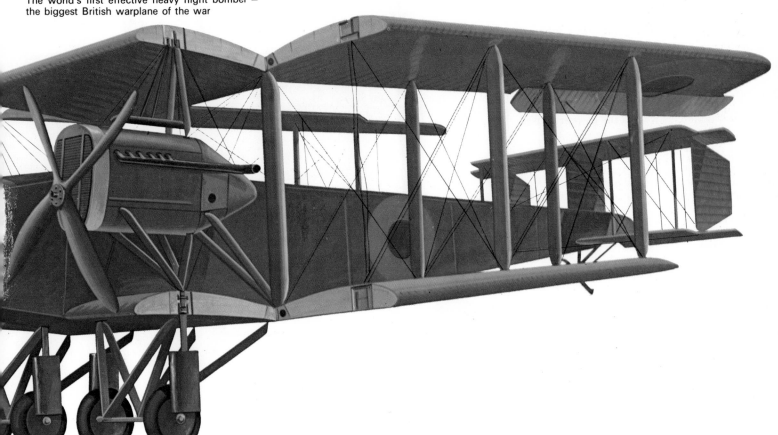

recalled. Samson's squadron was supposed to go with them, returning to one of the RNAS air stations that had been established along the east coast as part of Britain's defences. But this did not suit the fiery Commander who had pioneered flight 'from ships at sea. Using Channel fog as an excuse he landed his squadron at Dunkirk and enlisted the aid of the British Consul for him to stay on to support the French. Churchill agreed to the establishment of a naval air base on the French coast to help protect Britain from airship raids, and so 'Samson's boys' became a permanent feature at Dunkirk.

The RNAS squadron was intended to carry out reconnaissance and engage any Zeppelins or enemy aircraft sighted. But Samson preferred more vigorous action and decided to attack the Zeppelins at their actual bases. The first British air raid into German territory took place on 22 September 1914 but no damage was caused. Meanwhile, several of the aircraft had been sent to Antwerp to help in the battle to prevent the German Army reaching the sea. British forces were forced to withdraw on 7 October and a day later the last RNAS aeroplanes to leave the Belgian city were the two Sopwith Tabloids, flown by Squadron Commander Spenser Grey and Flt-Lt R. L. G. Marix.

Before returning to Dunkirk they were ordered by Samson to attack the Zeppelin sheds at Cologne and Düsseldorf. Spenser Grey was prevented by mist from seeing his target and dropped bombs on Cologne's railway station instead. But Marix was more successful and from 600 ft his 20-lb Hale high explosive bombs fell on the Zeppelin shed at Düsseldorf which exploded into flames, completely destroying the brand-new Zeppelin Z 9 inside. This was the first-ever strategic bombing raid, since it was designed to cripple the enemy's war effort by striking at a military target behind the front line rather than in the battle zone. A few weeks later, three Avro 504 biplanes made a similar raid on the Friedrichshafen Zeppelin works on Lake Constance, a mission requiring a flight of about 250 miles over hostile territory, from a take-off point at Belfort on the French-Swiss border. The Avros attacked by flying to within ten feet of the lake's surface – probably the first low-level bombing strike in history – destroying one Zeppelin under construction, as well as the gasworks used for filling the airships.

Heavier bombers
The success of these attacks led the Air Department of the Admiralty to issue a specification for a much larger twin-engined bomber able to carry much heavier bombs than the 20-pounders which were in general use at that time, and the biggest that most planes could carry. This resulted in the first of the famous Handley Page series of bombers, the 0/100.

At the same time, the Germans were developing large R-class bombers such as the Friedrichshafen and Gotha types. These also made their appearance in 1916, the latter being one of the finest bombers of the war. The French were slower in building heavy twin-engined bombers and it was not until 1917 that the first of the Letord series, designed by Colonel Dorand of the French Service Technique, came into operation. The Russians of course already possessed a number of Il'ya Muromets, but these were hampered by maintenance problems and

HANDLEY PAGE 0/400 (above)

Gross weight: 14,022 lb **Span:** 100 ft **Length:** 62 ft 10 in **Engine:** 2×250 hp Rolls Royce Eagle **Armament:** 5×·303 machine guns **Crew:** 4–5 **Speed:** 97 mph at ground level **Ceiling:** 8,000 ft **Range:** 4 hrs **Bomb load:** 2,000 lb

Improved version of the Handley Page 0/100 heavy night bomber (see page 25) and the most widely used by the British during 1917 and 1918 for raids on Germany

RE 7 (below)

Gross weight: 3,449 lb **Span:** 57 ft **Length:** 31 ft 10 in **Engine:** 150 hp RAF 4a **Armament:** 1 machine gun and small arms **Crew:** 2–3 **Speed:** 85 mph at ground level **Ceiling:** 6,500 ft **Range:** NA **Bomb load:** 336 lb

Introduced into service with the RFC early in 1916 and notable for its great weight-lifting capacity, in relation to its size

later operations were affected by the Russian Revolution. The Italians, who only joined the war in May 1915, were also well advanced in the development of the heavy bomber, and the Caproni Ca 32 was in service by the end of the same year. It was evident that 1916 would see the introduction of specialised bombers in the air services of all the major combatant powers.

In the meantime, however, they had to use the planes already in existence. From early in 1915, the Allies increased their raids, while the French, in retaliation for attacks on Paris, began to include targets in Germany itself. Much of the French strategic bombing effort was, in fact, based on a doctrine of retaliation. On 26 May, for instance, following a German poison-gas attack the previous month, Commandant Göys led three squadrons of Voisin bombers on a raid against the poison-gas factories near Mannheim, a flight of five hours. Considerable damage was achieved and only one Voisin failed to return. Unfortunately this was the one piloted by Göys, who had been forced to land in Germany because of engine trouble. He was taken prisoner but eventually escaped and found his way back to France.

By June the French had begun to penetrate as far as Karlsruhe. Much of the early success of these bombing missions was due to the fact that here was virtually no opposition from German aircraft. This meant that raids could be carried out in daytime and at relatively low altitudes, so that even by the primitive method of dropping bombs over the side of the cockpit, a surprising degree of accuracy could be achieved. The British and French crews had a healthy respect for the Germans' improvised anti-aircraft guns. Many of these had been hastily converted from other uses: the 3·7-cm *maschinen flak*, for example, which could fire three shots a second with an accuracy up to 9,000 ft, was originally used by the navy on torpedo-boats. But there was little to fear from German aircraft, whose only armament was the small arms carried by the crews.

Even with such relatively ineffective weapons, the Allied pusher aircraft had an advantage over the German tractor types for their gunners had a much less restricted field of fire. This was even more marked when, in late 1914, the French began to arm their Voisin bombers with machine-guns carried by the gunner/observer seated in front of the pilot. These would have been more effective still had they not been the heavy Hotchkiss 8-mm type, which hampered the plane's performance and were difficult to operate in the air. Nevertheless they were more than a match for the German aircraft and during the early period of 1915, French bombers were virtually unmolested as they raided German targets.

Wider fire power
Meanwhile, a better and lighter air-cooled machine-gun had been designed by Col Isaac Newton Lewis of the US Army, and experiments in its use were made as early as August 1914 by individual pilots such as Lt L. A. Strange of No. 5 Squadron RFC. Simple mountings were devised to enable the observer of a two-seater – or even the pilot of a single-seater – to fire over the side of the cockpit. This meant that an enemy plane had to be approached in a crab-like manner to make it a suitable target, but many victories were obtained in

this way, and aerial fighting became commonplace. An even more successful method in the case of single-seaters was to mount a machine-gun above the centre section of the top wing, so that it could be fired forwards above the propeller arc by means of a cable attached to the trigger.

This period of German docility, which gave the Allies supremacy in the air, came to an end in the spring of 1915 when the more powerful C-class planes of Rumpler, Albatros and Aviatik design came into service. These were armed with a Parabellum machine-gun, fired by the observer, who now sat behind the pilot so that he had a wider field of fire. It was now the turn of the slower pusher aeroplanes to suffer since they were blind from behind. The French followed the German example, but inexplicably, the British retained the old seating arrangement and the standard Farnborough-designed BE types of the RFC began to suffer disastrous losses. With the Germans fighting back, the Allied bombers no longer always got through.

An even greater blow to the Allies came in the summer of 1915 when the German single-seat Fokker monoplane (*Eindekker*) appeared. It was armed with a machine-gun placed directly in front of the pilot, and synchronised to fire between the blades of the revolving propeller. The aircraft itself could now be aimed at a target, making it much more effective than the free-swinging weapon that the observers on two-seater aircraft had to use. In spite of the lead that might have been achieved by the French, who had been the first to fit deflectors to propeller blades, and similar ideas that had been put forward and rejected in Britain, Allied fighter aircraft were not fitted with gun synchronising gear until 1916. The winter of 1915–1916 saw the Fokker achieving such supremacy in the skies above the Western Front that British pilots were angrily labelled 'Fokker fodder'.

Increasingly, the Allied bomber squadrons had to call on the faster and better armed single-seat scouts to provide fighter escorts, which severely restricted their range. To give themselves better protection the French bomber units developed the idea of formation flying, first realised by the remarkable Capitaine Happe of *Escadrille MF29* and later adopted by the British, while more and more raids had to be carried out at night, reducing the effectiveness of the bombing. By the autumn of 1915 it was apparent to the military leaders of all the combatant powers that air power was an important new element in warfare. Reconnaissance was still its most useful function, especially in view of the growing use of photography. But it was equally important to deny the enemy similar facilities for reconnaissance, and this involved not only fighters to patrol the battle zone, but also bombers to raid the enemy's airfields and bomb his planes on the ground.

The fighters had advanced considerably with the development of fast and manoeuvrable single-seat aircraft armed with machine-guns. But the bombers, by and large, were still the general purpose types which had been in existence when the war began. It was now necessary to design bombers especially adapted to the task, with the defensive armament to take on fighters. From this point onwards, the story of air warfare became a continual struggle, both in the air and on the drawing board, between bomber and fighter aircraft.

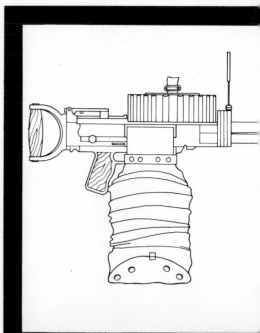

LEWIS ·303-in MACHINE-GUN

Invented by Col Isaac Newton Lewis of the US Army and adopted early in the war as their standard light machine gun by both the British Army and the RFC – and later by the French and Belgian forces. Gas-operated and fed at first by 47-round revolving drums – later by 97-round drums. For aerial use, a cartridge-case deflector and receptacle was provided to prevent ejected cartridges damaging the aeroplane, and electric heaters prevented freezing-up at height. Rate of fire was increased by 1918 to 850 rounds per minute

PARABELLUM 7.92-mm MACHINE-GUN

Weight: 22 lb **Cyclic rate:** 700 rpm

The most widely-used observers' machine gun in German aircraft from early 1915 until the end of the war. A lightweight form of Maxim with a firing rate of 700 rounds per minute, and a water-jacket slotted for air cooling in later models

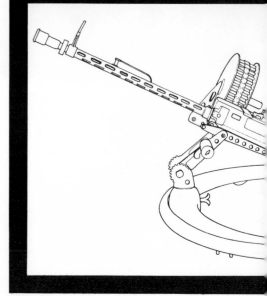

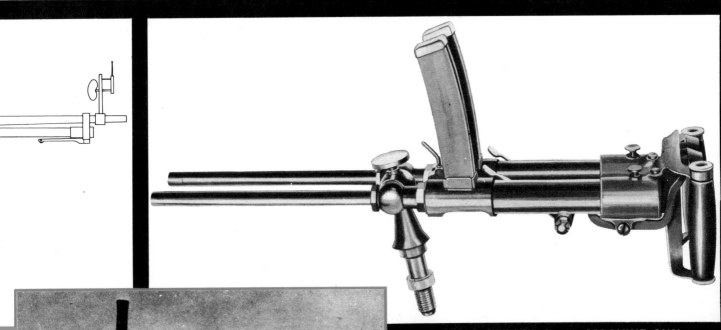

VILLA PEROSA 9-mm MACHINE-GUN

Weight: 8 lb approx. **Length:** 35·5 in **Calibre:** 9 mm
Magazine: RD.S **Muzzle velocity:** 1,250 fps **Cyclic rate:** 900 rpm

Double-barrelled machine-gun invented by Major B. A. Revelli, primarily for use in Italian aircraft, but not really suitable because of the lack of striking power of it's pistol-type ammunition. This was in spite of an extremely high rate of fire — 1,500 rounds per minute from each barrel, firing separately or simultaneously

British 3:6-in QF self-propelled anti-aircraft gun (left), developed during 1917–18. A very promising weapon but the war ended before it saw service

HOTCHKISS 8-mm MACHINE-GUN

This gas-operated air-cooled machine gun, fed by a belt wound round a drum and holding 25 rounds, was the most commonly-used type in French aircraft until 1915/16. It was replaced by the Lewis

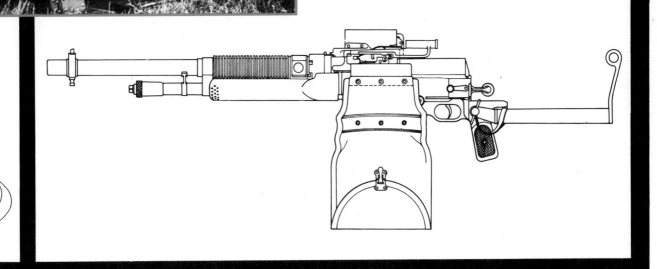

THE BOMBS

During the course of the First World War the shape of the bomb was modified to ensure stable and predictable flight. Bomb-fusing mechanisms and special bomb-release gear were developed, and more powerful aircraft were introduced to carry increasingly heavy loads. The bomb was developed into a devastating weapon

Hardly less important than the planes themselves were the bombs they carried and the techniques employed to drop them with some degree of accuracy. Both made very great advances during the war, to the point where high-explosive and incendiary bombs were beginning to resemble the weapons used to such devastating effect in the Second World War, and bomb-sights were taking into account not merely height and airspeed but also wind velocity and drift when flying across wind. Special telescopic sights were also developed for night raids.

The idea of launching a bomb from the air dated back to the early days of lighter-than-air craft and with the arrival of the Zeppelin as a practical means of bombing, the Germans in 1912 developed the first bomb intended specifically for aircraft use. This was the APK (Artillery Test Commission), a spherical cast-iron shell filled with high explosive and detonated by an impact fuse. It was produced in 5-kg and 10-kg sizes but was too light for effective aerial use and was not used in the war. From experiments with the APK, the more advanced Carbonit series of bombs was developed, ranging in size from 4·5-kg to 20-kg and widely used by the Germans until late 1915.

A similar type of bomb was designed by F. Martin Hale in 1913 for the RNAS which pioneered British bombing; the RFC possessed no bombs when the war began, since its function had been limited to reconnaissance. The first Hale bomb was a 20-pounder but by early 1915, 10 and 100-lb versions were being manufactured by the Cotton Powder Company and used by both the RNAS and RFC.

The Carbonit and Hale bombs represented the first attempts to modify the external shape to give stable and predictable flight. Both were pear-shaped and had tail-fins, although the Carbonit merely had a tin cylinder attached by stays which failed to provide sufficient accuracy in aiming at a target. The Carbonit did however have a steel-tipped nose for better penetration; this was one of the aims of later bombs which had a more streamlined shape, based on a study of ballistics.

From the beginning, one of the main problems was to ensure that bombs could be carried safely and jettisoned if necessary without exploding, but that when aimed at a target, they would arm themselves when

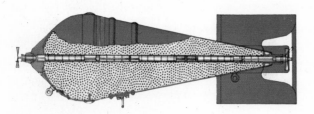

H.E.R.L. 520-lb

Actual weight: 525 lb **Case:** 180 lb **Explosive:** 340 lb **Case material:** steel **Dimensions:** 5 ft 1 in long × 1 ft 7½ in wide **Fuse:** nose and tail fuses

H.E.R.L. 16-lb

Actual weight: 16 lb **Case:** 9 lb **Explosive:** 7 lb **Case material:** M S steel **Dimensions:** 25·15 in long × 5 in dia. **Fuse:** tail fuse

H.E. 'HALE' 20-lb

Actual weight: 18·5 lb **Case:** 14 lb **Explosive:** 4·5 lb Amatol **Case material:** steel **Dimensions:** 23¼ in long × 5 in wide **Fuse:** tail fuse

FRENCH BOMB MADE FROM
75-mm SHELL AND TIN FIN

The French, early exponents and innovators of artillery, regarded bombing as essentially an extension of artillery, and it was not surprising that most of their bombs were modified artillery shells. This was one of the best and most widely used throughout the war

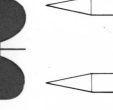

RANKEN ANTI-PERSONNEL
DARTS (flèchettes)

Approx 5 in long and made of steel, they were dropped from canisters each containing 500 darts. On reaching ground from 5,000 ft, they attained the speed of a rifle bullet

falling and detonate on impact. This led to a great deal of work on fuses, carried out all through the war. There was an analogy with artillery shells, which also had to be safe when transported and handled and had to withstand the shock of discharge from a gun without premature detonation, and yet still remain in a condition to function on impact. The advantage with the artillery shell was that the large translational and rotational forces arising on discharge could be used to arm the fuse. These forces were so great that fuses could be designed without any detachable safety devices. Aircraft bombs on the other hand were not subject to such forces on release and other means had to be found to arm their fuses.

After the initial use of steel darts and small Aasen bombs of Danish origin, the French solved this problem in 1915 by equipping their daybombing units with artillery shells fitted with tail-fins, a logical development since they regarded bombing basically as an extension of artillery. The most commonly used shells were 75, 90 and 155 mm calibre. Later in the war, more conventional bombs were manufactured by the French, such as the Gros-Andreau type made in 22, 55 and 110-lb sizes. But they were much less interested than the Germans or the British in the concept of strategic bombing with heavy bombers and had no need of larger bombs. In consequence, the modified 75-mm artillery shell became the most widely used and successful of the

French bombs, used right until the end of the war.

Before considering the development of bomb fuses, carried on mainly in Germany and Britain, it is first necessary to describe the nature and components of the high-explosive bomb of the First World War. All such bombs contained three different types of explosive. The main bursting charge was some safe and insensitive explosive such as TNT or amatol. Amatol was the most commonly used in the early stages of the war but thereafter, bomb fillings followed the development of explosives in general. The bursting charge could only be detonated by a violent explosion and therefore an exploder was required, usually tetryl which resembled TNT but was more sensitive. The exploder was set off by a detonator containing fulminate of mercury. This explosive was highly sensitive and had to be handled with extreme care. The exploder and detonator were fitted into the bomb before loading it into an aircraft. When the bomb hit the ground, the detonator was hit by a striking pin, igniting the exploder which, in turn, exploded the bursting charge.

In the case of the early Carbonit and Hale bombs, the fusing mechanism was armed by means of a small propeller mounted in the tail which unwound a spindle inside the bomb during flight and allowed the striker to come into contact with the detonator on impact with the ground. Thus the bomb was

not fused until the airscrew had been turned a certain number of times. In later, more sophisticated bombs, this meant that the distance they had to fall before becoming armed could be predetermined. A clip was attached as a safety device to prevent the propeller turning while in the aircraft, and this had to be removed before release. This was done by hand with the early bombs, which were carried loose on the floor of the cockpit and dropped over the side. But they rolled about on the cockpit floor and tended to get under the pilot's feet, interfering with the controls. A crude method of overcoming this was to carry two bombs, one attached to either end of a length of rope slung over the fuselage in front of the cockpit; the pilot released them by simply cutting the rope with a knife.

When special bomb release gear was developed for carrying bombs in racks, at first externally and later in bomb bays inside the aircraft, safety devices could either be removed by the automatic trigger mechanism on release, or retained if the bombs had to be jettisoned without exploding.

The propeller type of fuse in various forms was used in all the British bombs manufactured in wartime. From late 1914, the Royal Laboratory at Woolwich began designing a series of bombs, ranging in size from 16 lb to 550 lb, while during 1915–1916, the Royal Aircraft Factory also developed a range up to 585 lb for the larger aircraft then coming

H.E. COOPER 20-lb

Actual weight: 24 lb **Case:** 20 lb **Explosive:** 4 lb Amatol **Case material:** steel **Dimensions:** 24·4 in long × 5·1 in wide **Fuse:** nose fuse

H.E. RAF 336-lb

Actual weight: 336 lb **Explosive:** 70 lb compressed TNT **Case material:** cast steel **Dimensions:** 6 ft 9⅛ in long × 14 in dia. **Fuse:** nose fuse

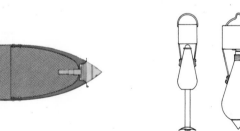
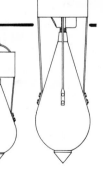

GERMAN 300-kg P.u.W.

Actual weight: 300 kg **Case:** steel **Dimensions:** 2,750 mm long × 365 mm diameter. **Fuse:** nose fuse

Its offset fins gave this bomb high speed rotation for penetration

CARBONIT H.E. BOMBS

A group of German bombs, left to right: 4·5 kg; 10 kg; 20 kg; 50 kg

into use. The 20-lb Hale became obsolete towards the end of the war and was replaced by the 20-lb Cooper bomb. Two main classes of fuse were developed and used in accordance with the type of target being attacked. The nose fuse had the arming propeller in the nose of the bomb and, since the striker spindle was the first portion to hit the ground, the explosion was instantaneous on impact so that the bomb did not enter the ground. Only a shallow crater was formed while fragments of the bomb were scattered over a wide area. In consequence, it was generally desirable to use nose fuses with thick case bombs to attack personnel and light targets such as road transport, aeroplanes on the ground, and military equipment. The weight of the case was sometimes three or four times the weight of the explosive it carried.

The tail fuse, on the other hand, involved a delayed action since the fuse was some distance from the exploder; the delay was at least 1/20th of a second but could be set to as long as 15 seconds. Even the smallest delay caused tail fuse bombs to bury themselves in the ground before exploding, producing a considerable crater but scattering no fragments. This type of bomb therefore was used with a light case where violent local destruction was needed, in attacking railways or buildings for instance. In this example the weight of the explosive carried could be up to 50 per cent more than the weight of the case.

Faulty fuses

Although each type of fuse had its particular advantages, it was not uncommon for bombs to fail to explode because of a faulty fuse mechanism. Another problem was the general shortage of steel which meant that some bombs had to be made of cast iron which was liable to break up on impact with hard surfaces before the tail fuse could operate. For this reason, many of the British bombs were fitted with both nose and tail fuses so that at least some result would be obtained if one failed to operate. Heavy and light case bombs were manufactured in varying sizes, the given weight including both the casing and the explosive material.

By the end of the war, four main types had become standard. These were the small 20-lb heavy case Cooper bomb, the medium 50-lb heavy case RL Mk IV, the large 112-lb heavy case RL Mks VI and VII, and the large 230-lb light case RFC. Heavier bombs such as the 550-lb heavy case RL Mk I/N were occasionally used during the last year of the war and a special series of heavy SN bombs was developed for the large Handley-Page bombers, ranging from 1,600-lb to 1,800-lb and finally to 3,360-lb. This last could only be carried by the V/1500 Handley-Page, although it was not, in fact, used.

The early German Carbonit bombs also used the propeller-actuated firing pistol but in 1915 the *Prüfanstalt und Werft der Fliegertruppe* (Test Establishment and Workshop of the Air Service) co-operated with the Görz company at Friedenau, already manufacturing bomb sights for use in Zeppelins, to produce a new type of bomb. The PuW bomb, as it became known, had a streamlined torpedo shape to give it better aerodynamic performance and was in many respects the true prototype of the modern aircraft bomb. It was made of high-grade steel rather than cast iron, which gave it superior penetration power. But of more

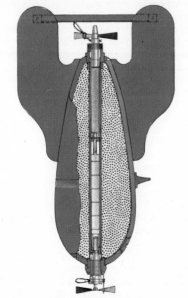

H.E.R.L. 112-lb **Actual weight**: 106 lb **Case**: 79 lb **Explosive**: 27 lb **Case material**: Cast steel **Dimensions**: 29·1 in long×9 in dia. **Fuse**: nose or tail fuse

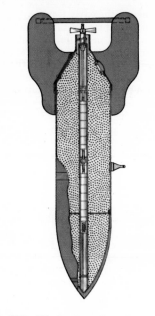

H.E. RFC 230 lb **Actual weight**: 230 lb **Explosive**: 140 lb **Case**: 90 lb **Case material**: Steel **Dimensions**: 50½ in long×10 in dia. **Fuse**: tail fuse

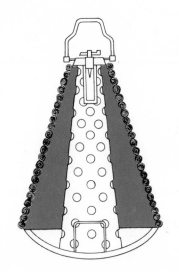

ROPE BOUND INCENDIARY with inertia fuse. The detonating material (in the perforated brass centre tube) and incendiary material around it only had to burn through rope – not a metal case

significance were the slanting fins fitted to the tail which gave a rotary motion to the bomb as it fell. In this way the fuses could be armed by centrifugal force instead of propeller devices, in a similar way to artillery fuses.

Unlike most Allied bombs at that time – which were carried vertically in racks either under the wing or fuselage in the case of British aircraft, or on the fuselage sides as favoured by the French – the PuW bombs could be suspended horizontally in racks, under the wing or fuselage at first and later in bomb bays inside the aircraft. This lessened wind resistance. A PuW type of bomb was also used in the latter part of the war by the Austro-Hungarian air services while the Italians used a light torpedo with thin casing for anti-personnel attacks and a heavy mine type with thick casing for raids on buildings.

The first incendiary

Incendiary bombs were also developed during the war, particularly by the Germans. These bombs, generally around 20 to 40 lb in weight, were in an entirely different category from high explosives and could be said to date back to the 'Greek fire' of ancient times, with aircraft outclassing all previous methods of launching them. The early British incendiaries were filled with petrol, carcass or black powder, with a propeller-actuated fuse firing a Very Cartridge. They were of little practical use, but a 40-lb phosphorous incendiary introduced in the last year of the war was more successful, often employed against kite balloons as the time fuse could be set to ignite at any height above ground and spread a shower of burning phosphorus over a circle of about 250 yards diameter.

The first French incendiaries were also phosphorus-filled but other fillings such as a mixture of celluloid, paraffin and resin, or cotton, potassium and resin were later developed. German incendiaries were first of all filled with petrol, kerosene and liquid tar, a highly inflammable mixture which was only loaded into the bomb shortly before take-off. This was later succeeded by a mixture of benzol, tar and thermite which burned at temperatures as high as 3,000°C. And by 1918, Germany had developed an even more advanced bomb of which the body itself, made of magnesium, formed the main incendiary material. This magnesium bomb weighed about 2 kg and was used mainly for anti-personnel attacks. A bomb rack containing twenty such bombs could be fitted to any two-seater aircraft.

As the war progressed, more powerful aircraft were introduced which could carry increasingly heavy bomb loads, from the 50 lb of the 1914 Maurice Farman and RE8 to the 4,500 lb load which could be carried by the Zeppelin-Staaken of 1918. It was, of course, with the later heavy bombers in mind that the larger sizes of high explosive bombs were designed, primarily by the British and Germans for strategic raids on each other's cities. But in practice, the big bombers usually carried a larger number of small size bombs rather than one giant bomb. One reason was the difficulty of loading and carrying such a weapon, but there was also the problem of being able to aim it with sufficient accuracy to make it worth risking an aircraft for a single bomb. The more bombs that could be dropped, even small ones, the better the chance that at least some would hit the target.

THE BOMB-SIGHTS

The first bomb-sights were very primitive, and more sophisticated methods were vital. With increasing understanding of bombing theory the sights of large bombers were developed to take account of the height of aircraft above the target, its airspeed and the wind velocity. Telescopic sights were introduced for night use, and the Germans devised an automatic-release mechanism

In the early days of the war, when bombs were mostly dropped by hand, the pilots had two advantages which partly made up for the lack of any mechanical sighting mechanism. Because of little opposition, except gunfire from the ground and even that was not well organised to begin with, they could fly by day and at sufficiently low altitudes to give a good visual appreciation of the target. They learned to make allowance for the effect of the speed of their aircraft on the trajectory of the bombs and from this experience, the first elementary system of sighting used by the Allies was simply three nails driven into the side of the aircraft, to be lined-up on a target.

Another simple method was to dive the aircraft at a target which gave the pilot a better view and increased the stability of the plane itself, making for a more accurate drop. This should not be confused with the specialised technique of dive-bombing

which was developed after the war, but it was a step in that direction.

As fighter aircraft were developed, and defences improved, more sophisticated methods of sighting were essential. German bomb-sights were initially the most advanced because of the thought that had been given to the Zeppelin as a bomber. Even before the war, the Zeiss optical firm had produced a telescopic device of this kind, intended for operation at altitudes higher than most aircraft could then fly. This sight was adopted for use in aircraft by the German Air Service and by 1916 it had been improved to take account of the fact that aircraft flew faster than airships. The observer noted with a stop-watch the time it took for a landmark on the ground to pass across a certain part of the sight and could set the sight at the correct aim by relating this to his altitude, based on a predetermined table of scales. A special Görz telescopic sight was devised for night use, protruding through the cockpit floor in some aircraft. Towards the end of the war, the Görz-Borjkow sight was introduced. By means of a built-in clockwork mechanism, this automatically determined the correct moment at which to release a bomb.

The first British bomb-sight was simply an arrangement of nails and wire, not dissimilar from that devised by Lt Scott of the US Navy in 1912, and evolved soon after the outbreak of war by Lt R. B. Bourdillon of No. 6 Squadron RFC. As a result, he was sent to the Central Flying School at Upavon and co-operated in designing the CFS bomb-sight which became standardised in the RFC and RNAS and remained in service until the end of 1917. Like the German Görz sight, it ascertained the speed of an aircraft by means of a stop-watch to measure the time taken for a landmark to pass two sightings, and the foresight was moved along a time-scale to obtain the correct angle for bomb-dropping.

A similar system was adopted by the French in 1915 with the Dorand and Lafay sights. By the following year it was general practice for sights to be mounted internally and viewed through glass panels in the floor, either in the nacelle of pusher or twin-engined aircraft, or in the rear cockpit of two-seaters for use by the observer or gunner.

More scientific

During the last eighteen months of the war, bomb-sights became vastly more complicated as more was understood about the theory of bombing. Sights fitted to the large bombers could take account of the height of an aircraft above the target, its airspeed, the wind velocity, and the amount of drift when flying across the wind. First spirit levels and then gyrostats were used to level the sight. In the case of single-seater aircraft, more simple sights were devised which the pilot could view through the floor of the cockpit but these did not give a high degree of accuracy. Usually they were calibrated for use only at three heights – about 6,000 ft, 10,000 ft and 15,000 ft – and the pilot had to guess the wind direction and velocity. This could either be done from a previous knowledge of the weather forecast – not reliable when flying above cloud where the wind could be blowing in a reverse direction from that on the ground – or by watching the smoke bursts of shells fired from the ground.

Left: A negative-lens bomb-sight calibrated for use at three heights. Aircraft must fly at a predetermined height for each of these altitude readings: 6,000 ft = 90 mph; 10,000 ft = 80 mph; 15,000 ft = 70 mph. Above: A detail of the calibration plate. Below: A bomb-sight installed in a DH 4 fuselage

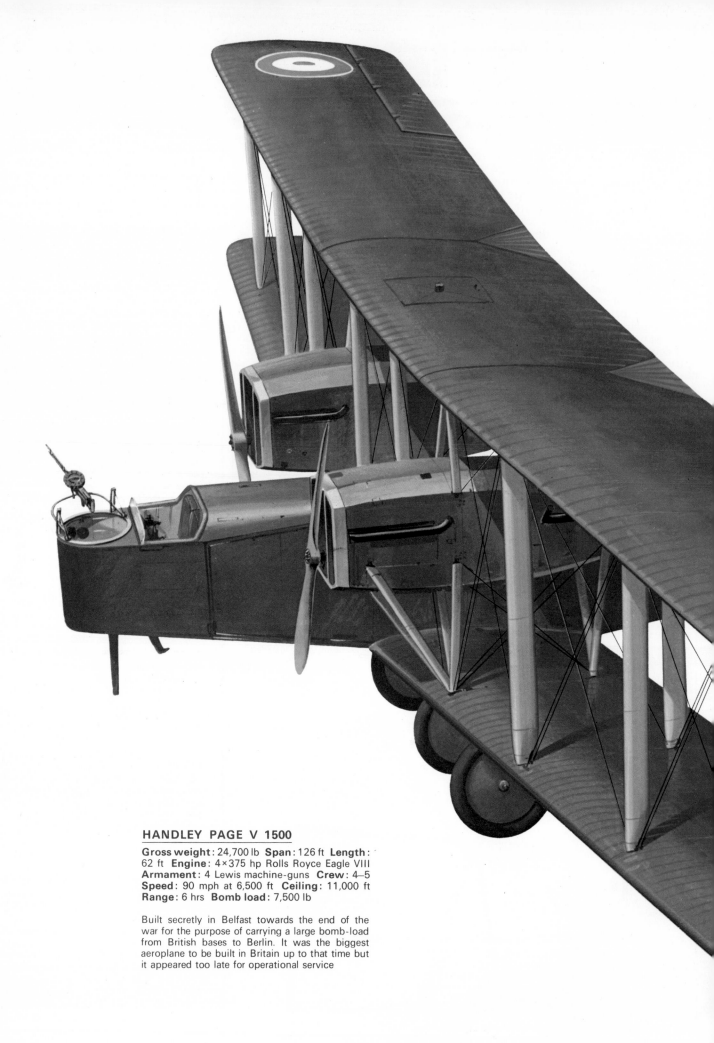

HANDLEY PAGE V 1500

Gross weight: 24,700 lb **Span:** 126 ft **Length:** 62 ft **Engine:** 4×375 hp Rolls Royce Eagle VIII **Armament:** 4 Lewis machine-guns **Crew:** 4–5 **Speed:** 90 mph at 6,500 ft **Ceiling:** 11,000 ft **Range:** 6 hrs **Bomb load:** 7,500 lb

Built secretly in Belfast towards the end of the war for the purpose of carrying a large bomb-load from British bases to Berlin. It was the biggest aeroplane to be built in Britain up to that time but it appeared too late for operational service

THE HEAVIES

The first bombers were little more than general purpose aircraft
adapted to carry indifferent bomb-loads. But in order to carry out
the growing number of strategic raids against effective fighter
opposition, armament, speed, range and ceiling all had to be
increased. The first country to develop large, multi-engined
bombers was Russia, but by 1916 most of the major powers were
working on their own 'heavies'

The first multi-engined heavy bombers to be used in the war were the Russian Il'ya Muromets with which the Squadron of Flying Ships of the Russian Imperial Air Service was equipped at the end of 1914. Operations started in February 1915 with raids on towns and military targets in East Prussia, well inside the Muromets' combat range of about 300 miles. Among the successful attacks was the destruction of the German seaplane base on Angern Lake and the virtual obliteration of the HQ of the German Commander-in-Chief, General von Bulow, at Shavli in Lithuania.

These bombers were tough enough to take considerable punishment and still keep flying, helped by specially designed fire-proof fuel tanks and some metal-plate protection under the pilot's cabin. The heavy armament they carried, normally three machine-guns, with up to seven on some models, was usually more than a match for the German fighters of the period. The Muromets were also equipped with excellent bomb-sights which gave them an average of 75 per cent successful hits on target. If it had not been for constant maintenance problems and difficulties in obtaining engines and spare parts, the Russian bombing offensive would have been even more effective. As it was, the morale of the German aircrews fell to a very low ebb when it seemed that nothing could prevent the Muromets getting through. It was in an effort to inspire morale that Oswald Boelcke, the German fighter ace who had become a national hero after scoring eighteen victories in France, was sent on a tour of the Eastern Front in the spring of 1916. But not until 12 September of that year was the first and only Muromets brought down in air combat – and only after it had shot down three of its opponents and damaged a fourth.

Enclosed cockpits

The first Muromets type to enter operational service was the IM-B, which carried a crew of four – pilot, co-pilot, bombing officer and air mechanic – in completely enclosed accommodation with glazed window panels in the nose and fuselage sides. Its bomb load was 1,120 lb and three machine-guns were mounted in the fuselage sides for shooting at ground targets. It was powered by two 200 hp and two 135 hp Salmson radial engines. The next and most widely used type was the IM-V which had a smaller wing span and 150 hp Sunbeam liquid-cooled engines, originally bought from England and later made under licence. The bomb load was increased by 600 lb.

As a result of the introduction of armed fighters by the Germans, the defensive armament of the later types, the IM-G1, G2 and G3, was increased to include machine-guns mounted on the upper wing section, under the fuselage, and in the nose and tail, for which the crew was increased to seven: two pilots, one navigator, one mechanic and three gunners. The wing chord was also increased and the 2,000 lb bomb load was stored internally and the bombs dropped either vertically or horizontally.

Largest of the Muromets was the IM-YeA, with a wing span of 113 ft 2¼ in and a gross weight of 15,432 lb, but it was not put into production. A few of the slightly smaller IM-YeI were built, armed with seven machine-guns and powered by four 220 hp Renault engines. Although the Muromets crews were the élite of the Russian Air

CAPRONI Ca 5

Gross weight: 11,700 lb **Span:** 77 ft **Length:** 41 ft 4 in **Engine:** 3×300 hp Fiat **Armament:** 2 machine-guns **Crew:** 3 **Speed:** 95 mph at ground level **Ceiling:** 15,000 ft **Range:** 4 hrs **Bomb load:** 1,188 lb

With the Ca 5 series in 1917, Caproni returned to a biplane configuration after the Ca 4 triplane. Widely used as a day and night bomber in 1918

Service, the plane itself was not easy to fly and considerable training was required before crews could be sent to the Front. About half of the eighty IMs built were used for training purposes. Most of the machines were destroyed by their crews after the Revolution and the German invasion to prevent them falling into enemy hands, but a few remained to inaugurate passenger services in Russia after the Civil War.

The next country to introduce large bombers into service was Italy, following its declaration of war against Austria-Hungary on 24 May 1915. These were the Caproni series, based on the original pre-war design of the Ca 31, but modified considerably as the war progressed. The first to enter operational service, in August 1915, was the Ca 32 biplane, powered by three 100 hp Fiat liquid-cooled engines. Its range of 340 miles enabled it to be used for strategic bombing attacks, but as the Austrian fighters improved in performance, the Ca 32 later had to be relegated to night bombing.

Meanwhile the most widely used type, the Ca 33, came into service towards the end of 1916 with a higher maximum speed of 94 mph. The two pilots sat side-by-side in the centre fuselage, a gunner operated a

Revelli machine-gun from the nose position, and a fourth crew member in the rear cockpit operated up to three similar guns, fixed to fire in different directions.

The Ca 3 series, as they were designated, were all biplanes but with the next (Ca 4) series, starting with the Ca 40, a triplane design was used with huge 100 ft wings. The main production model was the Ca 42, powered by three 270 hp Fiat, Isotta-Fraschini or American Liberty engines. It was a sturdy and reliable plane with a combat range of seven hours, and could carry a bomb load of 3,910 lb, made up of small bombs mounted externally under the bottom plane. But its size and relatively low speed made it an easy target for enemy fighters, and it was reserved for night-bombing operations. For the next (Ca 5) generation Caproni returned to a biplane layout and these were beginning to replace the Ca 3 series when the war ended.

Semi-rigid airships and smaller bombers were also used by the Italians throughout the war but by far the greatest bombing effort was made by the Capronis. The first raids, beginning at the end of August 1915, were against military targets to the rear of the Austrian armies, such as railways, supply depots, troop concentrations and

especially airfields. Tactical operations remained the prime objective of the Italian Air Service until the end of the war but early in 1916, mainly at the instigation of Gabriele d'Annunzio, long-range strategic raids were undertaken.

Daylight attacks

The Capronis did not have the range to reach Vienna, 260 miles from their main base at Pordenone, but targets were available some 100 miles away across the Adriatic, such as the Austro-Hungarian naval base at Pola and the industrial city and seaport of Trieste. Daylight attacks were made on these and other strategic targets, at first by Capronis flying in formation but later escorted by Italian-built Nieuports. One of the biggest raids was made on 2 October 1917 by nearly 150 Capronis and eleven flying-boats on the naval base at Pola. As a result of the Caporetto disaster later in the month, however, when the Pordenone base was captured by the Austrians after the Italian retreat, strategic bombing became too much of a luxury and for the rest of the war the Caproni squadrons concentrated on tactical operations, mainly against Austrian airfields. A number of American pilots were

attached to Caproni units to gain experience in bombing operations.

Just as the first British efforts at bombing were pioneered by the RNAS, so the first British heavy bomber was developed by the Admiralty for use by the navy's Air Arm. Following the success of the RNAS raids on Zeppelin sheds towards the end of 1914, the Air Department of the Admiralty was convinced of the value of air bombardment and laid plans for the creation of a strategic bombing force that could operate at long range from bases in France and England. There were, of course, no planes then available for such a purpose and engines were too scarce in 1914 and 1915 for a twin-engined layout to be attempted. As an interim measure a single-engined bomber was ordered from Sopwith, resulting in the introduction of the 1½ Strutter, while the Short company developed a single-engined landplane from their successful Short 184 seaplane. In the meantime, Captain (later Rear Admiral) Murray Sueter, Director of the Air Department, issued a specification for a large twin-engined aircraft capable of extended patrols over the sea.

The challenge appealed to Sir Frederick Handley Page who set about designing such a bomber, powered by two 120 hp Beardmore

engines. So impressed was Murray Sueter with the design that he asked Handley Page to improve on it in order to produce a 'bloody paralyser' of an aeroplane. The result was the Handley Page 0/100 biplane, one of the most famous bombers of the war, which went into service in November 1916. It was intended to have two 150 hp Sunbeam engines but as construction progressed so did work by Rolls Royce on two engines which were to become the renowned Eagle and Falcon. Both were water-cooled twelve-cylinder Vee types, the Eagle being the largest. This was chosen for the 0/100, its horsepower de-rated from 300 to 250 to increase reliability. They were enclosed in armoured nacelles, each with a separate armoured fuel tank. Unusual features included the facility for folding the huge 100-foot wings, so that the aircraft could be stored in canvas field hangars, and a biplane tail unit.

The crew of three sat in a cabin which was originally intended to be enclosed with bullet-proof glass and armour plate, but in the production models, the enclosure and much of the armour plate was removed. The maximum bomb load was 2,000 lb, consisting either of a single 1,650-lb bomb or eight 250-lb, sixteen 112-lb, or three 520 or 550-lb bombs. Defensive armament consisted of one or two Lewis guns on a ring-mounting in the nose cockpit, one or two Lewis guns in the upper rear cockpit, and a single Lewis gun mounted to fire rearward and downward through a hole in the fuselage floor just behind the wings.

More stability

While work on the Handley Page 0/100 continued, in the spring of 1916 the RNAS went ahead with the formation of two strategic bombing wings at Luxeuil in Belgium and Dunkirk in France, in preparation for the Sopwith 1½ Strutter and the Short Bomber which had been ordered the previous year. By that time it was apparent that bombers would have to fight their way past defending fighters, in particular the Fokker *Eindekker*. Coincidentally the British had at last developed interrupter gear to enable the fixture of fixed forward-firing machine-guns, either Lewis or the more successful belt-fed Vickers which was later generally adopted.

This gear, originally designed by Lt-Cdr V. V. Dibovsky of the Russian Imperial Navy, and developed by Warrant Officer F. W. Scarff of the Admiralty Air Department (who had also been responsible for designing one of the best ring-mountings of the war for use by observer/gunners) was first installed in the RFCs single-seat Bristol Scout. But the first two-seater to use this synchronised gun was the 1½ Strutter, in addition to the usual free-mounted Lewis gun in the rear cockpit. The Strutter had been designed as a bomber, capable of carrying a 130 lb bomb load with the emphasis laid on stability rather than manoeuvrability. However, its armament made it an excellent fighter as well, especially when German pilots attacked from the front to avoid the observer's gun, only to be met by a deadly hail of fire from the pilot's synchronised Vickers.

With the Battle of the Somme about to begin the RFC was desperately short of fighter aircraft, and after appealing to the RNAS for help, the Admiralty handed over a large number of Strutters for army use, thus delaying its own plans for a strategic bombing offensive against Germany.

The other plane which had been ordered

F9569

H9569

VICKERS VIMY IV

Gross weight: 12,500 lb **Span:** 67 ft 2 in
Length: 43 ft 6 in **Engine:** 2×360 hp Rolls
Royce Eagle VIII **Armament:** 6 Lewis machine-
guns **Crew:** 5–6 **Speed:** 103 mph at ground
level **Ceiling:** 7,000 ft **Range:** 985 miles
Bomb load: 2,476 lb

Initiated in 1917 as a heavy bomber to take part in
Britain's plan for the strategic bombing of Germany, but it arrived too late to see operational
service before the Armistice. After the war, the
Vimy distinguished itself for long-distance flights,
including the first non-stop crossing of the Atlantic
by Captain John Alcock and Arthur Whitten Brown
on 14/15 June 1919

was the Short Bomber, powered by a 250 hp
Rolls Royce engine and with a maximum
bomb load of 920 lb, twice that of the
Caudron G4 which the RNAS also used at
that time. With the introduction of the
Short Bomber in the autumn of 1916,
together with the Caudrons and a few
Strutters, the RNAS began a bombing
offensive against military and industrial
targets in Germany and on German naval
forces at Ostend and Zeebrugge, although
not on the scale that had been planned.

The Short Bomber had a range of over
400 miles, which enabled it to raid targets
far behind the front line, but its maximum
speed was only 77 mph and it was inade-
quately armed, with only a single Lewis gun
on top of the centre-section. Even to reach
that the observer had to climb out of his
cockpit and stand up on the fuselage. In
company with the Caudron bombers, the
Short had to be relegated to night bombing.

With the arrival of the Handley Page
0/100 in November 1916 however, the RNAS
was able to increase its operations. The first
two bombers were delivered to the 5th Wing
at Dunkirk; a third landed by accident
behind the enemy lines and was studied in
great detail by the Germans. The first raids
by the 0/100 were carried out in daylight,
and it proved to be a formidable bomber,
able to carry three times the load of the
Short Bomber and six times that of the DH 4
day-bomber which had also just been
brought into service. In the meantime the
capability of fighter aircraft had also ad-

vanced, and when one of the valuable
Handley Page bombers was brought down
into the sea (admittedly after sinking an
enemy destroyer), the type was used only
for night bombing. Raids were directed
mainly against U-boat bases, railway
centres and airfields, while four aircraft
were brought back to England for anti-
submarine patrols over the North Sea. One
machine made a remarkable flight from
England to the island of Lemnos in the
Aegean Sea, with stops in Paris, Rome and
the Balkans. In June 1917 it bombed the
Turkish capital of Constantinople, but on
a second attempt two months later it came
down into the sea with engine failure and
the crew were taken prisoner, including
the pilot, Flt-Lt J. Alcock (later one of the
first two men to fly the Atlantic non-stop).

New fuel system

In the spring of 1917 the Germans began a
systematic campaign to bomb London and
other targets in England, using large
bomber aircraft far more frightening than
the Zeppelins. In retaliation, the British War
Cabinet decided to launch a strategic
bombing offensive against German cities
and industrial targets. The task was given
to Major General Hugh Trenchard, then
commanding the RFC in France. In October
1917 he formed the 41st Wing at Ochey
from where it was possible to reach German
towns in the Saar, and such cities as Karlsruhe, Mainz, Koblenz, Cologne, Frankfurt
and Stuttgart. In addition to the RFC day-

bombers (FE 2bs and DH 4s), the Wing
included a RNAS squadron of Handley
Page 0/100s for night bombing. These were
more effective than the day-bombers and
led to the development of an improved
version, the 0/400, which became the most
widely used of the Handley Page types;
some 400 were delivered before the end of
the war, compared with less than fifty of
the 0/100.

One of the features of the 0/400 was a
completely redesigned fuel system, in which
the fuel tanks were moved from the engine
nacelles to a position above the bomb-bay,
thus enabling the nacelles to be considerably shortened. The crew consisted of
a pilot who sat in the main cockpit, a bomb-
aimer who doubled as front gunner and
observer from a cockpit in the extreme nose
of the fuselage, and one or two rear gunners
who occupied a cockpit in the mid-section
just behind the wings. The bombs were
suspended nose-upwards in separate honey-
comb cells in the bomb-bay, each covered
by a door which was pushed open by the
weight of the falling bomb and closed by a
spring. The bombs were released by cables
from the nose cockpit where a bomb sight
was mounted externally. One or two Lewis
guns were mounted in both nose and rear
cockpits; in the latter position, one gun was
fired sideways or backwards from a raised
platform while the other, when carried,
could be fired downwards and backwards
through a trapdoor in the floor.

Although starting the war with very

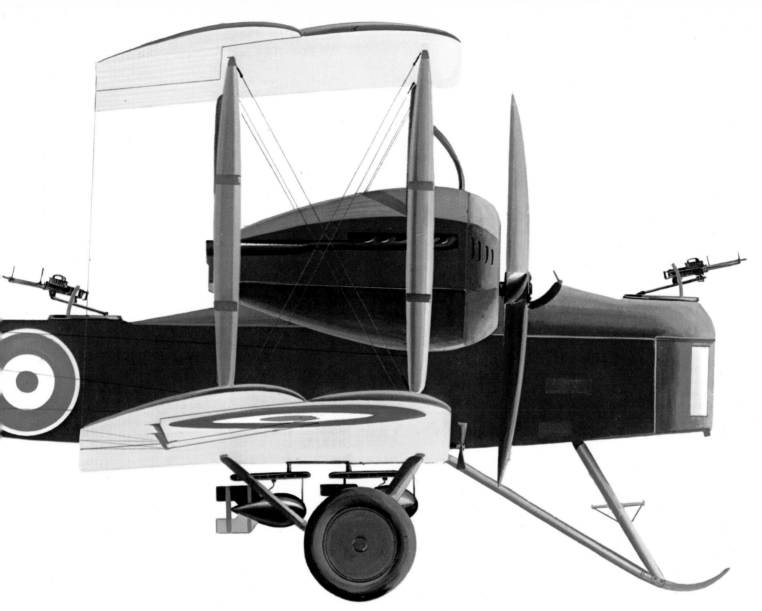

different functions, the RNAS and RFC had come to co-operate with each other for many operations, including Trenchard's strategic bombing wing which was later re-designated the VIII Brigade. During the last two years of the war there was a complete reorganisation of British military aircraft development in which the army followed the navy's policy of leaving aircraft design and manufacture to private industry. The Royal Aircraft Factory at Farnborough (which, in spite of some failures, produced in the SE 5a one of the best Allied fighters of the war) was directed to concentrate solely on research.

On 1 April 1918 the RNAS and RFC were merged into one service, the Royal Air Force, with the prime intention of pooling resources for a sustained strategic bombing campaign against Germany. Under the command of General (later Marshal of the RAF, Viscount) Trenchard, who was directly responsible to the newly formed Air Ministry, the RAF was the world's first major independent air service. On 6 June the strategic bombing wing he had previously commanded became the famous Independent Force of the RAF.

The Handley Page night bombers contributed a large proportion of the 665 tons of bombs dropped by the Independent Force and its predecessors the 41st Wing and VIII Brigade. One daring attack made was on the Badische Anilin factory at Ludwigshafen during the night of 25 August when the two Handley Pages came down to

200 and 500 feet respectively to place their bombs with the greatest accuracy, in spite of the searchlights and heavy anti-aircraft fire. This was no mean hazard by that stage of the war, considering the great advances made in the development of anti-aircraft defences. In raids during a single night the following month, six of the large bombers were brought down by anti-aircraft fire while attacking Saarbrücken and Trier. The five night bombing squadrons which were in operation during the last months of the war suffered eighty-seven crew members killed or missing and 148 aircraft destroyed. In the latter stages, the bombers were often employed against tactical targets to support the Allied offensives, and 220 tons of the bombs dropped were on enemy airfields, destroying many aircraft. From September onwards the Handley Pages often employed 1,650-lb bombs; one dropped on Kaiserlautern wiped out an entire factory.

Great secrecy

In order to carry an even bigger bomb load of 7,500 lb from bases in Britain to Berlin, including a single 3,300-pounder, the Handley-Page V/1500 was built in great secrecy in Belfast. Six had been delivered by the time the Armistice was signed, although none were used operationally. Nevertheless the V/1500 marked a triumph for British aeronautical development, with 126-foot wings which could still be folded, four 375 hp Rolls Royce Eagle VIII engines and a tail gun position which could be reached

by climbing along a cat-walk. With a combat range of 1,200 miles and a maximum speed of just under 100 mph, it showed how far the design of bomber aircraft had advanced since the days of the Avro 504 and symbolised the policy of long-range strategic bombing on which Trenchard set such importance. It was a policy which was continued after the war and culminated in the RAFs mighty Bomber Command striking force of the Second World War. Two other heavy bombers were also developed for use by the Independent Force but, like the V/1500, arrived too late to see operational service. These were the twin-engined three-seater DH 10 Amiens and Vickers Vimy. The Amiens operated as a mail carrier after the war while the Vimy achieved fame with a series of record long distance flights, including the first non-stop crossing of the Atlantic by Alcock and Brown and the first flight from Britain to Australia.

One of the myths of early aviation history was that the Handley Page 0/100 which had been captured after accidentally landing behind German lines in November 1916 was used as a model for Germany's own heavy bombers, the famous Gotha biplanes, which appeared shortly afterwards. This was certainly not true for even before the war German designers including Count von Zeppelin had drawn up plans for multi-engined aircraft. But the main effort was concentrated on building airships, and it was only with the realisation that lighter-than-air craft were too vulnerable that development was pushed ahead on heavy bombers.

Even earlier, however, the Germans had produced twin-engined aircraft which were used as bombers. Late in 1914 the Friedrichshafen company, though mainly concerned with the design and construction of naval seaplanes, built the GI bomber, a twin-engined pusher biplane with a biplane tail unit. This did not enter production, but it did lead to the G II, small numbers of which entered service in late 1916. Powered by two 200 hp Benz engines and able to carry a bomb-load of about 1,000 lb, it had two Parabellum machine-guns for defensive armament, one in the nose and the other in a dorsal position. A larger and more powerful development was the G III, with 260 hp six-cylinder water-cooled Mercedes engines, a monoplane tail unit, and the ability to carry over twice the bomb-load. This was the main production model of the Friedrichshafen G series which entered service in early 1917. It carried a crew of three in the central fuselage area and an interesting feature of its design was the steel-tube frame of the square-section fuselage, covered with wood at the nose and tail and fabric over the central part. Modifications to later models included a return to the biplane tail unit on the G IIIa and tractor propellers on the G IV.

The Friedrichshafen types were generally similar in design to the series of twin-engined bombers produced by the Gothaer company, and together they formed the mainstay of the German bomber units (*Bombengeschwadern*) from 1916 until the end of the war. The principle Gotha types were the G IV and G V and it was their ability to fly at a high altitude – over 20,000 feet – carrying a bomb-load of 1,000 lb in external racks that made them ideal for taking over long-range bombing duties from Zeppelin airships. Another asset was that in addition to the usual machine-gun in the front cockpit, they had a second machine-gun mounted behind the wings, which could fire not only upwards, but also downwards and rearwards beneath the tail, for defence against fighters attacking from behind and below.

Terrifying raids

Although the first aeroplane raid on London took place on 28 November 1916, when a single LVG CII dropped six 22-lb bombs near Victoria, it was the Gotha which introduced a new and terrifying form of warfare by a succession of day and night raids on the city from May 1917 to May 1918. The first attempt, by a formation of twenty-one bombers on 25 May 1917, ended when they had to turn back because of heavy cloud and dropped their bombs on towns in Kent instead, killing nearly one hundred civilians. There was an outcry from the British public who, congratulating themselves that the Zeppelin menace had been overcome, now had to face daylight raids with no warning of the enemy's approach.

Worse was to follow. On 13 June a formation of fourteen Gothas led by Hauptmann Brandenburg circled over London with contemptuous ease, in full view of people watching from below. They dropped nearly one hundred bombs, mostly in the region of Liverpool Street station, killing 162 people and wounding 438 – higher casualties than all the Zeppelin raids had caused, and more than any single bombing attack on Britain during the entire war. Although ninety-two fighter aircraft took off from various parts of England, the bombers were able to fly at an even greater altitude on the way home, lightened of their bombs, and had disappeared by the time the fighters could climb to that height. Not a single bomber was lost in the raid.

In spite of the serious situation in France, where every aircraft was needed, two squadrons of the latest fighters – SE5as and Sopwith Pups – had to be withdrawn to help protect London from bombing. It was this dissipation of the Allied war effort on the Western Front, together with the effect on morale at home, which was the greatest success of the Gotha raids. Gradually, with strengthened fighter units and a complete reorganisation of anti-aircraft gun defences, the British began to take a heavy toll of the Gotha bombers, and in September they were forced to turn to night bombing. By this time they were being supported by the R-class bombers, produced by several different companies, but generally known as Zeppelin Staaken 'Giants'. They were the

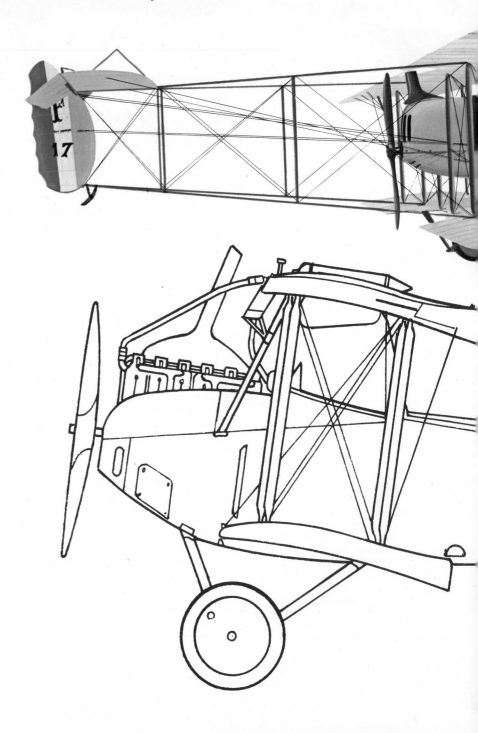

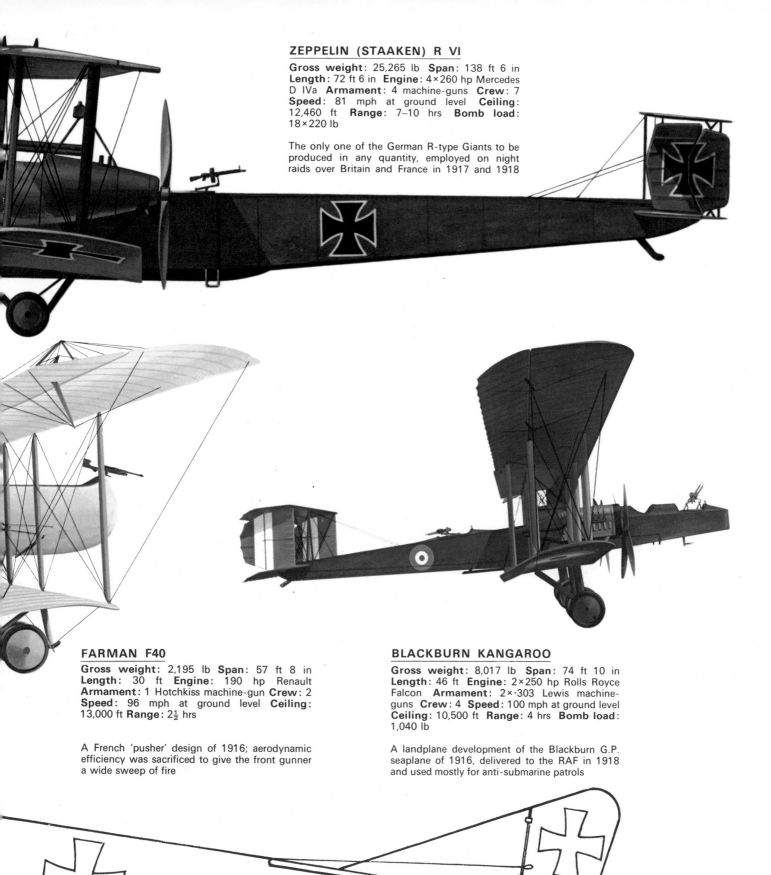

ZEPPELIN (STAAKEN) R VI

Gross weight: 25,265 lb **Span:** 138 ft 6 in
Length: 72 ft 6 in **Engine:** 4×260 hp Mercedes
D IVa **Armament:** 4 machine-guns **Crew:** 7
Speed: 81 mph at ground level **Ceiling:**
12,460 ft **Range:** 7–10 hrs **Bomb load:**
18×220 lb

The only one of the German R-type Giants to be
produced in any quantity, employed on night
raids over Britain and France in 1917 and 1918

FARMAN F40

Gross weight: 2,195 lb **Span:** 57 ft 8 in
Length: 30 ft **Engine:** 190 hp Renault
Armament: 1 Hotchkiss machine-gun **Crew:** 2
Speed: 96 mph at ground level **Ceiling:**
13,000 ft **Range:** 2½ hrs

A French 'pusher' design of 1916; aerodynamic
efficiency was sacrificed to give the front gunner
a wide sweep of fire

BLACKBURN KANGAROO

Gross weight: 8,017 lb **Span:** 74 ft 10 in
Length: 46 ft **Engine:** 2×250 hp Rolls Royce
Falcon **Armament:** 2×·303 Lewis machine-
guns **Crew:** 4 **Speed:** 100 mph at ground level
Ceiling: 10,500 ft **Range:** 4 hrs **Bomb load:**
1,040 lb

A landplane development of the Blackburn G.P.
seaplane of 1916, delivered to the RAF in 1918
and used mostly for anti-submarine patrols

LVG CII

Gross weight: 3,091 lb **Span:** 42 ft 2 in
Length: 26 ft 7 in **Engine:** 160 hp Mercedes
D III **Armament:** 1 or 2×7·92-mm machine-
guns **Crew:** 2 **Speed:** 81 mph at ground level
Ceiling: 10,000 ft **Range:** 4 hrs **Bomb load:**
150 lb

A light bomber, as well as one of the newly-
established C class of armed two-seater reconnaissance aircraft introduced by the Germans at
the end of 1915, this plane is credited with the
first daylight raid on London, which took place in
November 1916

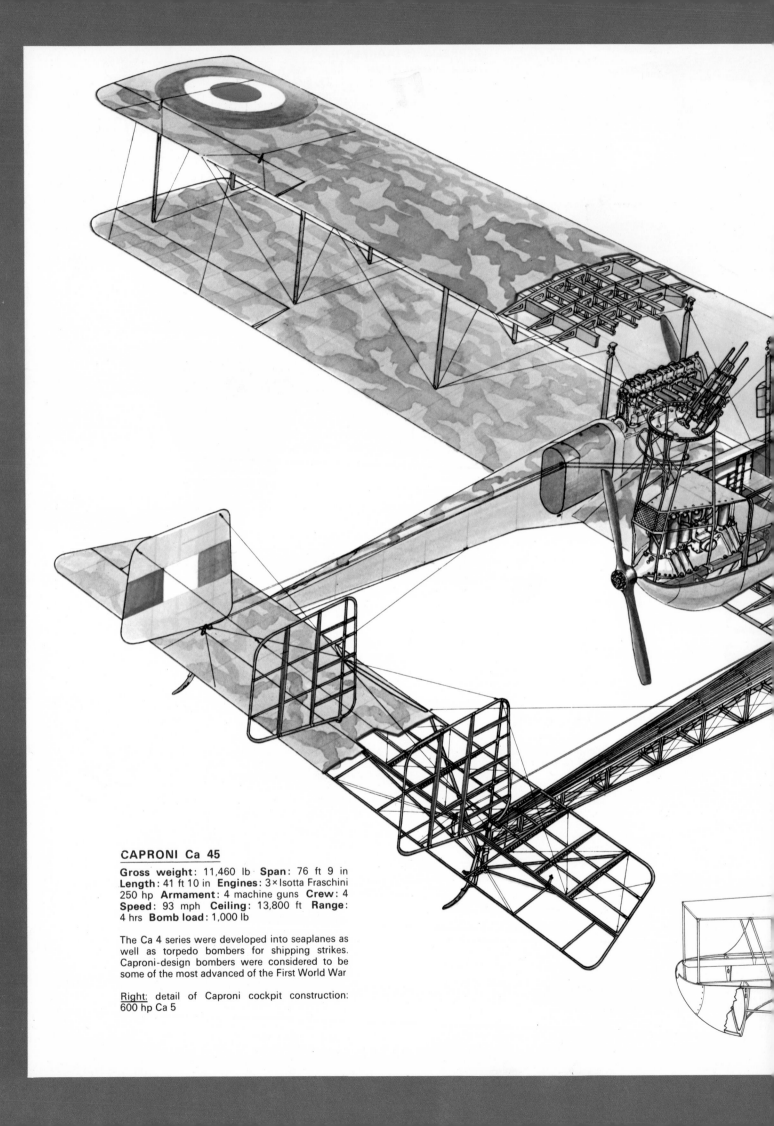

CAPRONI Ca 45

Gross weight: 11,460 lb **Span:** 76 ft 9 in
Length: 41 ft 10 in **Engines:** 3×Isotta Fraschini
250 hp **Armament:** 4 machine guns **Crew:** 4
Speed: 93 mph **Ceiling:** 13,800 ft **Range:**
4 hrs **Bomb load:** 1,000 lb

The Ca 4 series were developed into seaplanes as
well as torpedo bombers for shipping strikes.
Caproni-design bombers were considered to be
some of the most advanced of the First World War

Right: detail of Caproni cockpit construction:
600 hp Ca 5

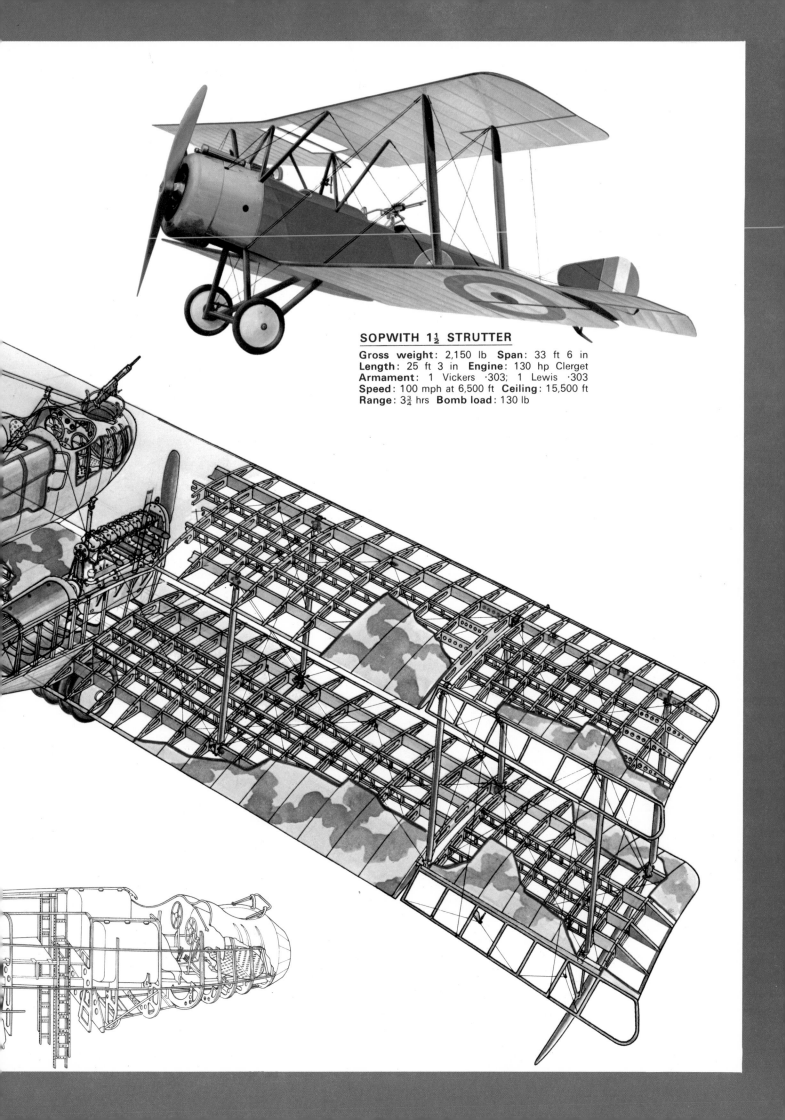

SOPWITH 1½ STRUTTER

Gross weight: 2,150 lb **Span:** 33 ft 6 in
Length: 25 ft 3 in **Engine:** 130 hp Clerget
Armament: 1 Vickers ·303; 1 Lewis ·303
Speed: 100 mph at 6,500 ft **Ceiling:** 15,500 ft
Range: 3¾ hrs **Bomb load:** 130 lb

biggest and in some respects the most remarkable aircraft of the war, and were produced only as single examples or in very small numbers.

The first of these leviathans to appear was the VGO I, with a wing span of over 138 ft, powered by three 240 hp Maybach engines, which flew for the first time in April 1915. The engine power was not sufficient for the huge, nine-ton aircraft and the later VGO III had six 160 hp Mercedes engines instead. Two of these were mounted in tandem in each of the port and starboard nacelles, driving pusher propellers, with the other pair side-by-side in the nose of the fuselage driving a single tractor propeller. After various modifications the R VI appeared in mid-1917 (the 'R' designation standing for *Riesenflugzeug* – giant aeroplane). This was the only type to be produced in any quantity.

The nose-mounted engines were abandoned and instead, four Maybach or Mercedes 260 hp engines were mounted in tandem pairs between the wings, driving tractor and pusher propellers. The nose cockpit was fitted with a machine-gun and the release mechanism for the eighteen 220-lb bombs carried internally. Two guns were located in a dorsal position and another two ventrally. The main cockpit was enclosed and the usual crew was seven. So great was the weight (nearly twelve tons fully loaded) that the undercarriage consisted of no less than eighteen wheels, two of which were under the nose.

In July 1917 the giant R-class bombers were first flown operationally on the Eastern Front, and gained some successes in attacks on railways and military installations. Between August and February the following year they were transferred to the Western Front and used initially for night raids on Britain, usually escorted by Gothas. In eleven such raids, during which single 2,200-lb bombs (the largest used in the war) were occasionally dropped, not one Giant was lost in action. The Gothas were less fortunate however, mainly because pilots of such improved fighters as the Sopwith Camel had learned to fly and intercept at night. After a raid on the night of 19 May 1918, when seven Gothas out of forty-three aircraft sent to attack London and Dover were shot down by fighters and ground fire, the German High Command ordered a stop to the bombing of Britain.

In fifty-two raids on Britain, one more than were carried out by airships, German aircraft achieved a statistically better result, killing 857 people and injuring a further 2,058. Just under £1,500,000 worth of damage was caused for the expenditure of only 2,772 bombs totalling about 196 tons.

Although the loss of life and amount of damage caused was hardly significant compared with what was happening in France, the psychological effect was considerable. This, however, operated to the detriment of Germany, for the anger aroused was directly responsible for retaliatory raids by the British, and was one of the factors which led to the merger of the RNAS and RFC to form the RAF.

The Giants continued to make bombing raids over Paris until those too were stopped. Thereafter they were used singly for tactical attacks on military targets a few miles behind the Allied lines, but it was a serious mishandling of machines that had been developed for long-range strategic bombing. They were too slow and made too big a target to operate successfully in the battle zone, and casualties were very heavy.

A better aircraft for tactical purposes was the other main type of twin-engined bomber built by the Germans, the AEG series.

This was a development of the K I three-seat general purpose biplane of 1915, later re-designated the G I when the Germans decided on the classification *Grossflugzeug* (big aeroplane) for all such types, irrespective of manufacturer. This model was used mainly on the Eastern Front during 1915 and, like the G II which followed, was only built in small numbers. The G III which began to appear in December 1915 carried a 660-lb bomb load and two machine-guns for defence. The major production model however was the G IV which came into service towards the end of 1916, powered by two 260 hp Mercedes engines driving four-blade opposite-rotating propellers. Neither its bomb load of 770 lb, nor its range – about 350 miles against the Gotha's 550 – could compare with those of the Gotha and other big bombers, but its speed of over 100 mph made it very suitable for attacking short-

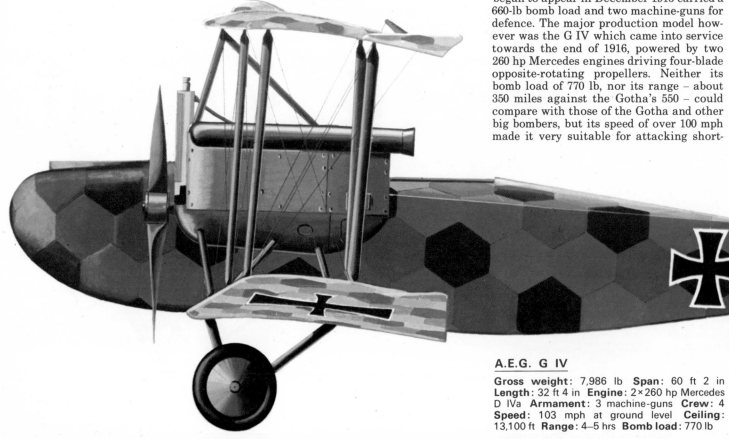

A.E.G. G IV

Gross weight: 7,986 lb **Span:** 60 ft 2 in
Length: 32 ft 4 in **Engine:** 2×260 hp Mercedes D IVa **Armament:** 3 machine-guns **Crew:** 4
Speed: 103 mph at ground level **Ceiling:** 13,100 ft **Range:** 4–5 hrs **Bomb load:** 770 lb

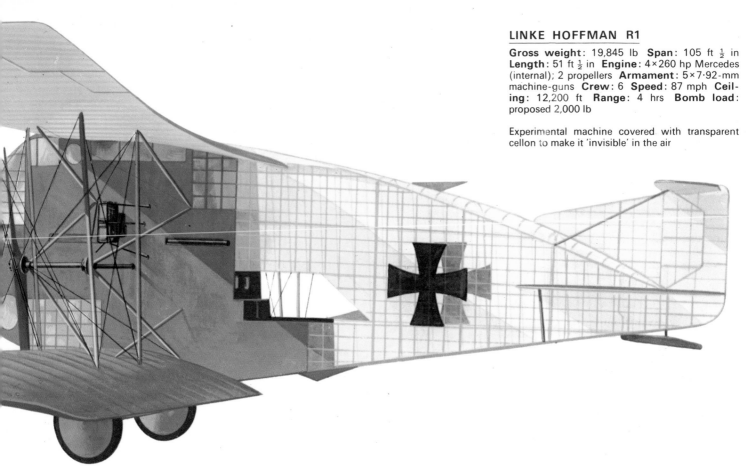

LINKE HOFFMAN R1

Gross weight: 19,845 lb **Span:** 105 ft ½ in
Length: 51 ft ½ in **Engine:** 4 × 260 hp Mercedes
(internal); 2 propellers **Armament:** 5 × 7·92-mm
machine-guns **Crew:** 6 **Speed:** 87 mph **Ceiling:** 12,200 ft **Range:** 4 hrs **Bomb load:**
proposed 2,000 lb

Experimental machine covered with transparent
cellon to make it 'invisible' in the air

range tactical targets and for photographic reconnaissance. A larger version, the G V, with a biplane tail unit and a bomb load of 1,320 lb was beginning to appear at the end of the war.

Although the French made a number of spectacular day and night bombing raids in the early months of the war, mainly through the efforts of enthusiasts like Laurens, Happe and Göys, the French High Command was not very impressed with the results.

Towards the end of 1915 the bomber groups which had been built up under the command of Commandant de Göys were split up and the aircraft dispersed among various army commanders. In fact, the French showed little interest in any long-range strategic bombing during the war, largely due to Marshal Foch's obsessive desire to win the war through ground attack alone. The Independent Force of the RAF was originally intended to include French bomber squadrons but these never materialised. Consequently, France was much slower than the other major powers in developing large twin-engined specialised bombers.

The first to appear, in mid-1917, was the Letord 3, one of a series of three-seat aircraft designed for reconnaissance, fighter and night bombing roles by Colonel Dorand of the French Service Technique, and built in relatively small numbers in the last two years of the war. The Letord 3 had the characteristic back-staggered wings of other types in the series, and was powered by two 200 hp Hispano engines. A better version was the Letord 5 which was of sesquiplane configuration (the lower wing being half the size of the upper) with 220 hp Lorraine engines giving a speed of nearly 100 mph. It could carry a bomb load of 440 lb and two machine-guns. The Letord 7 which appeared in 1918 had the same wing arrangement as the Letord 3 only larger, and was notable for the cannon mounted in the nose of the fuselage in place of a machine-gun. Only the Letord 9, with a wing span of 85 feet and two 400 hp Liberty engines, began to match the Handley Page bombers, and that only flew in prototype before the war ended.

The only big French bomber to see any service during the last months of the war was the two-seat Farman F50, powered by two 265 hp Lorraine engines mounted on the lower wing on either side of the fuselage and resembling the general lines of the Gotha. Eight 165-lb bombs could be carried under the fuselage between the legs of the

undercarriage, and the bomb aimer/gunner sat in the nose of the fuselage, in front of the pilot's cockpit. Only two Voisin units were re-equipped with F50s at the time of the Armistice, while a few were flown by the American Expeditionary Forces in France. The prototype of a larger bomber, the excellent Farman F60 Goliath, first flew in 1918 and, although too late for the war, it later became the standard French night bomber. Another type which was too late to see war service was the Caudron C23 powered by two 260 hp Salmson engines. In fact, a smaller Caudron twin-engined aeroplane, the G4, had been used for bombing since the spring of 1915, but it was too slow and poorly armed for daylight raids. Even in night bombing it suffered many casualties, and it was withdrawn the following year to be used mostly for training.

In general, all the big bombers that were built and brought into operation during the last two years of the war – the Capronis, Handley Pages, Gothas and Zeppelin-Staakens – were quickly transferred from day to night bombing as the capabilities of fighter aircraft improved and ground anti-aircraft defences became better organised. Such big aircraft, which after the war were to be of vital importance in the development of passenger airliners, were too expensive and in too short supply to be risked in hazardous daytime operations. Even at night they sometimes suffered heavy casualties – for instance, over one-third of the Handley Pages of the Independent Force were lost.

Night bombing inevitably was much less accurate than day operations but there were some targets, especially military installations, which required a high degree of accuracy if any success was to be achieved. There was an obvious need for smaller and faster bombers which could elude – or battle their way through – fighter opposition by day. These proved to be some of the best aircraft types produced during the war.

THE FIGHTERS MEET THEIR MATCH

Although large-scale strategic raids have always been the most dramatic form of bombing, it is debatable whether they have proved as valuable as local tactical raids in support of ground troops or against specific military objectives. This was certainly the case in 1914–18, and it was the small fast planes used in the latter role that made the most significant contribution

Bombing did not make a very great contribution to the First War and reconnaissance remained the most important use of aircraft. In spite of great technological advances, neither the bombers themselves, nor the bombs they carried were sufficiently powerful, or available in large enough numbers, to determine the outcome of any particular battle. Some of the bombing attacks were indeed spectacular, but it was the psychological fear they caused that created the spectre of terror bombing in the years after the war. This was reinforced by air force leaders who were to claim more for the power of strategic bombing than they could actually fulfil when the time came. But during the First World War, the most important contribution of both fighters and bombers was to control the air space over the battle zones by destroying the enemy's aircraft in the air and on the ground. Complete control could never be achieved, of course, and the balance swung to and fro depending on the quality and number of aircraft possessed by one side at any particular time.

In later wars, such as Germany's attack on Poland in 1939 and Israel's pre-emptive strike against the Arabs in the six-day war of 1967, complete control of air space was a decisive factor, but only in relation to the effort of ground forces and the strategic aims of the war. The much greater air superiority enjoyed by the Americans in Vietnam failed to achieve a decisive result because of the vagueness of the strategic aims. As the history of bombing has proved time and time again, attacks on military targets, especially airfields, are perhaps the most useful contribution that bombers can make in an overall war effort. The Luftwaffe's failure to maintain such attacks during the Battle of Britain, because the temptation to bomb civilian targets was too irresistible, altered the course of the Second World War. As the Germans, the British and – in another war – the Americans discovered, bombing civilians diverted an effort which might more usefully have been directed elsewhere. Not only did it fail to produce the expected psychological results, but it invariably strengthened a country's morale.

Shorter landing

During the First World War, therefore, in spite of the dramatic raids of heavy night bombers and their subsequent effect on the thinking of air force planners, it was the smaller and faster bombers, used for tactical raids in the battle areas, that made the most significant contribution. Some remarkable and highly successful aircraft were produced for that purpose. Although the British, through the efforts of the RNAS, were the first to carry out strategic raids, it was the French who employed bombing most widely during the early part of the war. The Voisin was the most predominant type of bomber aircraft at that time and it continued in service in various forms right up to the end of the war. It was very sturdy, due to the extensive use of steel in its construction, and was able to operate from small, rough fields, making for a short landing run. It was the first aircraft to be equipped with wheel brakes. But the early advantage of the pusher type of aeroplane was lost as soon as machine-guns were mounted in the rear cockpits of the faster tractor-driven types, and even more so with the development of fixed, forward-firing machine-guns.

The pusher was inevitably slower because of the drag created by the booms which carried the tail, the three-bay wing structure, and the complicated system of bracing struts and wires associated with such a configuration. By the autumn of 1915, the Voisin and the other pushers, with maximum speeds of little more than 70 mph, had to be relegated to night bombing. The resulting decrease in their effectiveness was largely responsible for the lack of interest shown by the French at this time in strategic bombing.

The first of a new family of Voisins, the Voisin VIII, with longer wings and distinctive streamlined fuel tanks mounted between them, appeared early in 1917. It was powered by a converted lorry engine, the 220 hp in-line Peugeot 8a, which gave it a speed of over 80 mph and a bomb load of 400 lb. Another feature was the replacement of the normal machine-gun with a 37-mm Hotchkiss quick-firing cannon. But the engine did not prove reliable, and the speed was still too low for it to be used for anything other than night bombing.

The Voisin X which appeared at the front early in 1918 had a much better performance and range, able to deliver 660 lb of bombs against a target 150 miles distant and return, but it too had to be confined to night bombing, for which purpose it was painted entirely in black.

Another pusher type of bomber which remained in service until the end of the war was the Bréguet-Michelin. This should have appeared in 1915, when its performance, superior to that of the Voisin, would have made it a useful day-bomber. In a competition with one of the early tractor biplanes produced by Paul Schmitt, the Bréguet-Michelin won hands down and promised to meet the specification for a powerful aeroplane capable of destroying enemy munition factories. But delays were caused by the initial failure of the 220 hp Renault engine, and by the time it appeared on the Western Front, in 1916, the development of fast fighter interceptors meant that it, too, had to be confined to night bombing. Meanwhile, Paul Schmitt had overcome his early difficulties and much was expected of the PS 7 single-engined tractor type. Again, how-

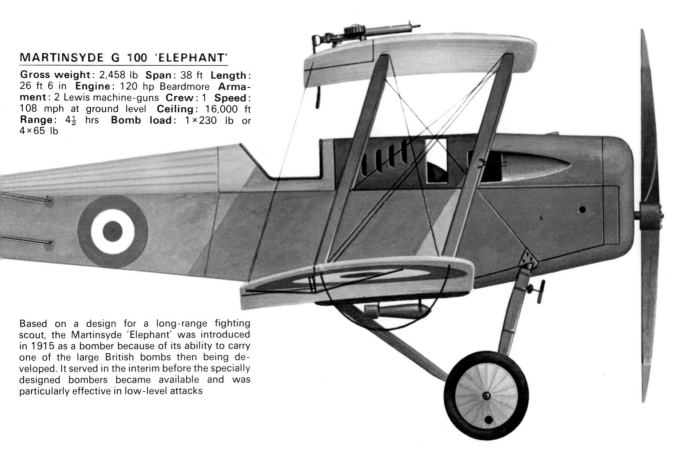

MARTINSYDE G 100 'ELEPHANT'

Gross weight: 2,458 lb **Span:** 38 ft **Length:** 26 ft 6 in **Engine:** 120 hp Beardmore **Armament:** 2 Lewis machine-guns **Crew:** 1 **Speed:** 108 mph at ground level **Ceiling:** 16,000 ft **Range:** 4½ hrs **Bomb load:** 1×230 lb or 4×65 lb

Based on a design for a long-range fighting scout, the Martinsyde 'Elephant' was introduced in 1915 as a bomber because of its ability to carry one of the large British bombs then being developed. It served in the interim before the specially designed bombers became available and was particularly effective in low-level attacks

ever, delays in production held back deliveries until 1917, and although it was used as a day-bomber, it was by then virtually obsolete.

The most successful of the single-engined French bombers, the Bréguet 14, was a remarkable aircraft in its own right, remaining in general service until 1930. It was a tractor type which first flew in November 1916 and was brought into service late in 1917. With a maximum speed of 112 mph at sea level, a service ceiling of 18,000 feet, a range of 435 miles and capable of carrying thirty-two 22-lb bombs, it at last provided the French with a first class day-bomber which could take on fighters on something approaching equal terms. It was built largely of light alloy and was powered by a 300 hp Renault engine which enabled it to climb to 16,500 feet in 39 minutes.

Of the seventeen versions produced, three were used as bombers – the B2 two-seater day-bomber, the BN2 two-seater night-bomber, and the B1 single-seater bomber. The Bréguet 14 enabled the French bombardment squadrons to resume daylight operations on a scale never before possible, and under the command of such men as Vuillemin and de Göys, the bomber crews took over from the fighter pilots as the élite of the French aviation groups. From early 1918 until the end of the war, the Bréguet formations of the First Air Division made daily raids on German military targets. A striking example of the power of mass-bombing was given on 4 June 1918, when a concentration of German troops in a ravine near the forest of Villers-Cotterets was virtually obliterated.

Also in June 1918, the first day-bomber squadron of the American Expeditionary Forces, the 96th Aero, commenced operations with Bréguet 14 B2s supplied three months earlier. The rest of the US bombing units, which flew day-bombers only, were

equipped with American-built DH 4s with Liberty engines, one of the most successful British planes of the war. In August 1918 all the American air squadrons at the front were grouped into the Air Service of the First Army, under the command of General W. Mitchell. In 150 American bombing raids before the end of the war, about 140 tons of bombs were dropped.

Early in 1915 the German C-class of two-seater tractor biplanes began to enter service with engines giving up to 180 hp, double that of the unarmed B-class machines. The new types were notable for the Parabellum machine-gun mounted in the rear cockpit giving them a 'sting in the tail', and which, for a period, turned the tables against the Allies. The British BE2c observation machine suffered particularly heavy casualties, because it retained the original layout with the pilot in the rear seat, leaving the observer/gunner hemmed in by wings, wires and struts. During the following year a number of the German C-class planes were developed as light bombers and formed into bombing groups (*kampfgeschwader*), but because of the shortage of aircraft they couldn't often be spared for strategic bombing. A raid on the night of 20 July 1916 showed what might have been achieved, when four machines bombed a British ammunition dump near St. Omer, destroying over twenty sheds and some 8,000 tons of ammunition.

Staff re-organisation

The Battle of the Somme in the summer of 1916 left the Germans even more desperately short of aircraft. Most of them were required to protect and escort the vital reconnaissance machines, leaving none to spare for bombing sorties. The aviation units at this time were divided among the various army groups with little co-ordination between them and this also

detracted from their operations. Accordingly, in October 1916, all the units were combined under one command, directly responsible to Army GHQ. General von Hoeppner was appointed commander of the new German Army Air Service with Major Thomsen as his chief of staff. The only aviation force not controlled by this new organisation was the Naval Air Service which continued to come under navy command. While the heavy multi-engined bombers began night bombing raids on both the Eastern and Western fronts, von Hoeppner built up C-class units for daylight sorties against military targets on the Western Front. In November 1917 the designation of the bombing groups was again changed to *Bombengeschwader*.

First of the C-class bombers to enter service was the Aviatik C III, with a maximum speed of 100 mph, a combat range of about 250 miles, and the ability to carry a bomb load of some 200 lb. The Albatros types used were the CIII, CVII and CX, the latter appearing in 1917 with a 260 hp Mercedes engine. All these were notable for their rounded tail units which had a 'fishtail' appearance. From the Rumpler firm came the CI and CIa, both of which were capable of carrying up to 220 lb of small bombs. The LVG C II, first appearing at the end of 1915, was credited with making the first daylight raid on London in November of the following year. During 1917, a CL category of plane was brought into service as a small, lightweight two-seater to undertake fighter escort duties. Two of these types, however, found additional employment in a ground-attack role in support of the infantry, when four or five 22-lb bombs could be dropped and enemy trenches machine-gunned. The Halberstadt CL II made its mark in attacking British troops during the Battle of Cambrai in November 1917. The other type, the Hannover CL IIIa, was unique among single-

SALMSON II (above)
Gross weight: 2,798 lb **Span:** 38 ft 7 in
Length: 27 ft 11 in **Engine:** 260 hp Salmson
Armament: 2–3 machine-guns **Crew:** 2
Speed: 116 mph at 6,500 ft **Ceiling:** 20,500 ft
Range: 3 hrs **Bomb load:** 200 lb

DH 4 (right)
Gross weight: 3,312 lb **Span:** 42 ft 5 in **Lengt**
30 ft 8 in **Engine:** 250 hp Rolls Royce Eagle **Arm**
ment: 1×·303 Vickers; 1×·303 Lewis **Crew:**
Speed: 117 mph at 6,500 ft **Ceiling:** 16,000 ft **Rang**
3½ hrs **Bomb load:** 4×112 lb

engined aircraft of the period for its biplane
tail unit. It was so small and compact in
design that Allied pilots often mistook it
for a single-seater until, coming up to attack
from behind in order to avoid the pilot's
forward-firing gun, they were met with an
unexpected hail of fire from the observer's
machine-gun.

As well as the Caproni heavy bombers,
the Italians also produced one of the fastest
light bombers of the war, the Ansaldo SVA
5, in the summer of 1917. This single-seater
biplane, powered by a 220 hp SPA in-line
engine and with twin synchronised Vickers
machine-guns mounted on top of the cowling, was originally intended to be a fighter.
Although its maximum speed of 136 mph
compared favourably with most fighters of
the time, its lack of manoeuvrability made
it unsuitable for fighting duties. However,
it possessed two attributes which made it
an excellent day-bomber; a range of over
600 miles, equal to that of the German Giants
and almost double that of the Capronis,
and the ability to carry a 200-lb bomb load.
The SVA 5 entered service as a bomber in
February 1918 and quickly established a
reputation for itself, enabling the Italians
for the first time to carry out long-range
strategic raids on cities as far away as
Innsbruck, Zagreb, Ljubljana and Friedrichshafen. A two-seater version, the
SVA9, was brought into service during the
last months of the war, and one of these
machines, with Gabrielle d'Annunzio as
observer, led six SVA 5s on a 625-mile
round journey from San Pelagio to Vienna
to drop leaflets on the Austrian capital.

Many different types of British aircraft
brought into service in the early days of
the war were used as bombers, even those
originally intended as fighters such as the
FE2b two-seat pusher biplane produced
by the Royal Aircraft Factory. Although
not fitted with interrupter gear, the FE2b
achieved considerable success as a fighter,
with its two Lewis machine-guns and
unobstructed view forward. One of its
successes was claimed to be the shooting
down of the German Fokker ace, Max
Immelmann.

During daylight fighter-reconnaissance
missions, eight 20-lb bombs could be carried,
and a few aircraft of the type, fitted with

Vickers one-pounder pom-pom guns, were
found to be ideal for attacking trains. This
kind of low-level ground-attack was primarily a British idea and was to lead later
to the development of strike aircraft
specifically designed for that purpose. By
the end of 1916, however, the FE2b had
been outclassed by the new Albatros and
Halberstadt single-seat fighters and was
used mainly for night bombing when up to
three 112-pounders were carried.

British fighters continued to carry small
bomb loads until the end of the war,
primarily for ground-attack duties in
support of the infantry. The two-seat Bristol
Fighter, one of the best general purpose
aircraft of the war, could carry up to twelve
20-lb bombs in racks under the bottom wing,
and even the fast and highly manoeuvrable

SE 5a and Sopwith Camel single-seat
fighters could carry four 20-lb bombs. It was
as a result of this experience that an
experimental version of the Camel was built
early in 1918 as an armoured trench fighter,
fitted with two downward-firing machine-
guns in addition to the one firing forwards,
and with a sheet of armoured plate to
protect the pilot from ground fire. The first
British aircraft to be built specifically for
this purpose was the heavily armour-plated
Sopwith Salamander which could carry a
remarkably heavy bomb load of nearly
650 lb in addition to its two machine-guns.
It was built in some numbers but did not
see active service before the war ended.

Meanwhile by 1915, the concept of
bombing had been accepted, and plans put
in hand for multi-engined heavy bombers.

DH 10 AMIENS Mk III

Gross weight: 9,000 lb **Span:** 65 ft 6 in
Length: 39 ft 7 in **Engine:** 2×400 hp Liberty
Armament: 4 Lewis machine-guns **Crew:** 3
Speed: 116 mph at 6,500 ft **Ceiling:** 16,500 ft
Range: 5 hrs **Bomb load:** 900 lb

One of several promising bombers being developed for the RAF, which arrived too late to see
operational service before the end of the war.
Later used for long-distance air mail services

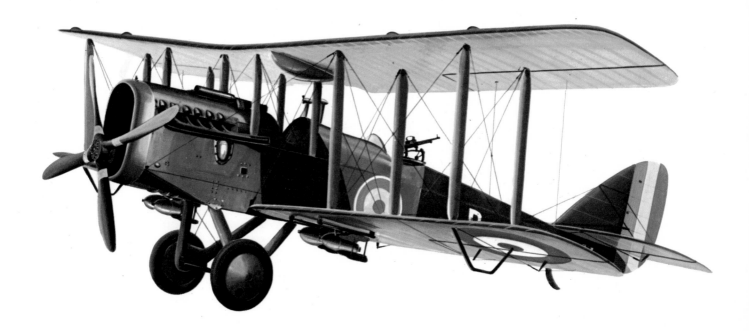

But there was also a need for fast day-bombers which could drop larger bombs than the four 20-pounders carried by most of the adapted fighters. The first answer was the Martinsyde G 102 Elephant which appeared late in 1915, so named because it was a relatively large aeroplane for a single-seater, and designed to have an endurance of 5½ hours. It could carry loads of up to a single 336-lb bomb. While it had a high speed for the time of 104 mph, it was not very manoeuvrable, its ceiling was limited to 16,000 feet and it was used most successfully as a low-level bomber. Another type which could carry the 336-lb bomb was the Farnborough-designed RE7 which came into service early in 1916. This was originally intended as a two or three-seater reconnaissance machine, and the crew were normally

armed only with rifles and pistols. The observer in the front cockpit had a very restricted field of fire, surrounded as he was by bracing struts and wires. The RE7 had a short-lived career, due to the development of fast and better-armed German fighters, but for a while its great weight-lifting capacity made it a useful bomber.

Early in 1917, there appeared in service with the RFC on the Western Front one of the best combat aircraft of the war and certainly the most outstanding day-bomber. This was the DH 4, designed by Geoffrey de Havilland and produced by the Aircraft Manufacturing Company (Airco). It was a straightforward two-seater tractor biplane, but unlike many aircraft coming into service at that time, part of whose construction was of metal, the DH 4 was

built almost entirely of wood. It was fabric-covered, except for the front half of the fuselage, which was covered with plywood, and this improved both its appearance and its strength. There was more than the usual distance between the two cockpits, giving the pilot an excellent view for bombing, while the observer/gunner was far enough back to have a wide field of fire for his Lewis machine-gun. The only drawback was the difficulty in communication between the two crew members during combat. A speaking tube connecting the cockpits on some machines was of little use in view of the noise of the engines and slipstream, and most crews worked out a satisfactory system of hand signals. The pilot was provided with a Vickers machine-gun synchronised by the Constantinesco system. Later models had two forward-firing Vickers and some, built for the RNAS, had two Lewis guns on pillar mountings in the rear cockpit. The normal bomb load was two 230-lb or four 112-lb bombs, carried on racks under the fuselage and lower wings.

The prototype DH 4, first tested in the autumn of 1916, was powered by a 230 hp Beardmore-Halford-Pullinger engine, but this proved troublesome and was soon changed for the excellent 250 hp liquid-cooled Vee-twelve Eagle produced by Rolls-Royce. This gave it a remarkable speed of about 130 mph at 10,000 feet, and it could climb to this height in nine minutes. When the 375 hp Eagle was fitted later, the performance of the DH 4, both in speed (143 mph at sea level) and ceiling (22,000 ft), outclassed all but a very few of the opposing German fighters. In addition to the Western Front, it saw service in Italy, the Aegean, Macedonia and Palestine. It was the only British aircraft to be built in any number by the Americans, who produced nearly 5,000 with Liberty engines and twin forward-firing Marlin guns. Some 600 were in service with the American bomber units in France at the end of the war.

From the moment of its introduction, the DH 4 was successfully used by the RFC for daylight attacks on military targets, while the RNAS used the type mostly for anti-Zeppelin patrols – it was a DH 4 which shot down the Zeppelin L 70 in August 1918. But the real impetus given to British bomber

production came after the Gotha raid on London in June 1917 when more damage was caused than during all the previous Zeppelin raids. It was decided to increase the strength of the RFC from 108 squadrons to 200, most of the new ones to be equipped with bombers to undertake a retaliatory strategic bombing campaign against German cities and industrial targets. Large numbers of the DH 4 were ordered, together with a new version, the DH 9, which had a longer range. This was basically similar to the DH 4, except that the pilot's cockpit was moved aft so that he could communicate more easily with his observer.

The DH 9 seemed to offer all the advantages of its predecessor and more, for it was expected to carry a heavier bomb load as well. But there were development problems with the BHP engine which had to be derated to 230 hp and further modified to facilitate production, at which point it was re-named the Siddeley Puma. The resulting loss of performance – the DH 9 could barely reach 13,000 feet with a full bomb and petrol load – rendered it considerably inferior to the older Rolls-Royce powered DH 4. By the time this was fully appreciated it was already being produced in large numbers and brought into service with the Independent Force. A marked improvement was achieved with the DH 9A, powered mostly by the 400 hp Liberty engine, although a few were fitted with the Rolls-Royce Eagle. This version could carry a maximum bomb load of 660 lb, and a normal load of two 230-lb bombs, at 17,000 feet without loss of height. It had a good enough performance to carry out daylight raids without escort, but unfortunately there were difficulties in obtaining the Liberty engine. Only four units had been re-equipped with 9As by the end of the war and they were only in active service for about two months.

The ill-fated DH 9 therefore had to bear the brunt of daytime operations with the Independent Force, with some pilots making as many as six sorties a day. Losses were high because of the reduced speed and ceiling, as well as the unreliability of the engines. During one raid against Mainz in July 1918, seven out of twelve DH 9s were shot down by German fighters and three had to turn back with engine failure. The day-bombers paid the highest price for the strategic bombing offensive against Germany; casualties among the four de Havilland squadrons were 25 killed, 178 missing and 58 wounded, with over 100 aircraft brought down over enemy territory and 201 wrecked in crashes on the Allied side of the lines.

This was a very different story from the early months of the war. It is fair to say that the bomber came of age during the First World War, proving all fears of its destructiveness to be well-founded. But defences against the bomber – fighters and anti-aircraft guns – had also developed. Some of the highest losses in men and aircraft were sustained by the bomber squadrons, especially those whose task it was to undertake precision bombing by day.

Light bombers on the production line of a French factory during 1918

Flight International

SHORT BOMBER

Gross weight: 6,800 lb **Span**: 85 ft **Length**: 45 ft **Engine**: 250 hp Rolls Royce Eagle **Armament**: 1 Lewis machine-gun **Crew**: 2 **Speed**: 77·5 mph **Ceiling**: 9,500 ft **Range**: 6 hrs **Bomb load**: 920 lb

A landplane development of the Short 184 seaplane, brought into service with the RNAS in 1916 to initiate the concept of strategic bombing behind the front line

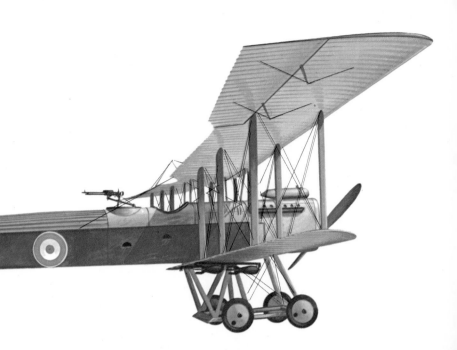

BETWEEN THE WARS

In the post-war years, de-militarisation and financial stringency put many obstacles in the way of the bomber's development. Private designs proliferated, but in the absence of any official policy, progress was haphazard and unco-ordinated. Some remarkable aircraft were produced nonetheless, and all the bombers used operationally during the Second World War were being developed by the mid-1930s

In many ways the most advanced plane of the First World War was the Junkers D 1 which embodied many of the features that were to become generally accepted in the 1930s. It was a cantilever monoplane with an all-metal airframe covered with thin sheet iron, resulting in such a strong structure that no struts or bracing wires were required to support the wings. Although the D1 was first flown in 1916, only a few were built during the war because of production problems. Under wartime conditions, aircraft were needed in such large numbers – France produced some 60,000, Britain 53,000, Germany 48,000, Italy 20,000 and the USA 12,000 – that preference often had to be given to simplicity of construction over ingenuity of design.

The large number of aircraft produced meant that there was a considerable surplus when the war ended, except in Germany. This ultimately turned out to Germany's advantage, since she had to build up a new air force from scratch, without the encumbrance of older types of aircraft. Meanwhile, a number of the large Allied bombers such as the DH 10 Amiens and the Il'ya Muromets, were used to pioneer civil transportation, opening up passenger, freight and mail routes around the world. Expenditure on military aircraft was severely cut back after the 'war to end wars', and it was not long before aircraft specifically designed as civil airliners had taken a technical lead over the bomber types from which they were originally developed.

Almost all the bombers used during the Second World War were the result of a technological revolution which took place in the early 1930s. This was led by the development of airliners in the USA and saw the increasing use of all-metal cantilever monoplanes with stressed alloy skins, retractable undercarriages, flaps, constant-speed propellers with variable pitch, and with radios among more efficient navigational aids. But for most of the period between the wars however, the biplane had remained the predominant type, and the first bombers to

be produced after the First World War continued to be constructed mainly of wood.

In Britain, for instance, the twin-engined Vickers Virginia, the main RAF heavy night bomber from 1924 to 1937, was of conventional wood and fabric construction, as was the Martin MB-2, in service from 1919 to 1927. This, the first American-designed bomber, was intended to improve on the performance of the Handley Page 0/400 then being built under licence in the USA. A similar French type was the Farman F 60 series, which appeared in the closing stages of the First World War, and remained in service until 1928, while a civil version developed from the Goliath was used with considerable success by French commercial fleets during the same period. In Italy, the large multi-engined Caproni bombers were replaced by the single-engined Caproni Ca 73 series, notable for their unusual inverted sesquiplane arrangement. Another single-engined bomber of conventional wood and fabric construction was the de Havilland R1, a Soviet version of the remarkable DH 9A – the first Russian aircraft to be mass-produced – which served from 1923 to 1935.

Limited service
The gradual change from wood to metal construction for military aircraft took place almost universally in the mid-1920s. Although the Avro Aldershot, one of the first new bombers to be designed for the RAF after the First World War, had only a single engine, it was intended as a heavy night bomber and could in fact carry a bomb load of 2,000 lb, equal to that of most twin-engined types of the period. But the Air Staff decided against the idea of single-engined heavy bombers and the Aldershot saw only limited service.

A similar policy decision was taken in the USA where the Huff-Daland bomber (the name was later changed to Keystone), brought into service to replace the Martin MB-2 in 1927, was changed from a single

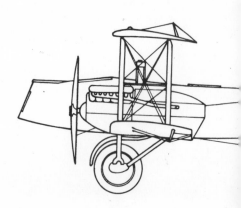

AVRO ALDERSHOT

Gross weight: 10,950 lb **Span:** 68 ft **Length:** 45 ft **Engine:** 650 hp Rolls Royce Condor III **Armament:** 1 Lewis machine-gun **Crew:** 3 **Speed:** 110 mph at ground level **Ceiling:** 11,500 ft **Range:** 652 miles **Bomb load:** 2,000 lb

Entered RAF service in 1924 with a bomb-load equal to that of many twin-engined bombers

VICKERS VIRGINIA

Gross weight: 12,467 lb **Span:** 86 ft 6 in **Length:** 50 ft 7 in **Engine:** 2×450 hp Napier Lion **Armament:** 2–4×·303 machine-guns **Crew:** 4 **Speed:** 104 mph at ground level **Ceiling:** 15,530 ft **Range:** 985 miles **Bomb load:** 3,000 lb

The main heavy night bomber in service with the RAF from 1924 to 1937

MARTIN MB-2

Gross weight: 12,064 lb **Span:** 74 ft 2 in **Length:** 42 ft 8 in **Engine:** 2×420 hp Liberty **Armament:** 5×0·3-in machine-guns **Crew:** 4 **Speed:** 99 mph at ground level **Ceiling:** 8,500 ft **Range:** 558 miles **Bomb load:** 2,000 lb

Designed by Glenn L. Martin, one of America's leading air pioneers, the MB-2 formed the bulk of the US Army's bomber force in the early 1920s

KEYSTONE B-4A

Gross weight: 13,209 lb **Span:** 74 ft 8 in **Length:** 48 ft 10 in **Engine:** 2×575 hp R-1860-7 **Armament:** 3×0·3 machine-guns **Crew:** 5 **Speed:** 121 mph at ground level **Ceiling:** 14,000 ft **Range:** 855 miles **Bomb load:** 2,500 lb

One of the final production series, for which orders were placed in 1931, of the long line of Huff-Daland/Keystone bombers

engine to a twin-engined type. One reason was safety, in that a multi-engined plane could keep flying even with one engine out of action; another was that by placing the engines on or between the wings, the nose was left clear, giving the gunner and/or bomb aimer a better field of vision.

There was still a need for light two-seater day-bombers powered by a single engine, although such a classification became obsolete in the 1930s, when many day-bombers were built with two engines. The first new day-bomber to be received by the RAF after the war was the Fairey Fawn, a wood and fabric biplane, in service from 1923 to 1926, whose performance was actually inferior to the wartime DH 9A. This was replaced by the Hawker Horsley which remained in service until 1934. The Horsley, of mixed wood and metal construction, had an excellent load-carrying ability – either 600 lb of bombs or a single 2,150-lb torpedo in the torpedo-carrier version – and was almost as manoeuvrable as the fighters of those days.

But undoubtedly the best of the light bombers of wood construction was the Fairey Fox. Part of the reason for the poor performance of the Fairey Fawn had been the stringent official specifications to which it had been built. Richard Fairey decided to build a much faster bomber as a private venture in the hope of obtaining a production order. In the early 1920s he had seen an American Curtiss seaplane win the Schneider Trophy at a speed of over 177 mph and he was so impressed that he obtained the right to use certain features of its design, particularly the slim Curtiss D 12 in-line engine which he built under licence as the Fairey Felix. The Fairey Fox, which appeared in 1926, was one of the most beautiful biplanes ever built and not only the fastest bomber of its day, with a speed of 156 mph, but faster and more manoeuvrable than most fighters. In fact, only one RAF squadron was equipped with this outstanding aircraft, and in the event, production models were powered by the Rolls-Royce F Kestrel. But it established a line of bombers which saw much use in Belgium, where both Kestrel and Hispano-Suiza engines were installed.

Japan's first

The first light bomber to be built in Japan for the Japanese Army Air Force was the Mitsubishi 2MB1, introduced in 1927, while two years later the Kawasaki Type 88 reconnaissance biplane was adapted to perform light bombing duties.

The transition in bomber design from wood to metal, though still fabric-covered to begin with, took place in the mid-1920s, with the final change to all-metal stressed-skin airframes beginning by the early 1930s. Before describing the introduction of these types, however, consideration has to be given to the other vital aspect of design, namely engine development.

In 1917 it had been decreed that the dominant British engine should be the ABC Dragonfly radial, a nine-cylinder air-cooled unit of modern design which was supposed to give over 400 hp. Had the war continued, this would have led to a crisis in British aviation, because by the time it was realised that it was a complete technical failure the Dragonfly was being produced on a large scale. It was not until after 1920 that the fine Rolls-Royce Eagle was backed up by two other outstanding engines, the Napier Lion and Bristol Jupiter.

The Lion, designed by Rowledge, had three banks each containing four water-cooled cylinders, the so-called 'W' or broad-arrow arrangement. It was rigid and refined, and though used at 450 hp in bombers such as the Handley Page Hyderabad (the last twin-engined bomber of wooden construction to be used by the RAF except for the Mosquito of the Second World War) it gave 1,320 hp in racing form. Roy Fedden's Jupiter, fitted originally in place of the Eagle in the Vickers Vimy, was the world-dominant engine of the 1920s, and was built under licence in no less than sixteen countries. Starting in 1918 as a 375–400 hp nine-cylinder radial, it grew to more than 500 hp and was then developed into the Pegasus, rated at more than 1,000 hp by 1938. Its history was one of strenuous effort to improve a basically sound mechanical design whilst introducing geared drive, super-charging, and better forms of low-drag aircraft installation.

Britain's prejudice

The Jupiter/Pegasus family took full advantage of the fact that there is always a great difference in temperature between an air-cooled cylinder head and the slipstream, whereas in the hottest countries there is less difference between the temperature of the air and the water passing through a radiator. Conversely, in the coldest climates, a water-cooled engine could freeze. Thus many British bombers designed for water-cooled engines were sold in very hot or very cold countries with air-cooled radials instead. But in Britain there was a prejudice in favour of the liquid-cooled engine, partly because of its success when used in Schneider Trophy racing. The belief grew that the supposedly 'streamlined' vee-12, exemplified by the 450–640 hp Rolls-Royce Kestrel and later by the 1,000 hp Merlin, was more efficient than the bluff-looking radial. No such belief was harboured in the USA, even though there was no lack of American in-line engines.

The vee-12 Hispano family, of 600–1,200 hp, was made in vast numbers, not only in France and other European countries but also in the Soviet Union where it was practically the standard engine for the most powerful military aircraft until after 1941. France's Lorraine Dietrich and Italy's Fiat and Isotta-Fraschini engines served to underline the European reliance on liquid-cooled vee types. In Germany the new *Luftwaffe* was born around the BMW VI (used in the prototypes of such bombers as the Dornier Do 17 and Heinkel He 111), some radials, and the unique opposed-piston diesel two-stroke, developed painstakingly by Junkers in the mistaken belief that it would give greater efficiency and longer range.

In the USA, in spite of extreme federal parsimony, the Curtiss D 12 was developed into the 575 hp Conqueror by 1926 and powered bombers well into the 1930s. Packard had a share of the business with a series of big vee-12 engines, some of which gave no less than 800 hp. But the Huff-Daland bomber, fitted with these big engines, was replaced by a model equipped with twin 400 hp Liberty engines, mounted upside down to raise the thrust axes to the correct levels. Increasingly, the air-cooled radial became dominant in the USA, especially after the emergence of the superb 425 hp Wasp, made by the newly-formed Pratt & Whitney company, late in 1925.

By 1930 nearly all American bombers were powered by various single-row and twin-row radials built by Pratt & Whitney and the Wright company. By 1937 the major engines of the future were seen to be the P & W R-1830 (radial, 1,830 cubic inches capacity) Twin Wasp, giving 1,000 hp, and the similarly powered Wright R-1820 Cyclone which, unlike the 14-cylinder Twin Wasp, had a single row of nine big cylinders. In 1937 the Cyclone entered combat service in the Boeing B-17 Fortress, the first really successful heavy bomber, and the Douglas B-18 derived from the DC-3. All the big American radials had one inlet and one exhaust valve in each cylinder head. They had geared drives and General Electric was nearing final success in its 20-year effort to perfect a turbo-supercharger spun by the white-hot exhaust gas. This was to prove of vital importance in the Second World War.

Meanwhile, Fedden's team at Bristol was looking keenly at the American radials which in turn owed so much to their own Jupiter engine. Fedden was daunted by the mechanical complexity of trying to devise valve gear for a two-row radial engine with four valves in each head. He had long used two inlet and two exhaust valves, giving better 'breathing' than the American engines, and was reluctant to halve the number. At the same time, though his Mercury (used in the Blenheim) and Pegasus engines were by 1930 showing great promise for a wide range of future aircraft, he wanted to look much further ahead. After extensive experiments with several schemes, he made the bold decision to try to develop a successful sleeve-valve engine. This type had been used in various forms since the turn of the century, but had never been completely successful. It nearly eluded his own team too, and vast effort and expense was needed. The problem lay not so much in perfecting the engine, but in making the engine a standard production type with interchangeable sleeves, instead of a hand-built engine

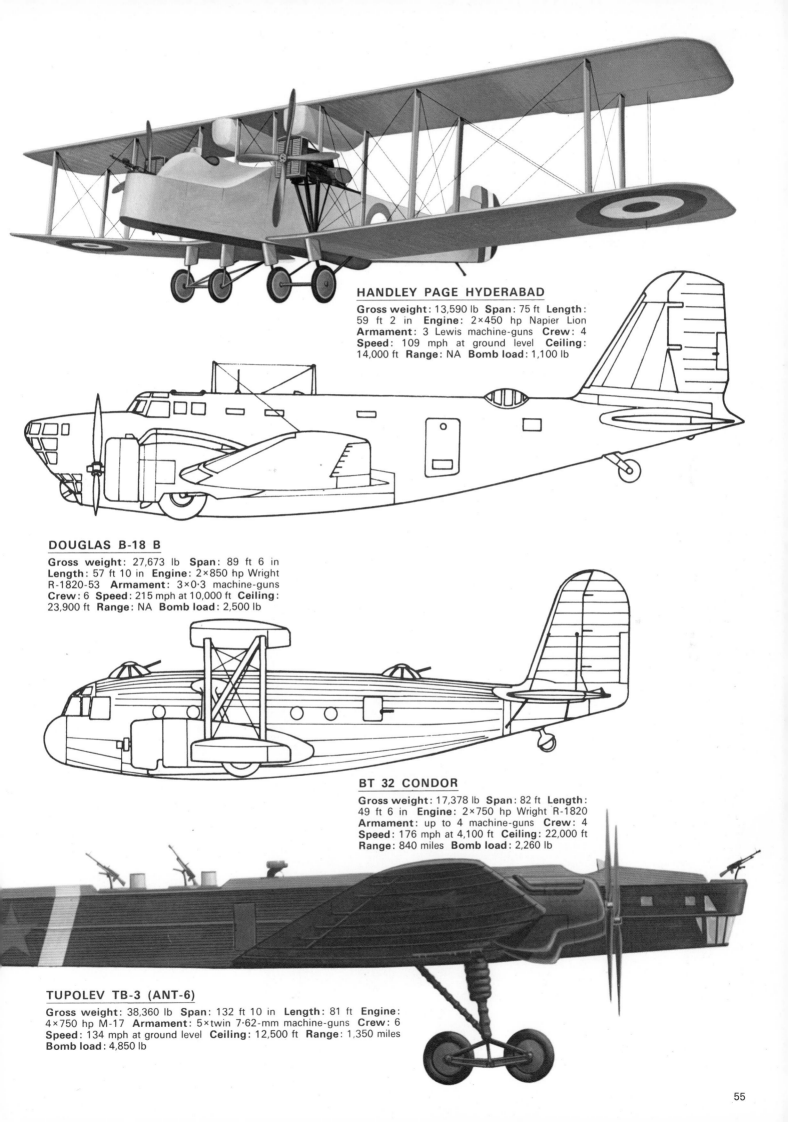

HANDLEY PAGE HYDERABAD

Gross weight: 13,590 lb **Span:** 75 ft **Length:** 59 ft 2 in **Engine:** 2×450 hp Napier Lion **Armament:** 3 Lewis machine-guns **Crew:** 4 **Speed:** 109 mph at ground level **Ceiling:** 14,000 ft **Range:** NA **Bomb load:** 1,100 lb

DOUGLAS B-18 B

Gross weight: 27,673 lb **Span:** 89 ft 6 in **Length:** 57 ft 10 in **Engine:** 2×850 hp Wright R-1820-53 **Armament:** 3×0·3 machine-guns **Crew:** 6 **Speed:** 215 mph at 10,000 ft **Ceiling:** 23,900 ft **Range:** NA **Bomb load:** 2,500 lb

BT 32 CONDOR

Gross weight: 17,378 lb **Span:** 82 ft **Length:** 49 ft 6 in **Engine:** 2×750 hp Wright R-1820 **Armament:** up to 4 machine-guns **Crew:** 4 **Speed:** 176 mph at 4,100 ft **Ceiling:** 22,000 ft **Range:** 840 miles **Bomb load:** 2,260 lb

TUPOLEV TB-3 (ANT-6)

Gross weight: 38,360 lb **Span:** 132 ft 10 in **Length:** 81 ft **Engine:** 4×750 hp M-17 **Armament:** 5×twin 7·62-mm machine-guns **Crew:** 6 **Speed:** 134 mph at ground level **Ceiling:** 12,500 ft **Range:** 1,350 miles **Bomb load:** 4,850 lb

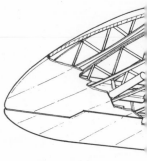

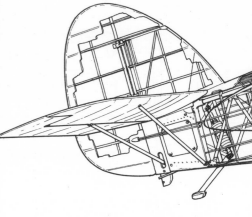

HAWKER HART (above right)

Gross weight: 4,554 lb **Span:** 37 ft 3 in **Length:** 29 ft 4 in **Engine:** 525 hp Rolls Royce Kestrel **Armament:** 1 Vickers machine-gun; 1 Lewis machine-gun **Crew:** 2 **Speed:** 184 mph at 5,000 ft **Ceiling:** 21,350 ft **Range:** 470 miles **Bomb load:** 520 lb

Section drawing of the RAF's standard light day bomber from 1930 to 1939. Its performance was better than most contemporary single-seater fighters. Used especially for colonial policing duties, for which many variants were produced

<u>Above</u>: armourers working on Browning and Lewis guns, aligning the gun sights

<u>Centre</u>: aligning gun sight

<u>Left</u>: apprentices receiving instruction on bomb preparation

Flight International

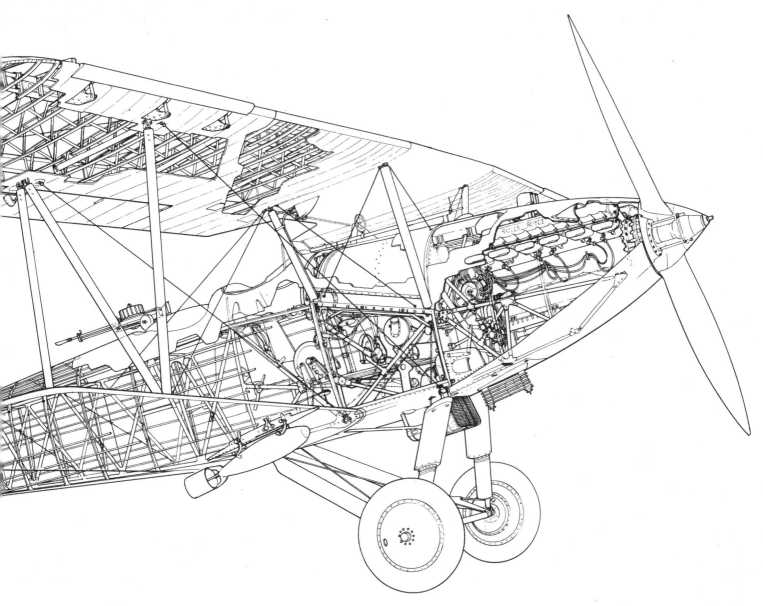

with each set of sleeves individually matched to its own set of cylinders and pistons.

In most of the aircraft-building countries, there were numerous companies making aero engines. Their efforts to make a living resulted in a profusion of engine types, when it would probably have been more cost/ effective to have concentrated on one or two designs in each broad power class. In the first half of the 1930s British bomber design would not have been notably handicapped if the Bristol Pegasus had been specified universally and all other engines in the 500–900 hp range had been cancelled. But no such decision was taken, and a diverse profusion of engines resulted, despite the fact that until 1935, when Hitler's announcement revealed the *Luftwaffe* to be among the foremost of the world's air forces, most governments cut bomber procurement to a minimum.

The atmosphere of economy largely explains why the big bomber with three, four, or even more engines, common in 1916–18, was almost non-existent in 1919–1938. Only in the latter year was a production order placed for an American four-engined bomber (the first B-17 Fortresses), and the RAF four-engined 'heavies' did not come into use until more than two years after the war began. The only nation to use fleets of four-engined bombers was the Soviet Union, whose Tupolev TB-3 monoplane came into service in 1931. This massive aircraft, powered by four Hispano-Suiza

vee-12 engines, had a greater loaded weight than any contemporary landplane. Experiments were even conducted into carrying two parasite fighters on the wings. The TB-3 and its derivatives were sufficiently reliable to play a major role in early Russian polar exploration in the era before the Second World War.

More metal structures
It was the use of metal in place of wood that gave large aircraft sufficient strength to enable them to be constructed in monoplane form. In France, the metal preferred by most designers was light alloy duralumin. This was used in the construction of the twin-engined Lioré and Olivier LeO 12, first exhibited at the Salon de l'Aeronautique in 1924 and later taken into squadron service on an experimental basis. Few machines of the type were actually built but a widely used development was the three-seat LeO 20, also built of duralumin, which equipped many French night bomber squadrons from 1927–1937, rivalling the Farman F 160 to 168 series. One of the most successful metal biplanes however was the single-engined Bréguet 19 two-seat light bomber which remained in service from 1925 for some fifteen years. It was also used by many foreign air forces, and built under licence in Belgium, Greece, Japan, Spain and Yugoslavia.

Another single-engined biplane of light alloy construction, which appeared in 1928

was the Amiot 122 BP3, the latter designation showing it to be a bomber-escort three-seater. The Amiot 122 had the handling characteristics of a light single-engined aircraft with the load-carrying ability of larger twin-engined types, and remained in service in various forms until 1935. Two other excellent single-engined biplane light bombers were the Czech Aero A11 and the Dutch Fokker CV-C, both introduced into service in 1923. The CV-C, one of the best combat aircraft ever designed by Anthony Fokker, had a welded steel-tube fuselage and wooden wings, and remained operational until the late 1930s.

The first British heavy bomber of metal construction was the Handley Page Hinaidi, a 1929 development of the Handley Page Hyderabad. The Hinaidi was replaced in 1933 by the Handley Page Heyford whose outstanding feature was the attachment of the fuselage to the upper instead of the lower wing. It also had a rotatable ventral turret which could be drawn up into the fuselage when not in use, its cylindrical shape quickly giving rise to the nickname 'dustbin'. These Handley Page twin-engined biplanes were built of a steel-tube structure with internal wire bracing. Another metal twin-engined biplane which came into service in 1928 was the Boulton Paul Sidestrand, but instead of being a night bomber, it was sufficiently fast and manoeuvrable to be used for daytime duties and was designated as the RAF's first medium bomber. It was replaced in 1934 by an improved version, the Boulton Paul Overstrand, which could carry a heavier bomb-load and was the first British bomber to have a power-operated enclosed gun turret in the nose. Apart from these two, British day-bombers were all single-engined two-seaters until the arrival of monoplanes in the late 1930s.

The usual metal in the early composite or metal-framed bombers was high-tensile steel, and there was a considerable reluctance on the part of designers to use light alloys. The steel was used both as tube and as strip, often welded at the joints. When aluminium alloys were brought in there was a great difference of opinion as to how they should best be employed. Sydney Camm, at the Hawker company, devised a patented form of 'bulb flange' in the shape of a tube assembled from sections of strip rolled to particular profiles. These flanges were then riveted to aluminium-alloy sheets to serve as spar booms – the strong top and bottom of the wing spars – in the way that later aircraft used booms of much thicker angle and T-sections.

Camm's fuselages were typical in having either circular-section tube with the sides flattened at the joints or else square-section tube throughout. The flat sides could then fit snugly against heavy bolted or riveted plates which were added to reinforce the main joints. Ways were also found of making strong streamlined struts from hollow light-alloy sections, though high-tensile steel wires were invariably still needed for bracing and for 'rigging' the structure (adjusting the tensions in different wires to obtain exactly the desired shapes, wing angles and tail incidence). It was because this new form of metal construction was easy to maintain in operational conditions that Hawker won a competition in the late 1920s when the Air Ministry decided to have a high-performance all-metal aircraft.

The Hawker Hart remained the standard RAF light day-bomber from 1930 to 1937, with a speed of 175 mph and a better all-round performance than most single-seat fighters of the period. The last RAF biplane bomber was the Hawker Hind. This type was in service from 1935 to 1938 as an interim replacement for the Hart, until the monoplane Fairey Battles and Bristol Blenheims began to enter service in RAF Bomber Command in 1937.

In Japan, the last biplane bomber to be produced for the Japanese Army Air Force was the Kawasaki Ki-3, a single-engined two-seater which entered service in 1933 as the Type 93 light bomber. By then, however, advances were being made in the production of bombers in monoplane form.

The big question

It was during the 1920s and 1930s that aircraft design became something of an exact science, though questions remained which caused endless arguments: should a bomber have air-cooled radial or liquid-cooled vee engines? Should it be a fabric-covered biplane or a fabric-covered monoplane – or, boldest of all, an all-metal stressed-skin monoplane? Fabric was used as the covering for the RAF's first twin-engined cantilever monoplane, the low-wing Fairey Hendon which entered service in 1936, and the Caproni Ca 101 and Ca 111 high-wing monoplanes, used extensively during the Italian campaign in Ethiopia. Some, such as the Handley Page Harrow and the Dornier Do 11, 13 and 23 bombers,

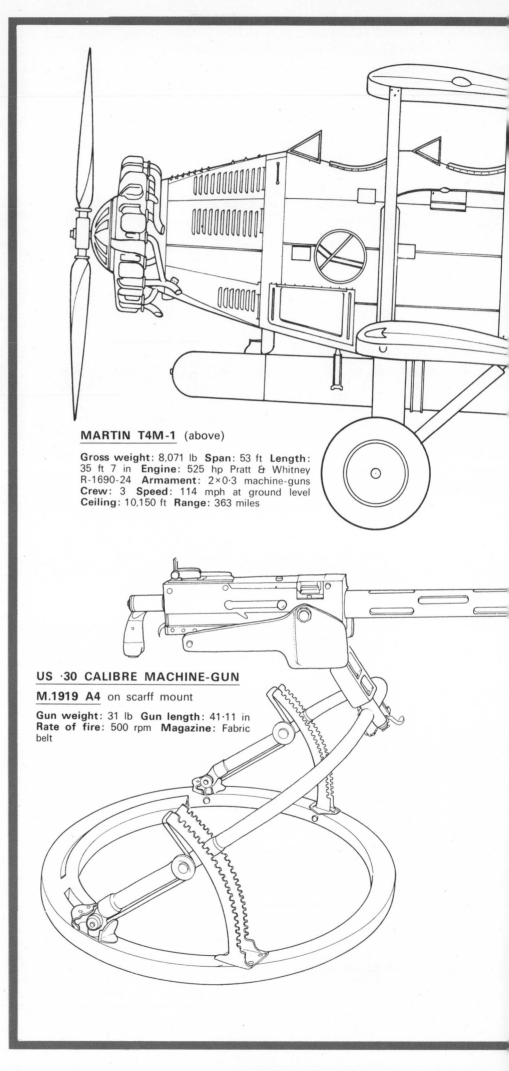

MARTIN T4M-1 (above)

Gross weight: 8,071 lb **Span:** 53 ft **Length:** 35 ft 7 in **Engine:** 525 hp Pratt & Whitney R-1690-24 **Armament:** 2×0·3 machine-guns **Crew:** 3 **Speed:** 114 mph at ground level **Ceiling:** 10,150 ft **Range:** 363 miles

US ·30 CALIBRE MACHINE-GUN

M.1919 A4 on scarff mount

Gun weight: 31 lb **Gun length:** 41·11 in **Rate of fire:** 500 rpm **Magazine:** Fabric belt

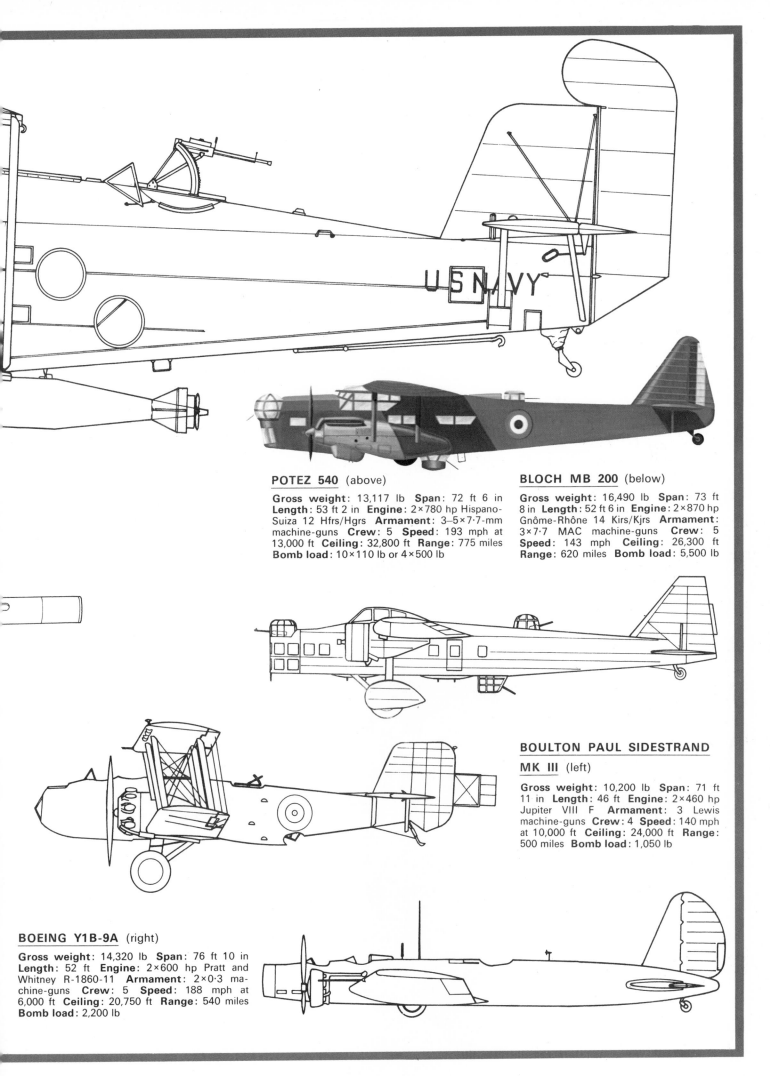

POTEZ 540 (above)

Gross weight: 13,117 lb **Span**: 72 ft 6 in
Length: 53 ft 2 in **Engine**: 2×780 hp Hispano-
Suiza 12 Hfrs/Hgrs **Armament**: 3–5×7·7-mm
machine-guns **Crew**: 5 **Speed**: 193 mph at
13,000 ft **Ceiling**: 32,800 ft **Range**: 775 miles
Bomb load: 10×110 lb or 4×500 lb

BLOCH MB 200 (below)

Gross weight: 16,490 lb **Span**: 73 ft
8 in **Length**: 52 ft 6 in **Engine**: 2×870 hp
Gnôme-Rhône 14 Kirs/Kjrs **Armament**:
3×7·7 MAC machine-guns **Crew**: 5
Speed: 143 mph **Ceiling**: 26,300 ft
Range: 620 miles **Bomb load**: 5,500 lb

BOULTON PAUL SIDESTRAND

MK III (left)

Gross weight: 10,200 lb **Span**: 71 ft
11 in **Length**: 46 ft **Engine**: 2×460 hp
Jupiter VIII F **Armament**: 3 Lewis
machine-guns **Crew**: 4 **Speed**: 140 mph
at 10,000 ft **Ceiling**: 24,000 ft **Range**:
500 miles **Bomb load**: 1,050 lb

BOEING Y1B-9A (right)

Gross weight: 14,320 lb **Span**: 76 ft 10 in
Length: 52 ft **Engine**: 2×600 hp Pratt and
Whitney R-1860-11 **Armament**: 2×0·3 ma-
chine-guns **Crew**: 5 **Speed**: 188 mph at
6,000 ft **Ceiling**: 20,750 ft **Range**: 540 miles
Bomb load: 2,200 lb

MITSUBISHI Ki-2I

Gross weight: 10,031 lb **Span:** 65 ft 6 in
Length: 41 ft 4 in **Engine:** 2×570 hp Nakajima
Armament: 2×7·7-mm machine-guns **Crew:** 5
Speed: 158 mph at 9,500 ft **Ceiling:** 22,890 ft
Range: 560 miles **Bomb load:** 660 lb

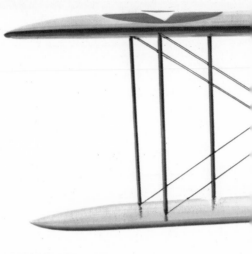

AMIOT 143 (left)

Gross weight: 19,568 lb **Span:** 80 ft 2 in
Length: 58 ft 11 in **Engine:** 2×870 hp Gnôme-
Rhône **Armament:** 4×7·5-mm MAC machine-
guns **Crew:** 5 **Speed:** 190 mph at 13,000 ft
Ceiling: 21,200 ft **Range:** 800 miles **Bomb
load:** 1,984 lb

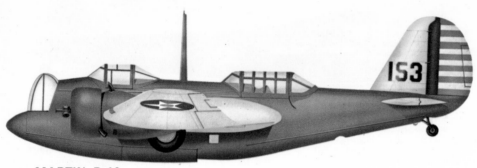

MARTIN B-10

Gross weight: 14,600 lb **Span:** 70 ft 6 in
Length: 44 ft 9 in **Engine:** 2×775 hp Wright
R-1820-25 **Armament:** 5×·303 Browning
machine-guns **Crew:** 4 **Speed:** 212 mph at
6,500 ft **Ceiling:** 24,200 ft **Range:** 1,240 miles
Bomb load: 2,260 lb

DH 9A

Gross weight: 4,645 lb **Span:** 45 ft 11 in
Length: 30 ft 3 in **Engine:** 400 hp Liberty
Armament: 1 Vickers machine-gun; 2 Lewis
machine-guns **Crew:** 2 **Speed:** 116 mph at
10,000 ft **Ceiling:** 17,000 ft **Range:** 3 hrs
Bomb load: 660 lb

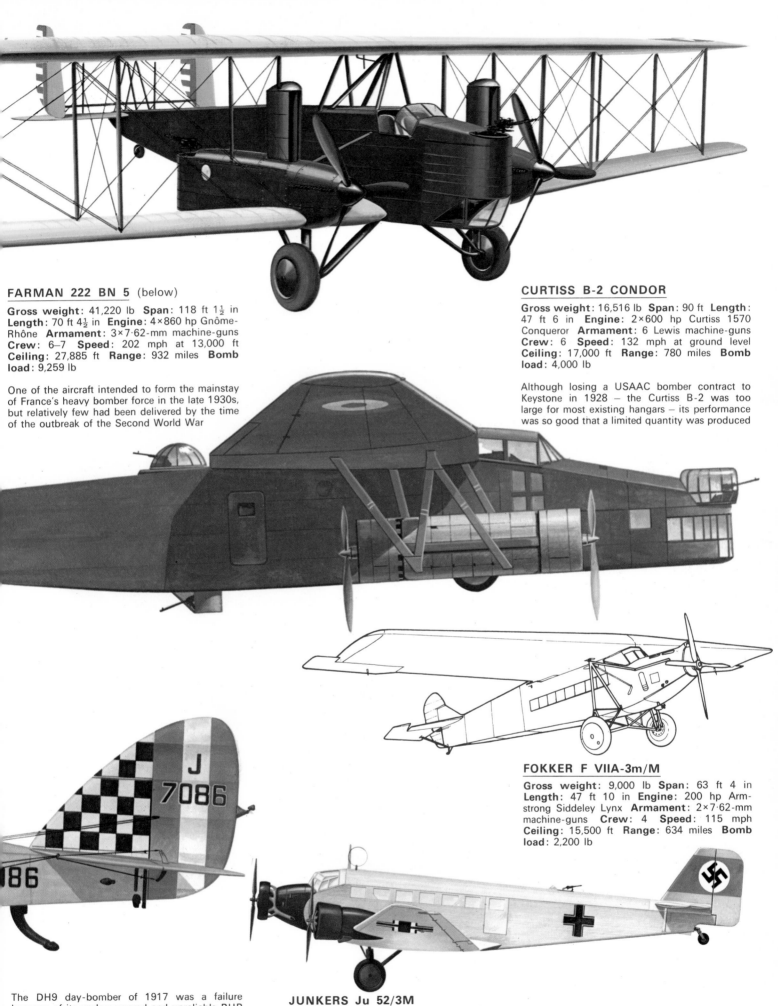

FARMAN 222 BN 5 (below)

Gross weight: 41,220 lb **Span:** 118 ft 1½ in
Length: 70 ft 4½ in **Engine:** 4×860 hp Gnôme-
Rhône **Armament:** 3×7·62-mm machine-guns
Crew: 6–7 **Speed:** 202 mph at 13,000 ft
Ceiling: 27,885 ft **Range:** 932 miles **Bomb
load:** 9,259 lb

One of the aircraft intended to form the mainstay
of France's heavy bomber force in the late 1930s,
but relatively few had been delivered by the time
of the outbreak of the Second World War

CURTISS B-2 CONDOR

Gross weight: 16,516 lb **Span:** 90 ft **Length:**
47 ft 6 in **Engine:** 2×600 hp Curtiss 1570
Conqueror **Armament:** 6 Lewis machine-guns
Crew: 6 **Speed:** 132 mph at ground level
Ceiling: 17,000 ft **Range:** 780 miles **Bomb
load:** 4,000 lb

Although losing a USAAC bomber contract to
Keystone in 1928 – the Curtiss B-2 was too
large for most existing hangars – its performance
was so good that a limited quantity was produced

FOKKER F VIIA-3m/M

Gross weight: 9,000 lb **Span:** 63 ft 4 in
Length: 47 ft 10 in **Engine:** 200 hp Armstrong Siddeley Lynx **Armament:** 2×7·62-mm
machine-guns **Crew:** 4 **Speed:** 115 mph
Ceiling: 15,500 ft **Range:** 634 miles **Bomb
load:** 2,200 lb

The DH9 day-bomber of 1917 was a failure
because of its underpowered and unreliable BHP
engine, but when the American Liberty engine
became available, the improved DH 9A proved
itself to be one of the most outstanding aircraft
in RAF service from August 1918 to 1931. The
'Nine-ack' as it was known was also put into
production in the USA and USSR.

JUNKERS Ju 52/3M

Gross weight: 24,320 lb **Span:** 95 ft 10 in
Length: 62 ft **Engine:** 3×830 hp BMW 132T
Armament: 1×13-mm machine-gun; 2×7·9-mm
machine-guns 15 **Crew:** 4 **Speed:** 189 mph
Ceiling: 18,000 ft **Range:** 930 miles **Bomb
load:** 3,306 lb

developed from the Do F mail and freight transport, at a time when the *Luftwaffe* was being secretly built up under the guise of civil aircraft, used a mixture of fabric and metal covering for different parts of the fuselage and wings. But structurally, military aircraft were conservative and all-metal stressed-skin airframes were rare until well after 1935.

This was surprising because, during the First World War, Junkers and other designers had shown that light-alloy skin could be used to bear part of the structural loads. A major advance was made in 1920 when at the London Aero Show, Oswald Short displayed the Silver Streak biplane which had a monocoque metal-covered fuselage, not only stronger and lighter than wood but easy to mass-produce.

The first Russian-designed metal bomber – the two-seat single-engined Tupolev R-3 biplane brought into service in 1926 – was also covered with corrugated Kolchug aluminium sheeting. This alloy was named after the Russian town where it was originally produced and claimed to be stronger than normal duralumin. A similar all-metal construction and covering was used in the Tupolev TB-1 twin-engined cantilever low-wing monoplane which was brought into service the following year. The TB-1 was a very large machine with an especially thick wing, capable of carrying a crew of six and a maximum bomb-load of 6,600 lb, and set the pattern for Soviet bomber design until the end of the 1930s.

'Iron Annie'

Germany had a long tradition of metal built and covered aircraft, and in 1926 the German designer Rohrbach perfected a complete system for making stressed-skin monoplanes with no bracing anywhere. Most German 'civil' aircraft of the middle and late 1920s were designed with military uses in mind, and such types as the three-engined Junkers Ju 52 'Iron Annie', which made its operational debut during the Spanish Civil War, served as interim bombers until the arrival of aircraft developed from airliners and specifically designed for bombing.

Some of the earliest mass-produced stressed-skin machines were the ugly, unstreamlined bombers of the French Armée de l'Air, such as the Amiot 143 multi-purpose battleplane and the Farman F 222, both twin engined high-wing monoplanes. Stressed-skin construction did not appear to do much either for the Bristol Bombay and Armstrong Whitworth Whitley, the two earliest large RAF aircraft of this type, though it was essential for faster machines like the Bristol Blenheim and Fairey Battle.

It was the USA in the early 1930s that led the switch to modern monoplane design. Stressed-skin construction made possible the rapid development of fast cantilever monoplane civil transports, notably the Boeing 247, Douglas DC-2 and Lockheed Electra, and stimulated the use of this form of construction for combat aircraft. The first of the new bomber designs was the twin-engined Boeing YB-9 low-wing monoplane in 1931, which incorporated such advanced features as semi-retractable undercarriage and variable-pitch propellers. Although not built in quantity and used only on a trial basis by the US Army Air Corps, the YB-9 offered, without any reduction of bomb-load, a dramatic improve-

JUNKERS Ju 52

Gross weight: 24,200 lb **Span:** 95 ft 10 in **Length:** 62 ft **Engine:** 3×830 hp BMW 132T **Armament:** 2×7·92-mm machine-guns 15; 1×13-mm machine-gun; **Crew:** 4 **Speed:** 165 mph at 3,000 ft **Ceiling:** 16,600 ft **Range:** 800 miles **Bomb load:** 3,300 lb or 10–15 paratroops

Although this, the famous 'Iron Annie' of the *Luftwaffe* made its operational debut as a bomber during the Spanish Civil War, it became better known as a military transport plane in the Second World War. It saw service in every major German invasion campaign. It is shown here in its Second World War colours

ment over the Keystone biplane bombers which were its predecessors.

An even greater advance was made with the Martin B-10, brought into service in 1934, with a fully-retractable undercarriage and enclosed cockpit. Its maximum speed of 212 mph at 6,500 ft made it faster than most fighters, and it was the first American monoplane bomber to be built in quantity. At the end of the 1930s, the MB-10 was being replaced by the Douglas B-18, developed from the DC-2 civil transport. Although an excellent aircraft, this was overshadowed by the four-engined Boeing B-17 Flying Fortress, produced from the Boeing 299 prototype of 1934.

Several of the American machines, especially the Northrop and Douglas types, had multi-spar wings with the advantage, not fully appreciated at the time, of being able to log large numbers of flying hours without suffering from any form of fatigue. Even if any structural member happened to crack, there were always alternative load-paths to bear the stresses.

It was partly in a search for a safer and

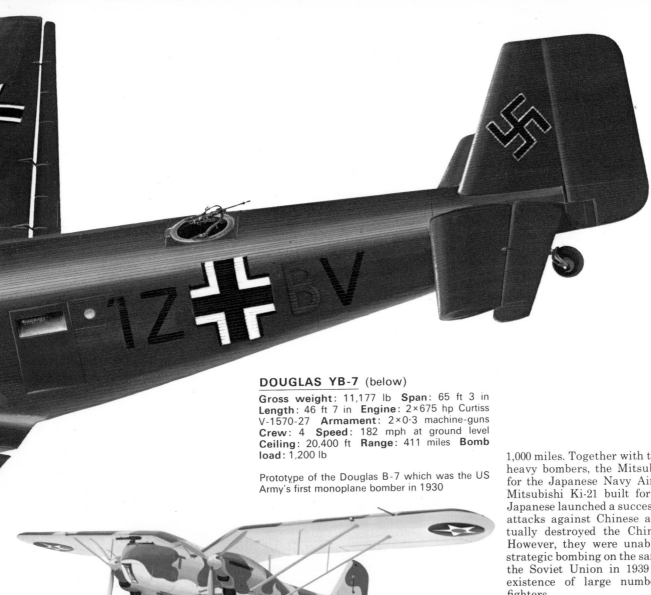

DOUGLAS YB-7 (below)

Gross weight: 11,177 lb **Span:** 65 ft 3 in
Length: 46 ft 7 in **Engine:** 2×675 hp Curtiss
V-1570-27 **Armament:** 2×0·3 machine-guns
Crew: 4 **Speed:** 182 mph at ground level
Ceiling: 20,400 ft **Range:** 411 miles **Bomb
load:** 1,200 lb

Prototype of the Douglas B-7 which was the US
Army's first monoplane bomber in 1930

more efficient form of metal construction that Barnes Wallis devised his 'geodetic' system in the early 1930s. Wallis had been chief designer of the Vickers airship R 100 of 1929, and he developed its structure into a completely new form of metal basketwork, assembled from large numbers of standard metal sections. Riveted together by small tabs and connectors, they formed a complete wing or fuselage. All the members had the shape of intersecting curves and each carried either tension or compression but no bending.

The first geodetic aircraft, the private venture single-engined Vickers Wellesley which ultimately went into service in 1937, showed its great efficiency compared with the rival types built to the official G 4/31 specification. Its high-aspect ratio wing helped the Wellesley set the world distance record in 1938, by which time Vickers were in production with the geodetic Wellington. One of the big advantages of geodetic construction was that battle damage could easily be repaired by cutting out and replacing the small pieces of basketwork. A feature of this type of structure was that the skin should be unstressed, so that all the geodetic machines had fabric covering.

Most of the bombers used operationally

during the Second Worlds War were being developed in the mid-1930s. Meanwhile, several modern all-metal cantilever monoplane types entered service towards the end of the 1930s but had been largely replaced by the time war broke out. One was the Bloch 200 which met a French specification for a five-seat night bomber in 1932. Unfortunately its top speed of 143 mph was some 30 mph slower than expected and by the time of the German offensive none of this type was in squadron service. The Bloch 210 was an improved version, with a speed of 186 mph at 13,000 feet, and saw operational service with the Republican forces during the Spanish Civil War. It was during that war of course that the Germans took the opportunity of testing their new aircraft in combat conditions, discovering for instance that the performance of the early Ju 86s was inadequate against contemporary fighter opposition.

Another war in which bombers were given their first important test in combat was the Sino-Japanese war which broke out in 1937. Two single-engined monoplane bombers had by that time been brought into service with the Japanese Army Air Force, the Kawasaki Ki-32 and the Mitsubishi Ki-30 which had a combat range of over

1,000 miles. Together with the twin-engined heavy bombers, the Mitsubishi G3M built for the Japanese Navy Air Force and the Mitsubishi Ki-21 built for the Army, the Japanese launched a succession of strategic attacks against Chinese airfields and virtually destroyed the Chinese Air Force. However, they were unable to undertake strategic bombing on the same scale against the Soviet Union in 1939 because of the existence of large numbers of Russian fighters.

The new generation

The disarmament policy of most of the Allied powers prevented the construction of aircraft to meet such policies as strategic bombing, until after 1935 when the threat of war spurred rearmament programmes. Design was dominated by the immediate needs of the customer. The wars of the 1920s were mostly colonial skirmishes in which European colonial powers needed little more than light single-engined bombers for their policing operations – hence the emphasis, especially in Britain, on building fighter-bombers. It was partly the success of bombing operations against ill-armed tribesmen that gave rise to exaggerated claims for the importance of strategic bombing.

The Second World War was to see the introduction of a completely new generation of bomber aircraft, flying at three times the speed of their First World War counterparts and delivering bombs ten times more powerful than the largest used in 1918, while the development of radar added a new dimension to aerial warfare. But the actual ways in which bombers were used differed little from the first war, except that they were on a vastly greater scale. The difference in the Second World War was that air power had become of such vital importance that without at least some degree of balance in the control of air space, battles would be lost and entire countries fall to an enemy who had mastery of the skies.

WAR! HOW THE WORLD'S BOMBERS LINED UP...

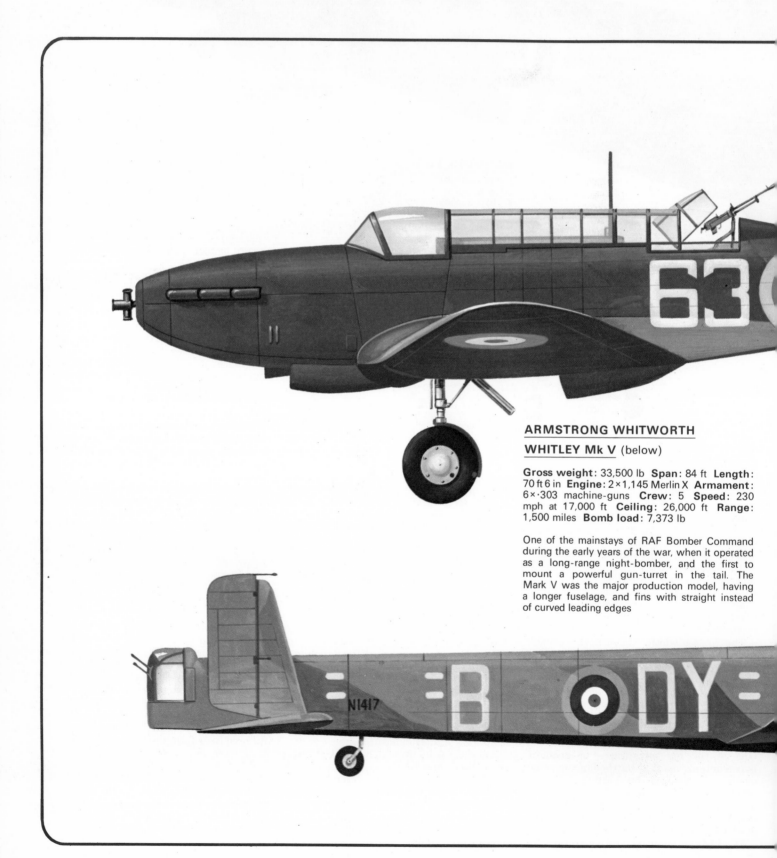

ARMSTRONG WHITWORTH

WHITLEY Mk V (below)

Gross weight: 33,500 lb **Span:** 84 ft **Length:** 70 ft 6 in **Engine:** 2×1,145 Merlin X **Armament:** 6×·303 machine-guns **Crew:** 5 **Speed:** 230 mph at 17,000 ft **Ceiling:** 26,000 ft **Range:** 1,500 miles **Bomb load:** 7,373 lb

One of the mainstays of RAF Bomber Command during the early years of the war, when it operated as a long-range night-bomber, and the first to mount a powerful gun-turret in the tail. The Mark V was the major production model, having a longer fuselage, and fins with straight instead of curved leading edges

Most of the bombers used in the Second World War were either flying before the start of the war or resulted from programmes initiated before 1939. Unlike fighters, which could be designed and put into production relatively quickly, heavy bombers were so complicated even in those days that it was a daunting task to develop a completely new one. Very few new types were designed and brought into service within the period of the war, and those initiated before were largely based on earlier developments

FAIREY BATTLE (above)

Gross weight: 10,792 lb **Span:** 54 ft **Length:** 52 ft 2 in **Engine:** 1,030 hp Rolls Royce Merlin **Armament:** 2×·303 machine-guns **Crew:** 3 **Speed:** 250 mph at 20,000 ft **Ceiling:** 25,000 ft **Range:** 1,050 miles **Bomb load:** 1,000 lb

Entered RAF service in 1937 as a fast day bomber. Already outdated when war broke out, it suffered heavy losses in France in 1939/40 when it formed the vanguard of the British Advanced Air Striking Force. Later relegated for training purposes

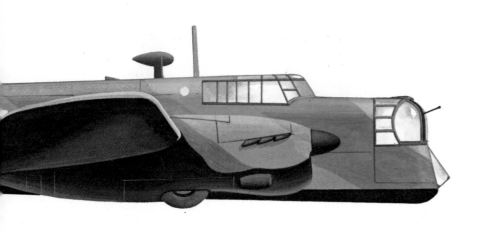

BRITAIN

Battle against time

The main bomber types in service with the RAF in 1939 were the Vickers Wellesley and Fairey Battle – the last single-engined bombers to be built in Britain – and the twin-engined Armstrong Whitworth Whitley, Bristol Blenheim, Handley Page Hampden and Vickers Wellington. These bore the brunt of operations in the early part of the war.

The Wellesley, first to use the geodetic form of construction, was brought into service in 1937 and was used operationally for the first two years of the war, especially from overseas bases against the Italians. An unusual feature was the method of carrying its bomb-load in containers under the wings. The Fairey Battle, powered by the same Merlin engine used by Spitfire and Hurricane fighters, though obsolete when the war started, was the only bomber available to form the vanguard of the British Advanced Air Striking Force in France during the winter of 1939–40. Heavy losses were suffered during daytime operations; during an attack on German pontoon bridges at Sedan on 20 May 1940, forty out of seventy-one were lost. The Battle was later withdrawn from bomber squadrons and used for training, especially in Canada under the Commonwealth Air Training programme.

Whitleys were the first British bombers to fly over Germany on the first night of the war, when they dropped some six million leaflets in an attempt to persuade the German people that the war could be avoided. Accompanied by Hampdens, they made the first bombing raid on German soil, on 19 March 1940, and were the first RAF

AVRO ANSON Mk I

Gross weight: 8,000 lb **Span:** 56 ft 6 in **Length:** 42 ft 3 in **Engine:** 2×350 hp Armstrong Siddeley Cheetah IX **Armament:** 2×·303 machine-guns **Crew:** 3 **Speed:** 188 mph at 7,000 ft **Ceiling:** 16,000 ft **Range:** 660 miles **Bombs:** 360 lb

Although Ansons first entered service in 1936 and were becoming obsolete by the outbreak of war, they continued in production until 1952, used for training and transport after 1941, and served with many other air forces

bombers to attack Italy. Early in 1942 they were withdrawn from front-line service, but they continued to be used for parachute dropping and glider-towing duties.

A smaller and much faster bomber was the Blenheim, which created a sensation when it entered service in 1937 with a speed of 285 mph, outpacing some of the best fighters. Many changes were made as the war progressed, particularly by fitting armour-plate and heavier armament, but these considerably reduced its speed and by 1942 the type was outdated. Blenheims had the distinction of being the only aircraft to serve in all the RAF wartime Commands – Bomber, Fighter, Coastal, Army Co-operation and Training. As a night-fighter, the Blenheim pioneered the use of the highly secret Airborne Interception radar in 1940, though it was not really fast enough.

The Hampden was the last medium bomber with only two engines to enter service with the RAF, in 1938. It had a serious deficiency in defensive armament and suffered very heavy losses in early daytime raids. Known as the 'Flying Suitcase' because of its deep forebody and slender tail, it was reserved for night operations from 1940–42, taking part in the first raid on Berlin and the famous 1,000-bomber raid on Cologne. At the end of 1942 it was withdrawn from bombing operations but continued as a torpedo-bomber.

Backbone of Bomber Command

Last and best of the pre-war bombers was the long-range Wellington. This plane formed the backbone of Bomber Command's offensive against Germany in the early years of the war, and was popular among its crews for its ability to return to base even after sustaining severe battle damage. Affectionately known as the 'Wimpey', it was generally used for night operations after early daylight bombing raids disproved the theory that the combined firepower of bombers flying in formation could beat off fighters. In April 1941, Wellingtons were the first to drop the new 4,000-lb 'block-buster' bomb during a raid on Emden, and

they were used to help start the Pathfinder tactics for indicating targets. Nearly 11,500 Wellingtons were built in many different versions, including reconnaissance, troop-carrying and transport as well as bombing. They remained in front-line service until the end of the war, by which time, because of the strength and lightness of the geodetic structure, the 21,000 lb all-up weight of the first models had been increased to 36,500 lb, with a maximum bomb-load of 6,000 lb.

A two-engined medium-heavy bomber, the Avro Manchester, was brought into service in November 1940, but constant trouble with the Rolls-Royce Vulture engine led to its being withdrawn from service in 1942, when only 200 machines had been built.

In 1936, when Germany's aggressive intentions were becoming obvious even to the pacifist British, the British Air Staff initiated a programme for three heavy, four-engined bombers. They were not ready when the war started, but later played the major role in RAF Bomber Command's strategic offensive against Germany. In spite of the

valiant efforts of the lighter bombers during the early years of the war, the use of air power built up very gradually; 83 per cent of all the bombs dropped on Germany by the Allies were delivered from 1944 onwards.

The first of the heavy bombers to enter service was the Short Stirling in 1940, with a maximum bomb-load of 14,000 lb at a range of 590 miles. But its usefulness was limited by the fact that the heaviest bomb it could carry was 4,000 lb. The first raid carried out by Stirlings was on 10 February 1941, against oil storage tanks at Rotterdam.

The Stirling was followed late in 1940 by the Handley Page Halifax medium-heavy bomber. Over 6,000 were built in several different versions and the Halifax proved itself a worthy successor of Handley Page's four-engined 0/400 'Bloody Paralyser' of the First World War. But it was inevitably overshadowed by the other heavy bomber with which it shared the major part of the RAF's night-bombing offensive against Germany – the Avro Lancaster. Whereas the Halifax flew 75,532 bombing sorties,

HANDLEY PAGE HAMPDEN Mk I

Gross weight: 18,750 lb **Span:** 69 ft 2 in **Length:** 53 ft 7 in **Engine:** 2×1,000 hp Bristol Pegasus XVIII **Armament:** 4×·303 Vickers machine-guns **Crew:** 4 **Speed:** 265 mph at 15,500 ft **Ceiling:** 22,700 ft **Range:** 1,990 miles **Bomb load:** 4,000 lb

BRISTOL BLENHEIM Mk I

Gross weight: 12,500 lb **Span**: 56 ft 4 in
Length: 39 ft 9 in **Engine**: 2×840 hp Bristol
Mercury VIII **Armament**: 2×·303 machine-guns
Crew: 4 **Speed**: 285 mph at 15,000 ft **Ceiling**:
27,280 ft **Range**: 1,125 miles **Bomb load**:
1,000 lb

Faster than the best fighters when it entered
RAF service in 1937, the Blenheim light bomber
later served in many wartime roles, including
night-fighting, ground attack, and anti-shipping

dropping 227,610 tons of bombs, the
Lancaster flew no less than 156,000 sorties,
and delivered 608,612 tons.

Although the most famous and successful
heavy night bomber used in Europe during
the war, the Lancaster did not have the
adaptability of the Halifax and was used
almost exclusively for bombing operations.
It went into service early in 1942 and by
mid-1943 had established its excellent all-
round performance – only one Lancaster
was lost for every 132 tons of bombs
delivered, compared with 56 tons for each
Halifax lost and 41 tons for each Stirling.

A major feature of the Lancaster –
described by the chief of RAF Bomber
Command as the greatest single factor in
winning the Second World War – was its
cavernous bomb-bay. This was initially
designed to take bombs of up to 4,000 lb,
with a maximum bomb-load of 14,000 lb, but
it was progressively modified to carry 8,000,

12,000, and eventually the 22,000-lb 'Earthquake' or Grand Slam bombs. The Lancaster
was also chosen to carry the remarkable
'spinning drum' bomb designed by Dr Barnes
Wallis for the famous raid on the Mohne
and Eder dams on 17 May 1943. Lancasters
were also responsible for sinking the *Tirpitz*
on 12 November 1944, using Barnes Wallis's
12,000-lb 'Tallboy' deep-penetration bomb.
Well over 7,000 Lancasters served in various
air forces, many until long after the end of
the war. A development of the Lancaster –
the Avro Lincoln, produced just after the
war – was the mainstay of RAF Bomber
Command as the last piston-engined heavy
bomber before the introduction of the jets.

The second most successful bomber used
by the RAF was the extremely versatile

twin-engined de Havilland Mosquito,
initiated as a private-venture light bomber
in 1938. One of its claims to distinction was
that it was built almost entirely of wood;
another was that it was so fast – 400 mph
plus – that it could generally avoid fighter
interception and therefore had no need to
be armed.

Mosquitoes were used for many purposes,
including night-fighting and photographic
reconnaissance. As a bomber it could
initially carry four 500-lb bombs, but more
than fifty Mark IVs were adapted to carry
4,000-pounders, previously taken only by
heavy bombers. The Mosquito first went into
service in 1941 and was the fastest type in
Bomber Command for nearly ten years until
the introduction of the Canberra jet.

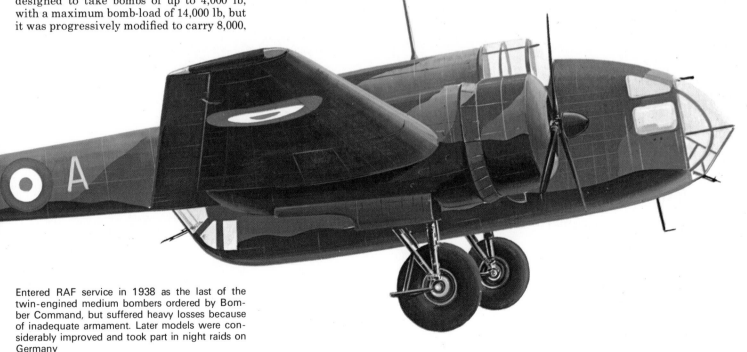

Entered RAF service in 1938 as the last of the
twin-engined medium bombers ordered by Bomber Command, but suffered heavy losses because
of inadequate armament. Later models were considerably improved and took part in night raids on
Germany

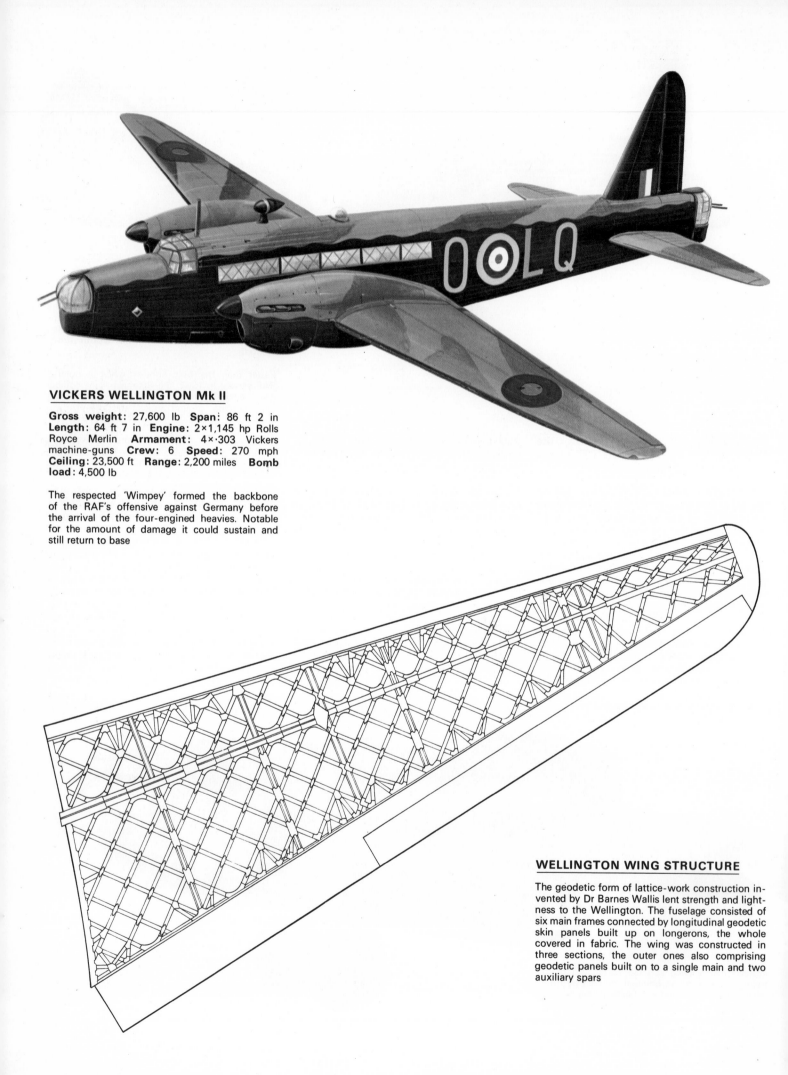

VICKERS WELLINGTON Mk II

Gross weight: 27,600 lb **Span:** 86 ft 2 in
Length: 64 ft 7 in **Engine:** 2×1,145 hp Rolls
Royce Merlin **Armament:** 4×·303 Vickers
machine-guns **Crew:** 6 **Speed:** 270 mph
Ceiling: 23,500 ft **Range:** 2,200 miles **Bomb
load:** 4,500 lb

The respected 'Wimpey' formed the backbone
of the RAF's offensive against Germany before
the arrival of the four-engined heavies. Notable
for the amount of damage it could sustain and
still return to base

WELLINGTON WING STRUCTURE

The geodetic form of lattice-work construction invented by Dr Barnes Wallis lent strength and lightness to the Wellington. The fuselage consisted of
six main frames connected by longitudinal geodetic
skin panels built up on longerons, the whole
covered in fabric. The wing was constructed in
three sections, the outer ones also comprising
geodetic panels built on to a single main and two
auxiliary spars

FRANCE

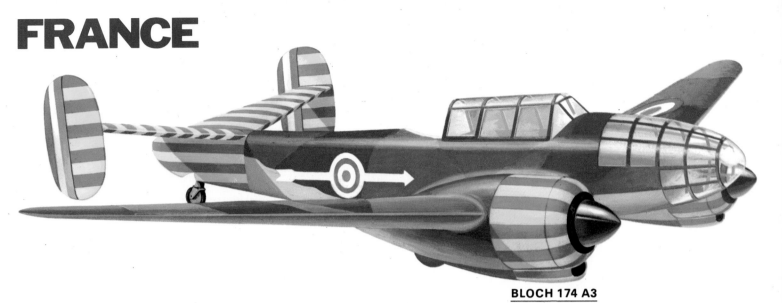

BLOCH 174 A3

Gross weight: 15,748 lb **Span:** 58 ft 9½ in
Length: 40 ft 1½ in **Engine:** 2×1,140 hp
Gnôme-Rhône **Armament:** 7×7·5-mm mach-
ine-guns **Crew:** 3 **Speed:** 329 mph at 17,060 ft
Ceiling: 30,090 ft **Range:** 1,025 miles **Bomb
load:** 1,500 lb

Too little, too late

Military aviation in France in the mid-1930s was in an even worse state than in Britain. At the start of the war, many French squadrons were equipped with such obsolete bombers as the Amiot 143, which undertook a few bombing missions over enemy-occupied territory, and the Bloch 210, used by the Republican forces in the Spanish Civil War but which, by 1940, was 100 mph slower than German bombers. A re-armament pro-gramme was under way in France but it was not due for completion until 1942 and France capitulated before very many of the new types had been delivered to the French Air Force. Even these suffered from a lack of equipment and serious engine problems, the result of government incompetence and refusal to take the German threat seriously

during the mid-1930s. The development of French bombers naturally ceased after the Armistice, but some of the new twin-engined types were used in the early months of the war, while others were taken over and used operationally by the Axis Powers.

One of these was the Bréguet 690 series which entered production in 1938 as a two-seater light assault bomber. The 693 version was used in May 1940 for low-level attacks on German trenches, and many were later used for the same purpose by the Italian Air Force. Another type which would have made an excellent bomber but which was developed too late was the Lioré et Olivier 451. Again there were problems with un-reliable and underpowered engines, although the prototype achieved a speed of 310 mph in level flight as early as 1937. The few that had been delivered before the Ger-man invasion of France in May 1940 were later used by the *Luftwaffe* as transports.

With the Potez 630 series, it was not only engine troubles but also a shortage of propellers which kept them grounded at the

This 1938 French design was switched to a reconnaissance role because of its limited bomb load, but from it was developed the Bloch 175. None saw action before the French surrender but the Germans continued production until 1942. French naval units used a torpedo-carrying version until 1953

time of the German attack. A greater degree of success was achieved by other countries which purchased machines of this type, including Greece, Rumania and Japan. One bomber which was kept in production by the Germans until the end of 1942 was the Bloch 175, a development of the 174, which had been given a reconnaissance role because of its limited bomb-load. Later, it was decided to use the self-contained engine-propeller-cowling units of the 175 in the huge Messerschmitt Me 323 transports. Finally, there was the Amiot 350 series which was being delivered to the French Air Force early in 1940. Lack of armament prevented these machines being used operationally, and many were destroyed to prevent them falling into German hands.

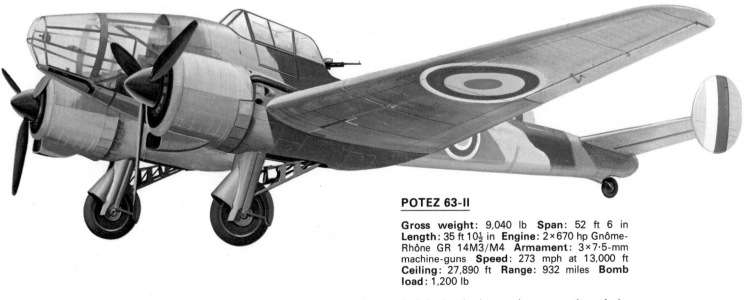

POTEZ 63-II

Gross weight: 9,040 lb **Span:** 52 ft 6 in
Length: 35 ft 10½ in **Engine:** 2×670 hp Gnôme-
Rhône GR 14M3/M4 **Armament:** 3×7·5-mm
machine-guns **Speed:** 273 mph at 13,000 ft
Ceiling: 27,890 ft **Range:** 932 miles **Bomb
load:** 1,200 lb

A light bomber/reconnaissance version of the Potez 630 day and night fighter

JUNKERS Ju 86K

Gross weight: 18,070 lb **Span:** 73 ft 10 in **Length** 57 ft 9 in **Engine:** 2×Swedish-built Bristol Mercury **Armament:** 3×7·9-mm machine-guns **Crew:** 5 **Speed:** 202 mph at 9,800 ft **Ceiling:** 22,300 ft **Range:** 1,240 miles **Bomb load:** 2,200 lb

Shown here in Swedish markings, the Ju 86 revealed deficiencies as a bomber during the Spanish Civil War and despite improvements it was used primarily as a reconnaissance aircraft by the *Luftwaffe* in the early years of the war

LeO 451

Gross weight: 26,000 lb **Span:** 73 ft 11 in **Length:** 56 ft 4 in **Engine:** 2×1,000 hp Gnôme-Rhône 14 N20/21 **Armament:** 1×20-mm cannon; 4×7·5-mm machine-guns **Crew:** 4 **Speed:** 310 mph at 18,000 ft **Ceiling:** 27,000 ft **Range:** 1,040 miles **Bomb load:** 3,080 lb

The only really modern bombers in the French Air Force in September 1939 were LeO 451s taken from an experimental squadron but they arrived too late to be of much value. A number were later used by the *Luftwaffe* and by the Vichy Government

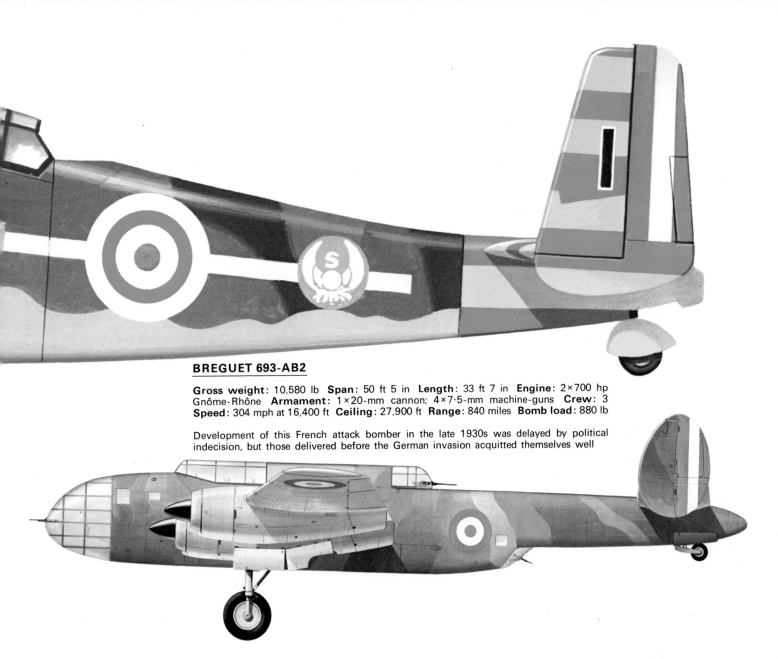

BREGUET 693-AB2

Gross weight: 10,580 lb **Span**: 50 ft 5 in **Length**: 33 ft 7 in **Engine**: 2×700 hp Gnôme-Rhône **Armament**: 1×20-mm cannon; 4×7·5-mm machine-guns **Crew**: 3 **Speed**: 304 mph at 16,400 ft **Ceiling**: 27,900 ft **Range**: 840 miles **Bomb load**: 880 lb

Development of this French attack bomber in the late 1930s was delayed by political indecision, but those delivered before the German invasion acquitted themselves well

CAO 700

Gross weight: 39,860 lb **Span**: 81 ft 7 in **Length**: 61 ft 6 in **Engine**: 4×1,140 hp Gnôme-Rhône 14N 14 cylinder air-cooled radial **Armament**: 1×7·5-mm nose; 2×7·5-mm ventral machine-guns; 1×20-mm cannon in power-operated dorsal turret **Crew**: 5 **Speed**: 330 mph at 17,000 ft

Flight trials were delayed and later cancelled by the French Armistice in June 1940 and development stopped

GERMANY

The Luftwaffe — born in secret

The three great German bomber manufacturers – Junkers, Heinkel and Dornier – were all gaining experience in the mid-1930s with aircraft either originally designed for civil use or disguised as such, a necessary deception in view of the Versailles Treaty which prohibited Germany from building military aircraft. Bombing operations during the Spanish Civil War provided the newly-formed *Luftwaffe* with valuable experience. Germany never showed much interest in long-range heavy bombers and concentrated from first to last on relatively small tactical machines for use within a European theatre of operations.

Towards the end of the Second World War, prototypes and even a few production models of larger aircraft appeared. The Junkers Ju 390, a very large six-engined machine which on one occasion flew to within ten miles of New York, could have formed the basis of a powerful night-bomber force. The Messerschmitt Me 264 was specifically planned as a bomber capable of striking the eastern seaboard of the USA, its four engines mounted on a wing of very high aspect ratio with a span of 141 feet. But little effort was put behind these developments and they eventually petered out.

With the exception of the four-engined Ju 290 maritime patrol and reconnaissance bomber, produced in small numbers from 1943 onwards, and the Heinkel He 177 which went into service at the same time, all the German bombers were limited to either one or two engines. In fact, the He 177 was the only long-range strategic bomber

put into production by Germany during the war, but persistent problems with the coupled engines – they were mounted in pairs in two nacelles, each pair driving a single propeller – and the fact that they caught fire easily made it far from efficient.

The main bombers in service with the *Luftwaffe* when war broke out were the twin-engined Do 17, Ju 88 and He 111, together with the single-engined Ju 87 dive-bomber. In addition, there was the Ju 86, whose poor performance in the

HEINKEL He 111H-6 (above)

Gross weight: 27,400 lb **Span:** 74 ft 1½ in **Length:** 54 ft 5½ in **Engine:** 2×1,340 hp Junkers Jumo 211 F-2 **Armament:** 6×7·9-mm MG 15 machine-guns; 1×20-mm cannon **Crew:** 6 **Speed:** 258 mph at 16,400 ft **Range:** 1,760 miles **Bomb load:** 5,510 lb or 2 torpedoes

The He 111 first proved itself during the Spanish Civil War, and gave excellent service with the *Luftwaffe* throughout the Second World War. The H-6 was a first-rate torpedo-bomber

JUNKERS Ju 87 B2 'STUKA' COCKPIT

1 Visual dive indicator
2 Gun sight
3 Artificial horizon
4 Compass repeater
5 Speedometer
6 Boost pressure
7 Altimeter
8 Rev counter
9 Flap indicator
10 Intercom connection
11 Crash pad
12 Manual engine pump
13 Engine priming pump
14 Electrics panel (radio)
15 Oil cooler flap control
16 Rudder bar pedal
17 Target view window
18 Control column
19 Target view window flap control
20 Fuel metering hand priming pump
21 Throttle
22 Starter switch
23 Main electrics switch
24 Coolant temperature
25 Fuel contents
26 Oil temperature
27 Oil contents
28 Compass
29 Oil pressure gauge
30 Clock
31 Dive pre-set indicator
32 Fuel pressure gauge
33 Radio altimeter
34 Rate of climb indicator
35 Water cooler flap indicator

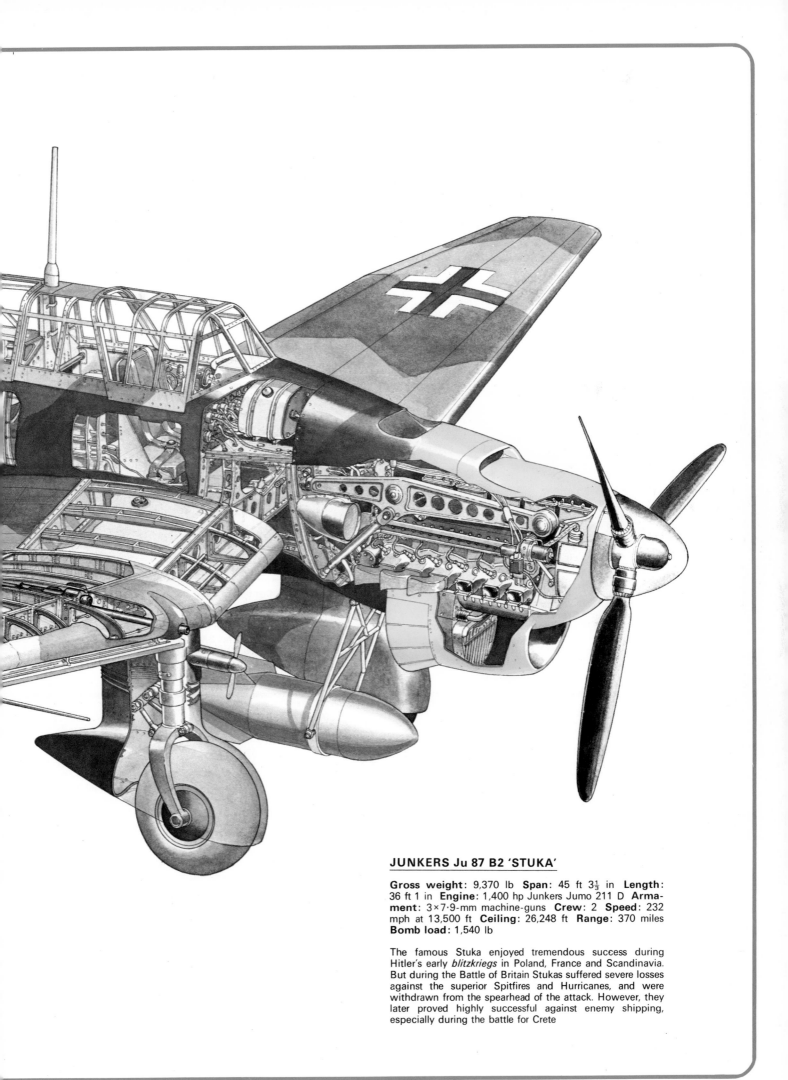

JUNKERS Ju 87 B2 'STUKA'

Gross weight: 9,370 lb **Span:** 45 ft 3⅓ in **Length:** 36 ft 1 in **Engine:** 1,400 hp Junkers Jumo 211 D **Armament:** 3×7·9-mm machine-guns **Crew:** 2 **Speed:** 232 mph at 13,500 ft **Ceiling:** 26,248 ft **Range:** 370 miles **Bomb load:** 1,540 lb

The famous Stuka enjoyed tremendous success during Hitler's early *blitzkriegs* in Poland, France and Scandinavia. But during the Battle of Britain Stukas suffered severe losses against the superior Spitfires and Hurricanes, and were withdrawn from the spearhead of the attack. However, they later proved highly successful against enemy shipping, especially during the battle for Crete

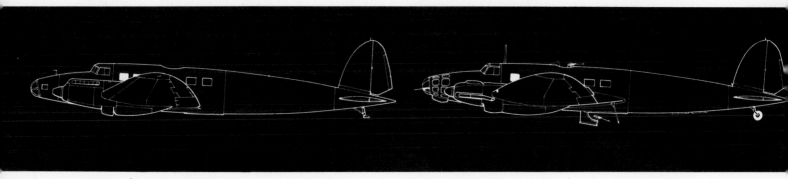

HEINKEL He 111/VI

The first prototype of the He 111 appeared at the end of 1934, fitted out as a bomber armed with three 7·9-mm machine-guns in nose, dorsal and ventral positions, powered by two 660 hp BMW VI liquid-cooled engines, and able to carry a 2,200-lb bomb load. Later prototypes were developed into commercial transports, and deliveries of the first military version, with more powerful DB 600A engines, began in 1936

HEINKEL He 111 E3

The E-series of the He 111, produced in 1937, was powered by Junkers Jumo 211A-3 engines which gave a maximum speed of 267 mph and a service ceiling of 22,900 ft. Semi-retractable radiators were adopted to reduce drag. Up until the beginning of the Second World War the He 111 was probably the best medium bomber flying, but improvements could not keep pace with changing requirements

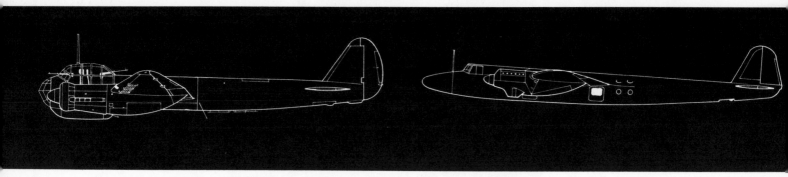

JUNKERS Ju 88 A-1

Gross weight: 27,500 lb **Span:** 59 ft 11 in **Length:** 47 ft 1½ in **Engine:** 2×1,200 hp Jumo 211B **Armament:** 3×7·9-mm machine-guns **Crew:** 4 **Speed:** 286 mph at 18,000 ft **Ceiling:** 30,675 ft **Range:** 1,550 miles **Bomb load:** 5,500 lb

DORNIER Do 17 V1

The Do 17 V1 first flew in 1934, and was quickly nicknamed the 'Flying Pencil' for its clean, slim lines. Intended as a high-speed commercial aircraft (a six-passenger mailplane was developed from it, and three built for *Lufthansa*), it was powered by two 660 hp BMW V1 liquid-cooled engines, and had two cabins for the passengers and a crew of two

Spanish Civil War had underlined its ineffectiveness against fighter opposition. Considerable improvements were made to later models, the Ju 86P and Ju 86R, which were still only really suitable for reconnaissance. Their main asset was an ability to fly at high altitudes, achieved by greatly increased wing span, supercharged diesel engines, and the installation of pressure cabins for the two-man crew. The service ceiling of the Ju 86R for instance, with its wing span increased from 74 to 105 ft, was over 49,000 ft.

Towards the end of the war, apart from the Ju 290 and He 177, the only other notable bomber to be brought into service was the Arado Ar 234 Blitz (Lightning), the world's first operational jet bomber, although only a few saw combat. The Messerschmitt Me 262 played a greater part. Though originally designed as a jet fighter, on Hitler's insistence it was pressed into service as a bomber, which delayed its introduction from early in 1944 as had been originally

planned to the end of that year.

Most of the German bomber effort during the war went into developing and improving the four major types already in service. One of the most successful early on was the Ju 87 'Stuka', the result of a German vogue in the late 1930s for dive-bombing as an integral part of the *blitzkrieg* tactics. It first appeared in 1938, and, during the early months of the war, achieved all that had been expected of it in helping the German armies blast their way across Poland, France, Belgium and Holland. The high-pitched scream made by the Ju 87's dive brakes (required to hold the speed steady enough to aim the bombs) brought a new terror to the confused armies and civilian populations of Europe. But when the Germans employed the Stuka to attack British airfields in the Battle of Britain, it proved highly vulnerable to the much faster Spitfires and Hurricane fighters and suffered heavy losses. Attempts to provide Me 109 fighter escorts were unsuccessful, because

in a dive they could not keep down to the speed of the Stukas and had to leave them behind to the mercy of the British fighters.

Later improvements included a doubling of engine power, an increase in bomb-load from 1,000 lb to 3,960 lb, and additional armour protection for the crew. Various Ju 87 types were used until the end of the war, with particular success on the Russian front and as a 'tank-buster' ground-attack machine during and after the Normandy invasion. Nearly 5,000 of all versions were completed during the war period.

The 'Flying Pencil'

The Do 17, originally designed as a fast six-passenger mail plane when the first prototype flew in 1934, earned itself the nickname 'Flying Pencil' for its slender appearance from the side. In 1937 it outstripped the best fighters then being produced in Europe, and was put into service with the *Luftwaffe* as a medium bomber. It was among the types selected to equip the

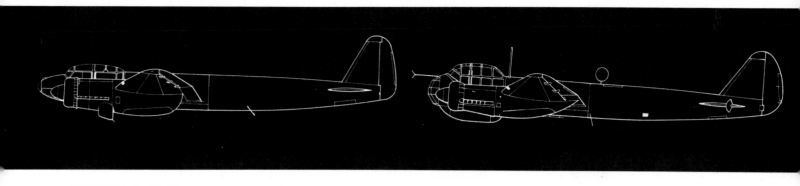

JUNKERS Ju 88 V1

Following the 1935 German specification for a fast twin-engined medium bomber, the Ju 88 V1 development proto-type made its maiden flight in December 1936, powered by two 900 hp DB 600 liquid-cooled engines

JUNKERS Ju 88 V4

Following the V1, six months later, the Ju 88 V4 had a redesigned cockpit to take a fourth crew member, and used 950 hp Jumo 211A engines. This set the pattern for the first models to be taken into service, the production Ju 88 A-1s arriving in time to take part in attacks on Britain in September 1939

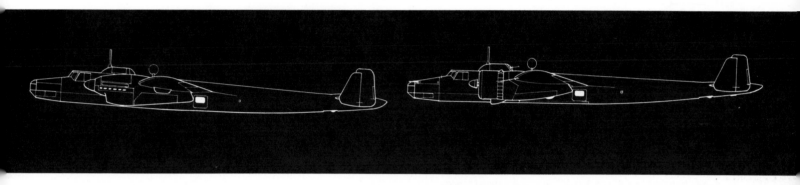

DORNIER Do 17 V8

Of a further series of prototypes, the V4 (1935) replaced the single fin-and-rudder with twin fins and rudders – a feature of all later models. The Do 17's military potential was revealed by the V8 model entered for the Military Aircraft Competition at Zurich in 1937

DORNIER Do 17K

One of the first orders for the Do 17 was received from the Yugoslav Government for an export model, the Do 17K, with two 986 hp Gnôme-Rhône 14N radial engines instead of the BMW engines in the earlier models

famous Condor Legion during the Spanish Civil War and, of the improved versions introduced by 1940, the Do 17Z was most commonly used in raids against England. This type had a completely new, more bulbous forward section for the crew of four or five, with extensive glazing. As further improvements were made, the original beautiful shape was gradually obscured by more pieces of equipment – the fate of many military aircraft. The Do 17Z series was followed by the Do 215, a number of which were used as night-fighters.

Last of the line was the Do 217 which first came into service in 1940, proving itself one of the *Luftwaffe's* most valuable bombers and used operationally until the end of the European war. It was powered at various times by both in-line and radial engines and carried out a wide range of operations, including dive bombing, mine-laying and torpedo bombing, as well as being used as a night-fighter with Lichtenstein airborne interception radar. The E-5 type

was developed with radio equipment to launch and guide the Henschel Hs 293 glider bomb.

The most versatile bomber

Although originally designed as a fast medium bomber when brought into service in 1939, the Ju 88 became the most versatile aircraft of the Second World War, even more so than the Mosquito. The standard bomber type of the early years of the war was the Ju 88A, with a maximum bomb-load of 5,500 lb and air brakes fitted for dive-bombing operations, although this was not its primary function. Later developments included increased armour protection, a longer wing-span, and increased power and defensive armament. With the last bomber version, the Ju 88S, speed was increased to 370 mph at 20,340 ft in an attempt to elude Allied fighters during daytime operations. Total production of the Ju 88, including day and night fighter versions, amounted to some 15,000 machines.

From this highly efficient basic design was produced the more advanced Ju 188 which first appeared in 1942, but relatively few were used purely as bombers. Development continued with the Ju 388 but the only version to go into service was for photographic reconnaissance. The final stage in development, the Ju 488, was still under construction at the end of the war.

The Heinkel He 111, which first flew in 1935, unconvincingly disguised as a commercial transport, was another German plane used by the Condor Legion in the Spanish Civil War. The success achieved then and during the bombing of Poland in 1939 was shattered when it came up against Spitfires and Hurricanes during daylight raids on Britain in 1940, and it had to be assigned to night raids. Nearly 1,000 He 111s had been built by that time and the production of numerous versions, although brought to a halt in Germany at the end of 1944 when over 5,200 had been built, continued for some years afterwards in Spain.

HEINKEL He 111 B-2

Gross weight: 22,046 lb **Span:** 74 ft 2 in **Length:** 57 ft 5 in **Engine:** 2×950 hp Daimler-Benz 600 **Armament:** 3×7·9-mm machine-guns **Crew:** 4 **Speed:** 186 mph at ground level **Ceiling:** 22,966 ft **Range:** 1,030 miles **Bomb load:** 3,307 lb

The B-2 version of the He 111 served with the Condor legion in the Spanish Civil War, outpacing all opposing fighters and carrying out unescorted raids at will. But the resulting over-confidence was shattered by opposition from Spitfires and Hurricanes in 1940 and the He 111 was soon relegated to night operations

FOCKE-WULF Fw 189

Gross weight: 8,700 lb **Span:** 60 ft 5 in **Length:** 39 ft 4 in **Engine:** 2×450 hp Argus As 410A-1 **Armament:** 2×7·9-mm MG 17; 2×7·9-mm MG 15 machine-guns **Crew:** 2 **Speed:** 221 mph at 8,500 ft **Ceiling:** 27,550 ft **Range:** 430 miles **Bomb load** 220 lb·

A light bomber/ground attack machine which entered service with the *Luftwaffe* at the end of 1940 and was later used primarily against the Russians

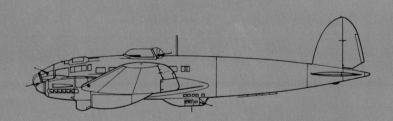

HEINKEL He 111 P-6

The He 111 P-series entered production in 1938. The P-6 was powered by 1,200 hp DB 601N engines, and had an oval nose section which gave excellent visibility. Three 7·9-mm machine-guns were mounted, and the maximum bomb load was 4,410 lb

HEINKEL He 111 H-6

The more effective H-series, with Jumo engines, was the most important bomber variant. The H-6 was used both as a bomber and a torpedo-carrier, some of which were fitted with a remotely-controlled 7·9-mm MG 17 in the extreme tail of the fuselage

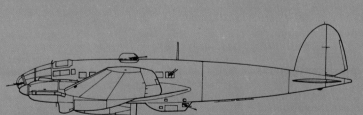

HEINKEL He 111 H-21

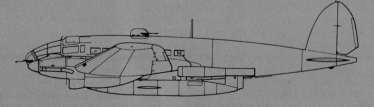

HEINKEL He 111 H-22

The H-21 and H-22 were basically similar, except in defensive armament. The H-21, the last bomber variant of the He 111, was produced in 1944 and powered by two 1,600 hp Jumo 213 E1 engines which gave a maximum speed of 295 mph and a service ceiling of 32,800 ft. Its defensive armament consisted of one 13-mm hand-held MG 131 in the nose, an electrically-operated dorsal turret with an MG 131, a similar gun in a heavily-armoured ventral gondola and twin 7·9-mm MG 81s in each beam position. Intended exclusively for night-bombing, it had large flame dampers on the exhaust pipes

ITALY

The development of one of the war's best bombers

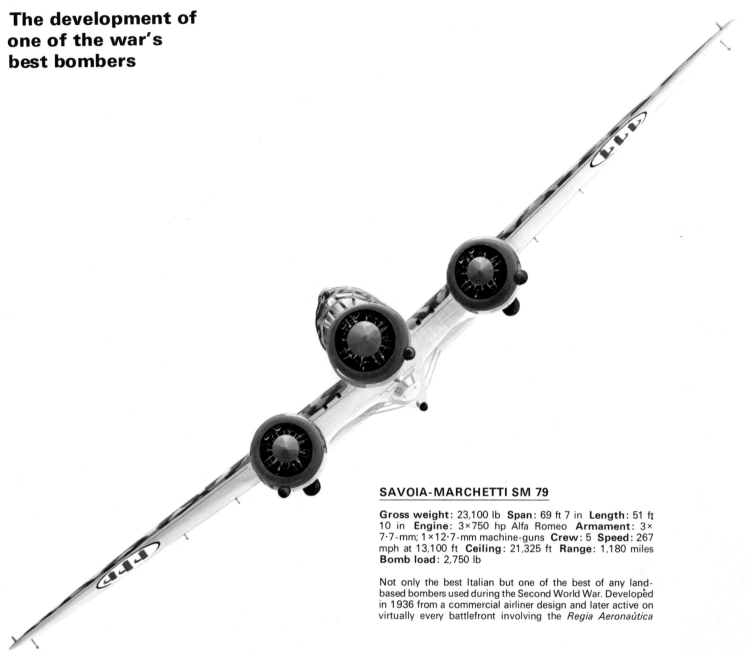

SAVOIA-MARCHETTI SM 79

Gross weight: 23,100 lb **Span:** 69 ft 7 in **Length:** 51 ft 10 in **Engine:** 3×750 hp Alfa Romeo **Armament:** 3× 7·7-mm; 1×12·7-mm machine-guns **Crew:** 5 **Speed:** 267 mph at 13,100 ft **Ceiling:** 21,325 ft **Range:** 1,180 miles **Bomb load:** 2,750 lb

Not only the best Italian but one of the best of any land-based bombers used during the Second World War. Developed in 1936 from a commercial airliner design and later active on virtually every battlefront involving the *Regia Aeronautica*

When Italy entered the war in 1940, a large number of Caproni Ca 133 high-wing medium bombers were still in service with the *Regia Aeronautica*, and although these were too outdated for bombing duties, they gave excellent service as transports throughout the war. The much faster Ca 135 mid-wing medium bomber, first flown in 1935, was a great improvement but it was not taken into service as better machines were available from other Italian manufacturers. In fact, it would have been superior to the Ca 309 to 314 series of bombers which were used in the early years of the war, and for which Caproni adopted a low-wing arrangement after trying all the other positions.

The closest Italian bomber to the German and British ones of the time was the Fiat BR20 Cicogna (Stork) which was used both in Ethiopia and Spain. It was the only Italian bomber to operate against Britain (from bases in Belgium) and was later used in the Italian invasion of Greece in 1941. A number of improvements were made, including increased defensive armament, and there were plans to produce it in large numbers before the Italians surrendered. The Caproni and Fiat bombers were twin-engined types, but several three-engined bombers were also produced and used with even greater success. The CRDA Cant Z 1007 *bis* Alcione (Kingfisher), brought into service in 1939, was constructed mostly of wood, but even so it stood up well to the extreme climatic conditions experienced during operations in North Africa and Russia, as well as serving throughout the Mediterranean and Aegean theatres.

Three-engined Hawk

But undoubtedly the best of the Italian bombers, and one of the best of all land-based bomber aircraft of the Second World War, was the three-engined Savoia-Marchetti SM 79 Sparviero (Hawk). This was also built largely of wood and came into service in 1937, two years after the SM 81 Pipistrello (Bat). The SM 81 was used in Ethiopia and in a wide range of areas after 1940, but because of its relatively slow speed it had to be relegated to more mundane duties towards the end of the war. The SM 79 was much faster, although the clean lines of the eight-passenger commercial airliner from which it was developed in the late 1930s were somewhat marred by the addition of a dorsal hump in the bomber version, housing two 12·7-mm Breda-SAFAT machine-guns. It was active throughout the war on almost every front, including the Mediterranean, North Africa and the Balkans, and a number served in a transport or training role until 1952.

The only heavy four-engined bomber produced by Italy during the war was the Piaggio P.108B, first used in action in 1942 over Gibraltar. It could carry a maximum bomb-load of 7,700 lb and was notable for its defensive armament of eight 12·7-mm machine-guns. In addition to single guns in nose and ventral turrets and in sideways-firing barbettes amidships, two remote-controlled pairs were installed in the rear upper cowling of each outboard engine nacelle.

FIAT BR 20

Gross weight: 22,266 lb **Span:** 70 ft 9 in
Length: 52 ft 9 in **Engine:** 2×1,000 hp
Fiat A80 RC41 **Armament:** 2×7·7-mm;
1×12·7-mm machine-guns **Crew:** 4
Speed: 267 mph at 13,120 ft **Ceiling:**
24,935 ft **Range:** 1,700 miles **Bomb
load:** 3,500 lb

A fast, well-armed light bomber which
came into service with the *Regia Aeronautica*
in time to see combat during the Spanish
Civil War. Used for night raids until Italy's
surrender in the Second World War

SAVOIA-MARCHETTI SM 81

Gross weight: 23,000 lb **Span:** 78 ft 9 in
Length: 58 ft 5 in **Engine:** 3×680 hp
Piaggio P IX **Armament:** 6×7·7-mm
machine-guns **Crew:** 5 **Speed:** 200 mph
at 3,280 ft **Ceiling:** 22,965 ft **Range:**
930 miles **Bomb load:** 2,200 lb

A 1935 military version of the SM 73
commercial airliner which followed the
current Italian vogue for three engines. It
took part in the Ethiopian campaign and the
Spanish Civil War; outdated by the outbreak of the Second World War, it was
quickly relegated to night operations

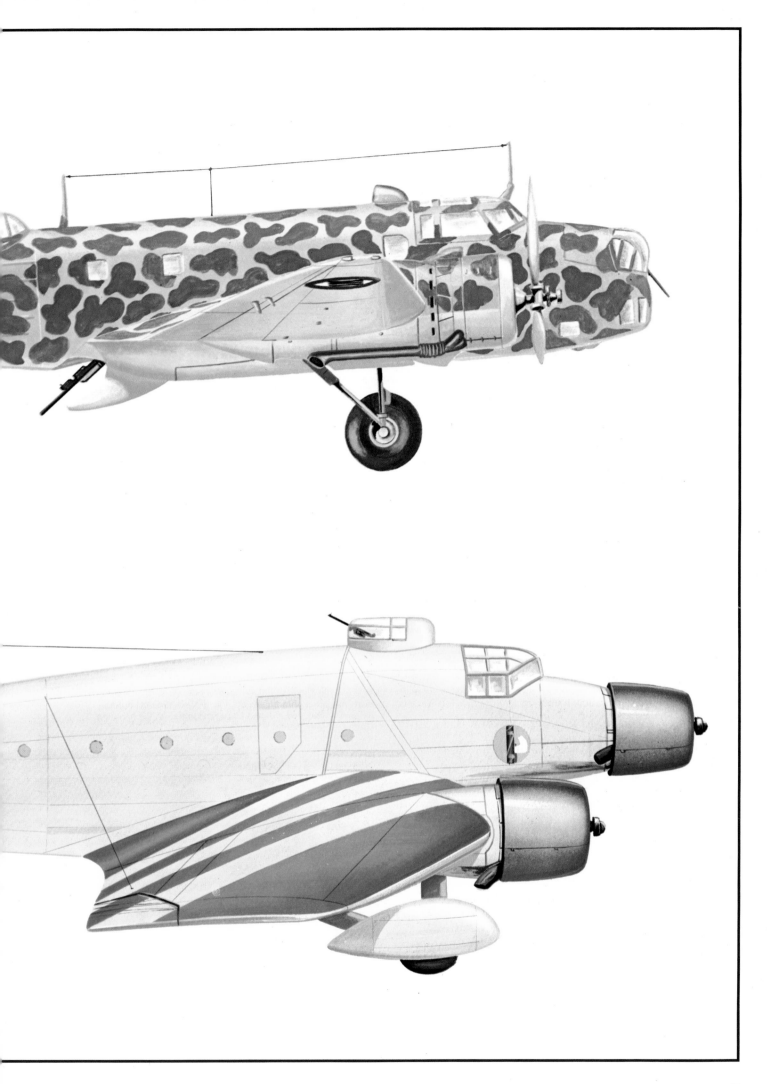

OTHER EUROPEAN NATIONS

Fighters lose to bombers

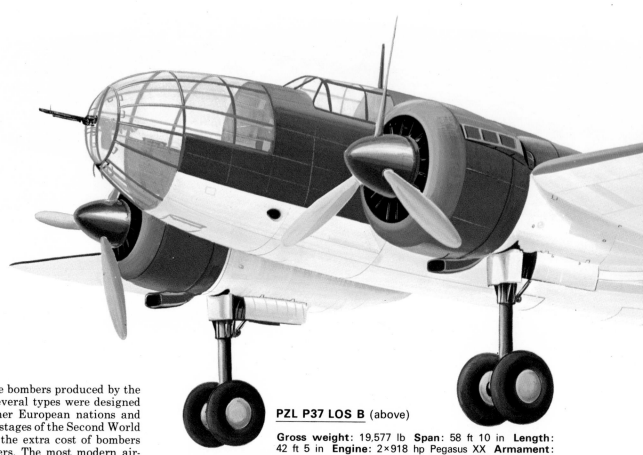

In addition to the bombers produced by the major powers, several types were designed and built by other European nations and used in the early stages of the Second World War, in spite of the extra cost of bombers as against fighters. The most modern aircraft type in the Czechoslovak Air Force in 1938 was the Aero A 304 bomber, based on the prototype for a civil airliner. The A 304 was a three-seat reconnaissance/light bomber, able to carry up to 660 lb of bombs. After the German occupation, the few machines that had been built were handed over to the Bulgarian Air Force for training purposes. In the case of the Fokker TV twin-engined fighter-bomber, which came into service in small numbers with the Netherlands Air Force in 1938, none remained to be taken over by the Germans after their invasion on 10 May 1940, the nine then operational having all been destroyed in attacks on enemy installations. Another Fokker aircraft used for bombing, although it was designed primarily as a bomber-interceptor, was the twin-engined GIA.

The most outstanding bomber produced by the small European nations, the Polish twin-engined PZL P 37 Lós, first flew in 1936, and in spite of being one of the smallest and fastest aircraft of its kind, it could carry up to 5,688 lb of bombs – equal to its own unladen weight. About forty of the type were operational with the Polish Air Force in 1939 and they inflicted heavy casualties on the Germans before Poland finally succumbed. The remaining machines were taken over by the Rumanian Air Force and used throughout the war against Russia.

PZL P37 LOS B (above)

Gross weight: 19,577 lb **Span:** 58 ft 10 in **Length:** 42 ft 5 in **Engine:** 2×918 hp Pegasus XX **Armament:** 3×7·7-mm machine-guns **Crew:** 5 **Speed:** 276 mph at 11,154 ft **Ceiling:** 19,685 ft **Range:** 932 miles **Bomb load:** 5,688 lb

This all-metal stressed-skin medium bomber was one of the best machines produced by the Polish aircraft industry before the war, and inflicted heavy casualties on the invading German armies before Poland's capitulation

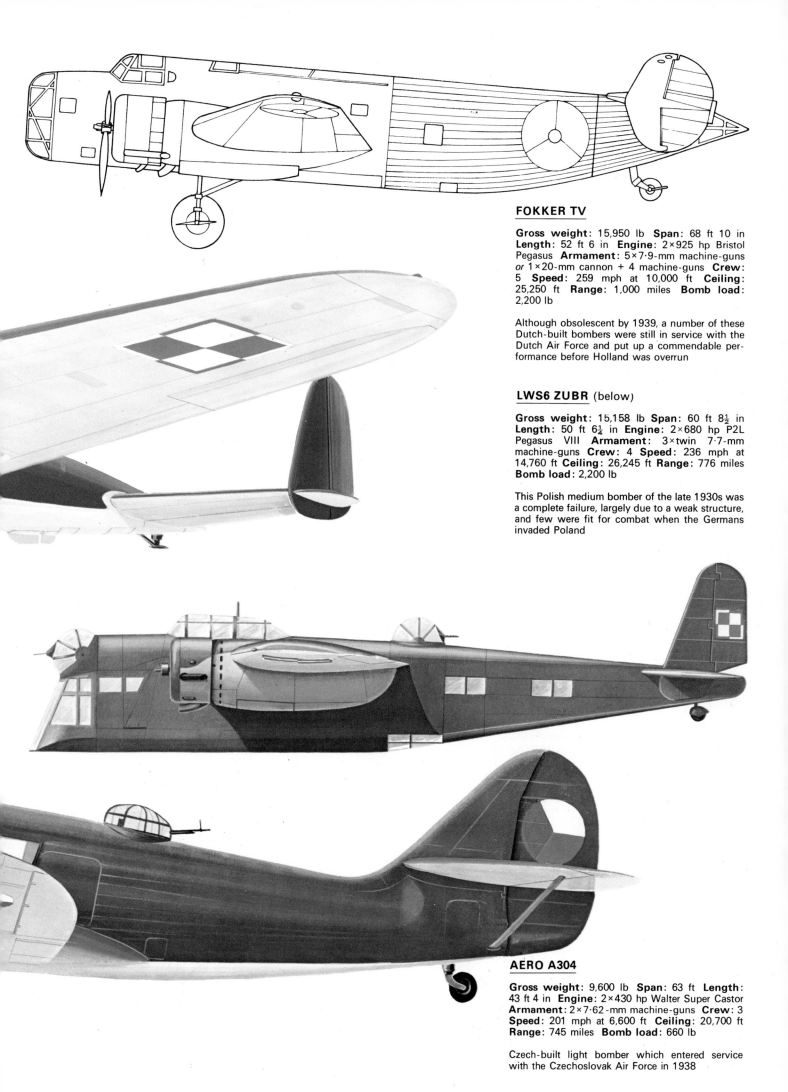

FOKKER TV

Gross weight: 15,950 lb **Span:** 68 ft 10 in
Length: 52 ft 6 in **Engine:** 2×925 hp Bristol
Pegasus **Armament:** 5×7·9-mm machine-guns
or 1×20-mm cannon + 4 machine-guns **Crew:**
5 **Speed:** 259 mph at 10,000 ft **Ceiling:**
25,250 ft **Range:** 1,000 miles **Bomb load:**
2,200 lb

Although obsolescent by 1939, a number of these
Dutch-built bombers were still in service with the
Dutch Air Force and put up a commendable per-
formance before Holland was overrun

LWS6 ZUBR (below)

Gross weight: 15,158 lb **Span:** 60 ft 8½ in
Length: 50 ft 6¼ in **Engine:** 2×680 hp P2L
Pegasus VIII **Armament:** 3×twin 7·7-mm
machine-guns **Crew:** 4 **Speed:** 236 mph at
14,760 ft **Ceiling:** 26,245 ft **Range:** 776 miles
Bomb load: 2,200 lb

This Polish medium bomber of the late 1930s was
a complete failure, largely due to a weak structure,
and few were fit for combat when the Germans
invaded Poland

AERO A304

Gross weight: 9,600 lb **Span:** 63 ft **Length:**
43 ft 4 in **Engine:** 2×430 hp Walter Super Castor
Armament: 2×7·62-mm machine-guns **Crew:** 3
Speed: 201 mph at 6,600 ft **Ceiling:** 20,700 ft
Range: 745 miles **Bomb load:** 660 lb

Czech-built light bomber which entered service
with the Czechoslovak Air Force in 1938

SOVIET UNION

Obsolescent air force

PETLYAKOV Pe-8

Gross weight: 63,052 lb **Span:** 131 ft 1 in **Length:** 73 ft 9 in **Engine:** 4×AM-35A **Armament:** 2×20-mm; 2×12·7-mm; 2×7·62-mm machine-guns **Crew:** 5 **Speed:** 234 mph at ground level **Ceiling:** 32,972 ft **Range:** 2,038 miles **Bomb load:** 4,400 lb

Designed by A. N. Tupolev to meet a 1934 specification for a fast long-range bomber able to carry a heavy bomb-load, the Pe-8 was overshadowed by the very successful Ilyushin 11-4 and the Yer-2, and relatively few were built

During the early months of the war, until production of more advanced designs got under way, Russian bomber squadrons were equipped largely with obsolete aircraft. The most out-dated was the Tupolev TB-3, first brought into service in 1931, which for some years constituted the only really effective four-engined bomber force in the world. Later models took part in operations against the Japanese in 1938 and in Poland and Finland in 1939. After Germany's invasion of the Soviet Union in 1941 they were used for a short period as night-bombers. Thereafter they continued to see service as transports throughout the war.

A more advanced type was the twin-engined Tupolev SB-2 which first flew in 1934 and served on the Republican side in the Spanish Civil War. Like the Bristol Blenheim, with which it was comparable in performance, the SB-2 was too slow and too poorly armed for daytime operations and in the early stages of the war with Germany it was relegated to night bombing duties.

Apart from the TB-3, the only other Russian four-engined bomber to be introduced during the war was the Petlyakov Pe-8. It was actually designed by A. N. Tupolev as a fast long-range bomber, capable of carrying a heavy bomb-load, but V.M. Petlyakov was responsible for preparing it for series production in 1939. The top speed of the Pe-8 at altitudes between 26,000 and 29,000 ft was faster than the Messerschmitt

Bf 109 fighter. With a range of over 2,000 miles and carrying a bomb-load of 4,400 lb, it undertook many raids deep into Germany. It remained in production until 1944, but relatively few were built as the Russians found the performance of their twin-engined bombers satisfactory.

Backbone of Russia's air force
The two which were produced in the largest numbers and formed the backbone of the Russian air force during the war were the long-range Ilyushin Il-4 and the Petlyakov Pe-2 tactical bomber, both introduced in 1940. The Il-4 was a development of the all-metal Ilyushin DB-3 of the early 1930s, with a completely redesigned forward fuselage and an elongated nose section to accommodate the navigator/bomb-aimer. Due to a metal shortage in Russia after the German attack, later models were built largely of wood, but this had only a slight effect on their high performance. The Il-4 saw service on every front on which the Russians were engaged against the Axis Powers, but was best known as a long-range bomber, taking part in continuous raids on Germany – including the first Russian attack on Berlin in August 1941.

The Petlyakov Pe-2 was based on an original design for a fast twin-engined fighter and a number were used for that purpose. Some versions were used for dive-bombing, with dive-brakes fitted under the

wings, but the Pe-2 also carried out level bombing and as such has to be considered a true bomber. Bombs could be carried not only internally in the fuselage and rear of the engine nacelles but also externally under the wings.

Another tactical bomber which was mass-produced from 1942 onwards, although not in the quantity of the Pe-2, was the Tupolev Tu-2, which had a maximum speed close to that of a fighter and could be adapted for either level- or dive-bombing. It continued in production after the war and served with the Soviet, Polish and Chinese air forces until the mid-1950s, seeing combat in Korea. In 1941, the Yermolayev Yer-2 long-range bomber was introduced as an intended replacement for the Ilyushin Il-4, but relatively few were built. This also applied to the only other Russian bomber of note in the Second World War, the Archangelskii Ar-2, which saw limited use during the German invasion in 1941.

Mention should be made, however, of the Ilyushin Il-2 Shturmovik, a ground-attack aircraft capable of carrying a bomb-load of up to 1,325 lb, built in single and two-seater versions, and in a class by itself. With its strong armour protection and remarkable handling characteristics at low levels, it was one of the Soviet Union's most effective weapons and was certainly superior to any other ground-attack machine used during the war.

UNITED STATES
Armoury of
the allies

The American aircraft industry made a tremendous contribution to the war effort, both in terms of numbers and different types of aircraft produced. Total production rose from about 18,000 machines in 1941, when the re-armament programme began to get under way, to 48,000 in 1942, over 90,000 in 1943 and a peak of more than 100,000 in 1944. Not only were the needs of the US armed forces satisfied but thousands of aircraft were supplied to Britain and Russia under lend-lease. Only in the USA was a sustained effort made throughout the war to develop more powerful long-range strike aircraft, and the design work on some of the later types was actually started after the war began.

This achievement was all the more remarkable in view of the fact that when war broke out in Europe, the US Army Air Corps (which became the US Army Air Force in 1942) was equipped largely with obsolete machines owing to the unwillingness of Congress to allocate adequate funds for military expenditure in the 1930s. The US Navy Air Force was in a better position, although even so it was not until 1942 that it received the Curtiss SB2C Helldiver, its most successful dive-bomber, which was also supplied to the Army as the A-25. But as far as USAAC was concerned, the only modern bomber being developed in the mid-1930s was the Boeing B-17.

One of the most remarkable four-engined

bombers of the war, the B-17 ultimately bore the brunt of the massive high-altitude daylight raids on Occupied Europe by the USAAF, operating from bases in England. When design work on the B-17 started in 1934, however, it was intended as a purely defensive weapon for offshore anti-shipping operations. It began to enter service in 1939 and was flown operationally for the first time by the RAF in 1940. Although its bomb-load was less than that of the Lancaster, it had the advantage of being able to operate at much greater heights.

The first Flying Fortress
Armament was less than adequate to begin with and it was only with the introduction of the more heavily armed E series that the type merited the name 'Flying Fortress'. With eight or more guns to each aircraft and flying in close formation to give covering fire, it was hoped that B-17 squadrons would have sufficient protection to fight their way through German air defences and carry out precision bombing by day. Some excellent results were achieved, but at a very heavy cost; as the British had learned in 1939 and the Germans in 1940, heavy bombers were vulnerable to determined fighter opposition, no matter how well armed they were.

Support for the American aircraft industry in the late 1930s was given by the British Purchasing Commission, which was concerned to meet those needs of the RAF

which could not be provided by Britain's own industry. In 1938 an order was placed for the twin-engined Lockheed Hudson coastal reconnaissance bomber which was coming into RAF service at the outbreak of war. A Hudson from No. 224 Squadron had the distinction of being the first RAF aircraft to destroy a German aircraft in the war, during a coastal patrol on 8 October 1939. Under the American designation A-28, Hudsons also served with the USAAC. Another Lockheed bomber purchased for the RAF was the Ventura, of which deliveries began in 1942.

Meanwhile, from 1938 onwards, the US Army began holding competitions for aircraft designs to replace the mainly obsolete types then in service. It was in that year that Douglas won the award for a light bomber with its DB-7 Boston. This was ordered in large numbers by the French and British, entered service with the RAF in 1942 and turned out to be one of the best light bombers of the war. It was also built as a fighter under the name Havoc.

In 1939 a competition for medium bomber designs resulted in contracts being awarded for the North American B-25 Mitchell and the Martin B-26 Marauder. The Mitchell became an outstanding aircraft, flying for the first time only one year after its design had been accepted. It was taken into service in 1941, operating mainly in the Pacific to begin with and scoring its first success on

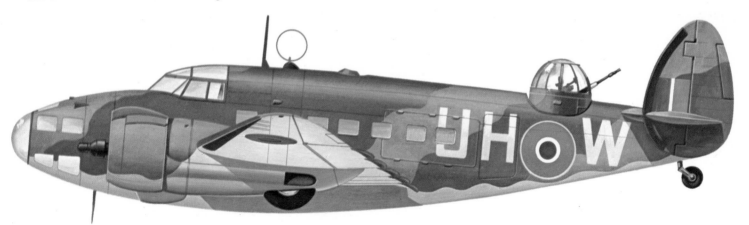

LOCKHEED HUDSON

Gross weight: 20,500 lb **Span:** 65 ft 6 in **Length:** 44 ft 4 in **Engine:** 2×1,200 hp Wright Cyclone GR-1820 **Armament:** 7×·303 machine-guns **Crew:** 4 **Speed:** 253 mph **Ceiling:** 26,500 ft **Range:** 2,160 miles **Bomb load:** 1,400 lb

Purchased by the British in 1938 and used extensively by RAF Coastal Command from 1939 to 1943, especially carrying four 325-lb depth charges against submarines. A Hudson with No 224 Squadron was the first RAF machine to shoot down a German aircraft in the Second World War, on 8 October 1939

24 December 1941 against a Japanese submarine. The epic raid on Tokyo in April 1942, led by Lt-Col 'Jimmy' Doolittle, was made by sixteen Mitchells flying from the deck of the aircraft carrier *Hornet*, although they were never intended for such a purpose. The Martin Marauder was also a fine aircraft although its very high wing loading caused several early accidents. It came into service in 1941, mainly in the Pacific, and in 1943 became operational in Europe with the US 8th Air Force. It was also flown by the RAF under the lend-lease programme, as were the two other twin-engined Martin bombers produced during the war, the Maryland and the Baltimore.

While deliveries of the B-17 were starting in 1939, it was decided to design a new four-engined bomber with a higher performance. The resulting Consolidated B-24 Liberator showed little actual improvement on the Boeing, but it served with great distinction in many roles, particularly in the Pacific where its long range – nearly 3,000 miles in later versions – proved of immense value. This was achieved mainly because of a new type of high aspect ratio wing, named Davis after its inventor. The Liberator was also used by RAF Coastal Command as a patrol bomber over the Atlantic, in areas previously out of range to land-based bombers, and joined the B-17 in the USAAF's historic raids over Occupied Europe.

Early in 1940, an official requirement was issued for a 'Hemisphere Defense Weapon', having a very long range and the ability to carry a much greater bomb-load than previous American aircraft. Of the four designs submitted, that of the Boeing B-29 Superfortress – conceived as early as 1938 – was judged to be the best.

Pressurised cabins
From the outset, the B-29 was planned to have pressurised cabins for its crew to allow it to operate at very great heights. The main factor which made the B-29 possible was the development of the large (3,350 cu in displacement) Wright R-3350 Duplex Cyclone 18-cylinder two-row radial engine, which had been launched as a bold private-venture programme by Wright Aeronautical in 1936. By 1940, prototypes of this engine were being provisionally rated at 2,200 hp, enabling Douglas to build the enormous but unsuccessful B-19, flown in 1941, and

opening the way for more capable and useful four-engined aircraft such as the B-29 (first flown on 21 September 1942) and the Lockheed Constellation.

The B-29 engines were each fitted with two General Electric turbo-superchargers, very similar to the single units fitted to the engines of the B-17 and B-24, to give high power at altitudes up to 35,000 ft. The propellers were four-blade Curtiss electrically controlled units, bigger than any previously used in a production aircraft. Operations of the B-29 by the USAAF began in the summer of 1944, initially from bases in India and China against the Japanese, and it was responsible for most of the devastating attacks on the Japanese mainland, including the two atomic bombs dropped on Hiroshima and Nagasaki in August 1945.

One of the companies which submitted designs for a Hemisphere Defense Weapon was Consolidated. Although it did not win, its XB-32 was felt to be promising enough to be given an order, resulting in the Consolidated B-32 Dominator which was first flown two weeks before the B-29. Smaller than the Boeing, the Dominator was adapted for a lower-altitude role in the Pacific, but relatively few were built.

Meanwhile, in 1941, as a result of the 'Atlantic Charter' meeting between the leaders of the USA and Britain, the USAAF planned a bomber far larger even than the B-29. This was intended for the almost incredible task of bombing Germany from bases in North America, should Britain capitulate. The required range of more than 7,500 miles, combined with a bomb-load of 10,000 lb – and a maximum of 72,000 lb over shorter distances – was almost beyond the limit of what was possible in the Second World War. Eventually, Convair won the design competition with its XB-36, designed around six as-yet-undeveloped Pratt & Whitney R-4360 engines in the 3,500 hp class, arranged inside a huge wing to drive pusher propellers. These propellers had to have a diameter of 19 ft, even larger than those of the B-29. So enormous was the task of creating the B-36 that it was not completed until after the war was over, first flying on 8 August 1946. Deliveries to the US Strategic Air Command began in 1947; the last version was retired from service with SAC in 1959.

One bomber which was brought into

combat service before the end of the war, even though the prototypes were not ordered until mid-1941, was the twin-engined Douglas A-26 Invader, intended to replace the Boston attack bomber. Operational use began at the end of 1944, first in the European theatre and later in the Pacific. The Invader lasted in operational service much longer than originally expected; it was used not only in Korea but also in Vietnam in the 1960s.

Finally, another Douglas aircraft which deserves mention is the single-engined SBD Dauntless, the most successful American dive-bomber of the Second World War. Although this was built primarily for the US Navy, beginning operational service at the end of 1941, it was also used by the USAAF.

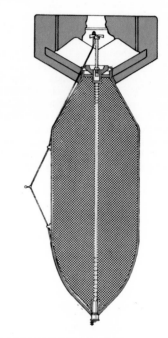

US LIGHT CASE BOMB

Total weight: 4,000 lb **Length:** 117·25 in **Fin width:** 47·62 in **Charge/weight ratio:** 80%

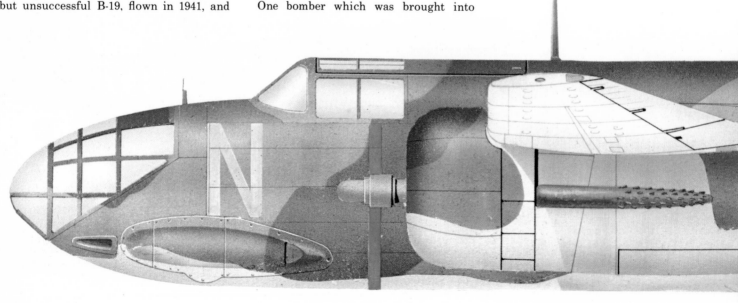

US ARMOUR PIERCING BOMB

Total weight: 1,000 lb **Length:** 73 in **Fin width:** 16·6 in **Charge/weight ratio:** 14·5%

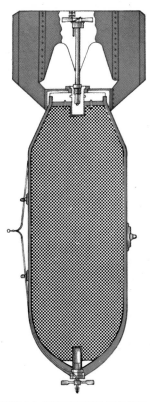

US GENERAL PURPOSE BOMB

Total weight: 500 lb **Length:** 59·16 in **Fin width:** 18·94 in **Charge/weight ratio:** 51%

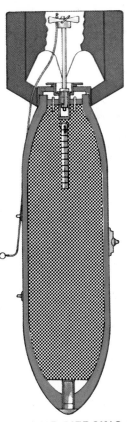

US SEMI-ARMOUR PIERCING BOMB

Total weight: 1,000 lb **Length:** 70·4 in **Fin width:** 20·72 in **Charge/weight ratio:** 31%

US FRAGMENTATION BOMB

(dropped in clusters of 6)

Total weight: 19·8 lb **Length:** 21·8 in **Fin width:** 5·13 in **Charge/weight ratio:** 13%

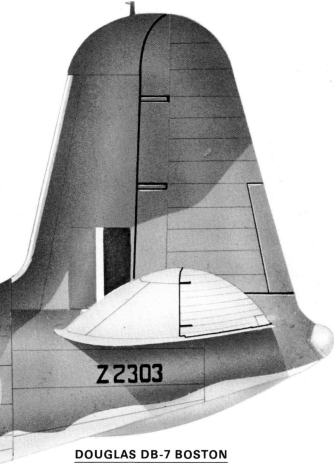

DOUGLAS DB-7 BOSTON

Gross weight: 15,150 lb **Span:** 61 ft 4 in **Length:** 46 ft **Engine:** 2×1,100 hp Pratt & Whitney R-1830 **Armament:** 7× ·303 machine-guns **Crew:** 3 **Speed:** 322 mph at 12,500 ft **Ceiling:** 33,800 ft **Range:** 462 miles **Bomb load:** 2,080 lb

One of the most widely used light bombers of the Second World War, the Boston was also developed as a fighter under the name Havoc

JAPAN

MITSUBISHI Ki-30 (left)

Gross weight: 7,324 lb **Span**: 47 ft 9 in
Length: 33 ft 11 in **Engine**: 1×850 hp 14 cyc.
Nakajima **Armament**: 2×7·7-mm machine-guns
Crew: 2 **Speed**: 263 mph at 13,125 ft **Ceiling**:
28,120 ft **Range**: 1,056 miles **Bomb load**:
660 lb

The Ki-30 light bomber made its debut in the Sino-
Japanese War and was still in JAAF service in the
Pacific in 1942, although it was seldom used after
the Philippines campaign

MITSUBISHI Ki-21 IIB (opposite top)

Gross weight: 21,407 lb **Span**: 73 ft 10 in
Length: 52 ft 6 in **Engine**: 2×1,450 hp Mitsubishi
Ha-101 **Armament**: 5×7·7-mm; 1×12·7-mm
machine-guns **Crew**: 5 **Speed**: 297 mph at
13,100 ft **Ceiling**: 32,810 ft **Range**: 1,350 miles
Bomb load: 2,205 lb

An improved version of the Ki-21 heavy bomber.
First entered service in 1937, with a dorsal turret
and a more powerful engine. Like most Japanese
so-called heavy bombers, the range and bomb
load were inadequate

Less than the best

While Japanese carrier-based aircraft, such
as the Mitsubishi A6M Zero-Sen fighter
and the Nakajima B5N torpedo-bomber,
were among the best of their kind used
during the war, the same could hardly be
said of Japanese bombers. Although the
Japanese might have been expected to
gain a great deal from a force of heavy
long-range bombers, only one four-engined
type ever entered service (the Nakajima
G5N1, code-named 'Liz' by the Allies) and
though much larger than any other of its
generation, with a 138 ft wing-span, it was
never used as a bomber at all. All the
Japanese bombers brought into service just
before and during the war had two air-
cooled radial engines, the major constructor
being Mitsubishi.

Mainstay of the Japanese Navy Air
Force's land-based bomber force was the
Mitsubishi G3M, first flown in 1935 as a
major step forward in Japanese aviation
and making its combat debut in the war
against China in 1937. It was code-named
'Nell' under the Allied identification system
and together with the later Mitsubishi G4M
'Betty' which was brought into service in
1941, took part in the attack and sinking
of the Royal Navy battleships *Prince of
Wales* and *Repulse* on 10 December 1941.
The G4M had an impressive range of more
than 3,000 miles but its necessarily large

load of gasoline, carried in unprotected
tanks, made it even more vulnerable than
most Japanese aircraft, and it became
known as the 'one-shot lighter' among
American pilots. Heavy losses were suffered,
especially in the battle for the Solomon
Islands in 1942, but only towards the end
of 1943 was an attempt made to provide
smaller, fully-protected fuel tanks. A large
number of G4Ms were equipped to carry
and launch the Ohka piloted suicide bomb
which caused considerable damage in the
later stages of the war.

The Japanese Army Air Force's standard
heavy bomber at the time of the attack on
Pearl Harbour on 7 December 1941 was the
Mitsubishi Ki-21 ('Sally'). This was too
slow and poorly armed to be very effective,
but its intended replacement, the Nakajima
Ki-49 ('Helen'), which began to enter
service in 1941, suffered from poor range
and inadequate bomb-load in trying to
achieve higher speed with heavier armament. It was not until 1944 that the JAAF
received a really first-class bomber, the
Mitsubishi Ki-67 Hiryu (Flying Dragon),
code-named 'Peggy', which first saw combat
in the Battle of the Philippine Sea. Unlike
most Japanese bombers, which had too light
an armament, the Ki-67 was formidably
armed with four heavy machine-guns and a
20-mm cannon. Its speed and manoeuvrability also showed a marked improvement
on previous types. Towards the end of the
year several of these aircraft were converted
into three-seater suicide bombers.

A smaller and lighter machine was the
Kawasaki Ki-48 ('Lily') which entered

service with the JAAF in 1940 and was
used both for level and dive-bombing. It
had the range to bomb Port Darwin,
Australia, from bases in New Guinea, but
its bomb-load of 660 lb (1,764 lb in later
models) was too modest.

The last and best of the Japanese bombers
to see combat before the war ended, although
limited by a shortage of skilled pilots and
high-octane fuel, was the Yokosuka P1Y1
Ginga (Milky Way), code-named 'Frances'.
It had a speed in excess of 345 mph at
19,300 ft, was well armed with a 20-mm nose
cannon and one or two dorsal heavy
machine-guns, had a high rate of climb, and
a combat range of nearly 3,000 miles. It was
used for both level and dive bombing by
the JNAF, while torpedo-bomber and night-
fighter versions were also developed. During
1945, one of the machines was used to
flight-test a turbo-jet engine, but the war
ended before further advances in jet-
propulsion could be made.

The only long-range strategic bomber
with a pressurised cabin to be produced in
Japan during the war was the Tachikawa
Ki-74 ('Patsy'), originated in 1939 for the
JAAF. Little interest was shown in its
possibilities until after Pearl Harbour, and
its maiden flight was not made until May
1944. With a range of 4,350 miles, a maximum
speed of 360 mph at 28,000 ft, and an internal
bomb-load of 2,200 lb, the Ki-74 could have
been of considerable value to the Japanese,
but although a small number had been
delivered by the summer of 1945, the war
ended before combat operations could be
carried out.

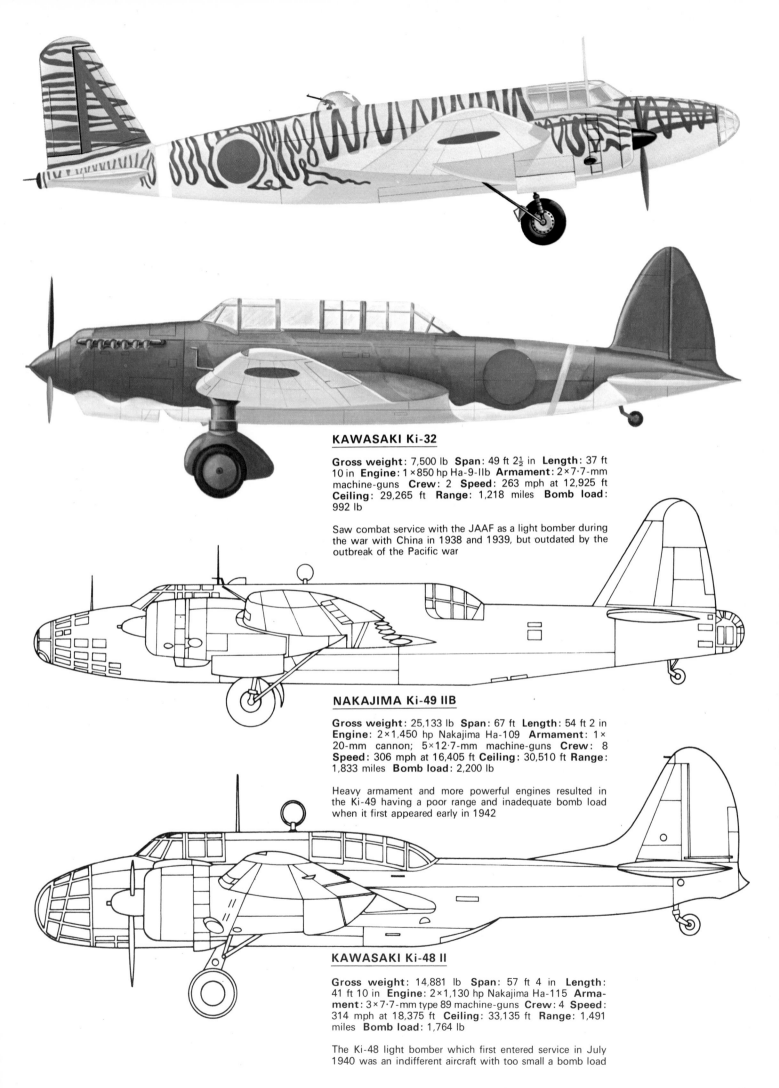

KAWASAKI Ki-32

Gross weight: 7,500 lb **Span:** 49 ft 2½ in **Length:** 37 ft 10 in **Engine:** 1×850 hp Ha-9-IIb **Armament:** 2×7·7-mm machine-guns **Crew:** 2 **Speed:** 263 mph at 12,925 ft **Ceiling:** 29,265 ft **Range:** 1,218 miles **Bomb load:** 992 lb

Saw combat service with the JAAF as a light bomber during the war with China in 1938 and 1939, but outdated by the outbreak of the Pacific war

NAKAJIMA Ki-49 IIB

Gross weight: 25,133 lb **Span:** 67 ft **Length:** 54 ft 2 in **Engine:** 2×1,450 hp Nakajima Ha-109 **Armament:** 1× 20-mm cannon; 5×12·7-mm machine-guns **Crew:** 8 **Speed:** 306 mph at 16,405 ft **Ceiling:** 30,510 ft **Range:** 1,833 miles **Bomb load:** 2,200 lb

Heavy armament and more powerful engines resulted in the Ki-49 having a poor range and inadequate bomb load when it first appeared early in 1942

KAWASAKI Ki-48 II

Gross weight: 14,881 lb **Span:** 57 ft 4 in **Length:** 41 ft 10 in **Engine:** 2×1,130 hp Nakajima Ha-115 **Armament:** 3×7·7-mm type 89 machine-guns **Crew:** 4 **Speed:** 314 mph at 18,375 ft **Ceiling:** 33,135 ft **Range:** 1,491 miles **Bomb load:** 1,764 lb

The Ki-48 light bomber which first entered service in July 1940 was an indifferent aircraft with too small a bomb load

STRUCTURE AND DESIGN

The structure of most Second World War bombers conformed to a conventional pattern, and the high-speed de Havilland Mosquito was one of the very few to introduce innovations in material and design and yet be highly effective and successful

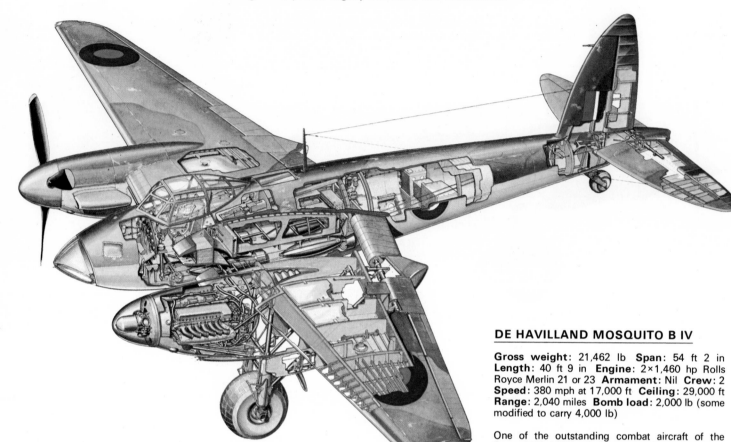

DE HAVILLAND MOSQUITO B IV

Gross weight: 21,462 lb **Span:** 54 ft 2 in **Length:** 40 ft 9 in **Engine:** 2×1,460 hp Rolls Royce Merlin 21 or 23 **Armament:** Nil **Crew:** 2 **Speed:** 380 mph at 17,000 ft **Ceiling:** 29,000 ft **Range:** 2,040 miles **Bomb load:** 2,000 lb (some modified to carry 4,000 lb)

One of the outstanding combat aircraft of the Second World War, built mostly of wood and too fast to be intercepted on bombing missions; guns were only carried on fighter variants. The B IV was the first bomber version to enter RAF service

The Second World War was delayed just long enough for almost all of the old aircraft with fabric-covered airframes of wood, mixed wood and metal or steel-tube, to have been withdrawn from service and replaced by modern types. The redoubtable Fairey Swordfish carrier-based torpedo-bomber was the only aircraft of the older type to serve throughout the war in the European theatre, its low performance being balanced by robust construction, ease of repair, good weight-lifting ability from small carrier decks and general utility except in the face of lethal defensive fire. Among other fabric-covered machines to survive were the Vickers Wellington and Warwick twin-engined bombers which remained in production until 1945.

But as a rule, bombers of the Second World War had light-alloy stressed-skin construction, built in cantilever monoplane form with monocoque fuselages. Under-carriages were made to retract into the wing, engine nacelles, or other compart-ments, at first by laborious winding of a hand-wheel and later by directing hydraulic power to a ram or electric power to a motor. The original hydraulic systems were crude and heavy, filled with oil at 1,000 lb/sq in.

Later aircraft had more complex systems operating at 2,500 lb/sq in and serving undercarriage retraction, wheel brakes, landing flaps, bomb doors and sometimes propeller pitch or gun-turret drive. American aircraft favoured all-electric systems, with as many as one hundred and eighty motors to drive various items of equipment.

More powerful flaps

With wing loadings rising from around 10 lb/sq ft, typical in 1930, to 40/65 lb/sq ft, the wings needed powerful flaps to increase lift at take-off (when they were depressed to about ten degrees) and at landing (depressed to the maximum of perhaps forty-five degrees to give both extra lift and extra drag). The Armstrong Whitworth Whitley, designed as a troop carrier around 1932, was redesigned as a bomber in 1934. The original design had no wing flaps and the wing was accordingly set at a large angle of incidence. The flapped Whitley always flew in a characteristic nose-down attitude, and would probably have been faster with the wing made thinner and set at a shallower angle.

Junkers devised a 'double wing' type of flap comprising a completely separate

auxiliary surface hinged well behind the main wing trailing edge. This was fitted to the Ju 86 and Ju 87, but the far more effective Ju 88 had powerful conventional slotted flaps. Both the Ju 87 and Ju 88 had special dive-brakes hinged under the wings and extended broadside-on to the airflow to permit very steep attacks (almost ninety degrees) without reaching excessive speeds.

In the USA, Lockheed used the advanced Fowler flap, still in evidence today. This extended backwards on wheeled carriages running on fixed tracks to give extra area on take-off. When fully extended, the tracks pulled the carriages sharply down to give very high drag as well. This was a useful feature of the Lockheed Hudson and Ventura, designed specifically for British requirements, which would otherwise have been difficult to land. Even with full flap, the Martin B-26 Marauder was not easy to land, and this hastened the development of the modern type of aircraft which is driven on to the runway at high speed and stopped with powerful brakes.

Special mention should be made of the four-engined Consolidated B-24 Liberator, possibly the first of the modern bombers. This was based on the Davis wing, a design of very high aspect ratio giving great efficiency and capable of heavy loading to well over 60 lb/sq ft. Such a wing was a radically new innovation when the Liberator first flew, as the Model 32, in 1939. It was only possible because of its advanced stressed-skin structure, which allowed a large quantity of fuel to be carried inside the slender wing as well as the main units of the landing gear and the Fowler flaps. Compared with British bombers such as the Avro Lancaster, which had thin skin and heavy highly-stressed spar booms, the wing of the Liberator was uniformly loaded throughout with slimmer spars and thicker skin, reinforced by many long stringers.

There was little that was unconventional about the structures of most of the main Second World War bombers. Nearly all had stressed-skin airframes, with quite thin skin, held by flush riveting and with large, high-tensile steel pins securing the fork fittings where wings joined the fuselage or where outer wings joined the centre section. Compared with earlier aircraft the smooth, regular skin made performance higher and more precisely predictable, and the time-consuming task of airframe rigging receded into the background. Yet occasionally, there were still maverick aircraft which did not conform to the general pattern. Either they consistently flew slower than the others, or suffered from disconcerting and

sometimes dangerous flight characteristics – or they proved themselves to be among the most successful aircraft of the war.

In the latter category, apart from the geodetic Vickers bombers, an outstanding example was the de Havilland Mosquito. This cantilever mid-wing monoplane, initiated as a private venture in 1938 and nearly cancelled before it first flew in November 1940, ultimately became one of the most versatile combat aircraft of the war. It was planned purely as a high-speed unarmed bomber fast enough to avoid interception, and for various reasons, including the metal shortage, it was built of wood. The de Havilland company had devised a method of making the main sections from a sandwich

CONSOLIDATED B-24 LIBERATOR

Gross weight: 64,500 lb **Span:** 110 ft **Length:** 67 ft 2 in **Engine:** 4×Pratt & Whitney R-1830-65 **Armament:** 10×·50 Browning machine-guns **Crew:** 9 **Speed:** 300 mph at 25,000 ft **Ceiling:** 28,000 ft **Range:** 2,100 miles **Bomb load:** 12,800 lb

One of the best-known American aircraft of the Second World War, the Liberator served with distinction in many different roles. It was of particular value to RAF Coastal Command in covering that part of the Atlantic formerly out of range of land-based bombers

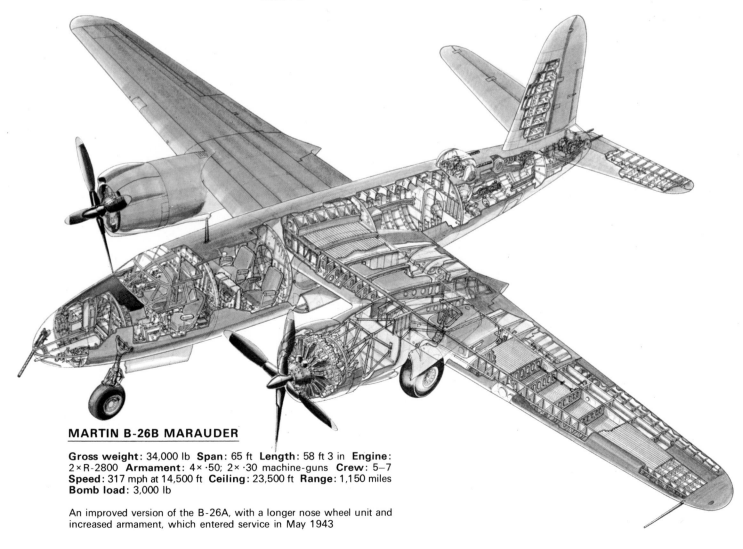

MARTIN B-26B MARAUDER

Gross weight: 34,000 lb **Span:** 65 ft **Length:** 58 ft 3 in **Engine:** 2×R-2800 **Armament:** 4×·50; 2×·30 machine-guns **Crew:** 5–7 **Speed:** 317 mph at 14,500 ft **Ceiling:** 23,500 ft **Range:** 1,150 miles **Bomb load:** 3,000 lb

An improved version of the B-26A, with a longer nose wheel unit and increased armament, which entered service in May 1943

of hardwood ply veneers with a thick core of light balsa wood, which gave a robust, rigid and smooth-surfaced airframe. Light alloy and steel fittings were used at the main stress areas and joints, and fabric formed a top skin over the entire airframe, including the control surfaces which were generally of light alloy.

Since a wooden structural member has a larger section than a metal one, the Mosquito had an outstanding ability to absorb battle damage. Shell splinters and bullets which would have severed a metal structure merely left a hole in the wooden one. This ability, combined with its speed of over 400 mph, made Mosquito losses towards the end of the war by far the lowest of any RAF bomber – only one per 2,000 sorties. As wood structures are inherently heavier than metal, the efficiency and weight-lifting power of the Mosquito was remarkable, and it was the only light bomber capable of carrying a 4,000 lb block-buster bomb. It was particularly effective against pin-point targets, but its manoeuvrability and performance at altitudes of up to 40,000 ft also made it an outstanding night fighter.

Apart from the Fi 103 Flying Bomb, produced by the Germans towards the end of the war with a predictably simple structure assembled from welded steel sheet, the only other bomber to make a major break with tradition and still be put into large-scale production was the Boeing B-29 Superfortress, brought into operation in 1943. Planned as the ultimate strategic bomber that could be created with the technology of 1940, it brought together every available new advance that appeared worthwhile. The great range (3,250 miles) and payload (16,000 lb of bombs) demanded led to an unprecedented size and weight, and this in turn led to the use of light-alloy sheet several times thicker (up to 0·188 in) than anything used in such machines as the Heinkel He 111 or Lancaster.

Absolute precision

This at once precluded the kind of workshop practice that had been common since the start of stressed-skin construction. No longer could sections of skin be filed to fit, or ill-fitting rivets be put into re-drilled holes. Each hole had to be a precision job,

in exactly the correct place to mate with the underlying structure, and countersunk to take a large rivet or screw fitting flush with the surface. It was no longer sufficient merely to bend the skins around the wings or fuselage as they were riveted on. They had to be formed in three dimensions by large press-tools. Though far stronger and more robust than any earlier airframes, the B-29 wing structure did have the drawback of being difficult to repair without special equipment.

The B-29 also marked a great increase in complexity. For example, it had five electrically-driven gun-turrets, four of them remotely controlled from sighting stations, with an override system to give a gunner control of all four turrets if he should have a good target. A further notable advance was that the crew were accommodated in a pressure cabin, linked by a pressurised tunnel to the smaller pressurised compartment of the two rear-fuselage gunners and the pressurised tail turret. All in all, the B-29 was a tremendous stride forward towards the even more complicated jet bombers of today.

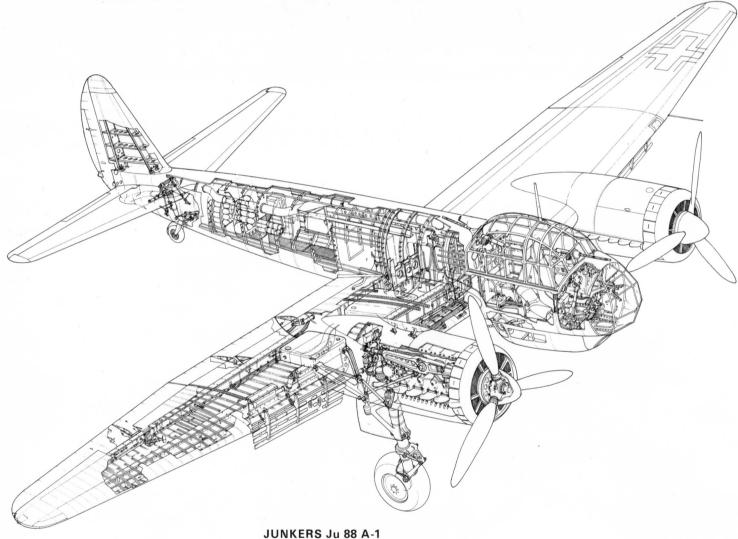

JUNKERS Ju 88 A-1

Gross weight: 27,500 lb **Span:** 59 ft 11 in **Length:** 47 ft 1⅓ in **Engine:** 2×1200 hp Junkers Jumo 211 **Armament:** 3×7·92-mm MG 15 machine-guns **Crew:** 4 **Speed:** 286 mph at 18,000 ft **Ceiling:** 30,150 ft **Range:** 1,550 miles **Bomb load:** 5,510 lb

Probably the most versatile aircraft of the war, more Ju 88s were built between 1939 and 1945 – over 15,000 in all, of which 9,000 were bombers – than all other German bombers combined. It was the subject of more modifications than any other combat aircraft of the war

ARMAMENT

The British and American power-driven turrets — increasingly situated in the tail of the plane — gave them a strong advantage over the hand-held guns of the *Luftwaffe* bombers. By the end of the war some of the US bombers commanded a tremendous concentration of firepower

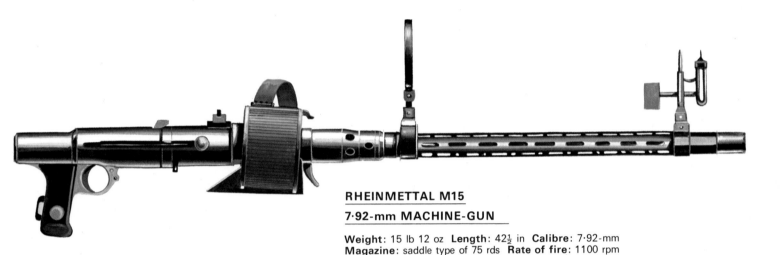

RHEINMETTAL M15

7·92-mm MACHINE-GUN

Weight: 15 lb 12 oz **Length:** 42½ in **Calibre:** 7·92-mm
Magazine: saddle type of 75 rds **Rate of fire:** 1100 rpm

The atmosphere of extreme financial stringency that surrounded armaments in most countries during the 1920s tended to restrict the pace of development and efforts were concentrated on making the best and most economical use of available equipment. This was invariably similar to that used in the First World War, if not actually ex-wartime stock. Thus the dominant aircraft guns in the RAF were the manually trained Lewis and the fixed Vickers, while the Marlin remained the chief American gun, despite the fact that both the rifle-calibre Browning and the 20-mm Hispano had completed their initial development before November 1918 and were available for use.

In the inter-war period, the Scarff ring, usually carrying single or twin Lewis guns, was almost universal for RAF bomber defence and was widely used elsewhere. Much heavier guns were carried in some aircraft, but only in a somewhat ineffectual and experimental way. For example, several British machines such as the Vickers and Westland COW-armed designs, the Bristol Bagshot and the Westland Westbury, had fitted the big 37-mm (1·46-in) Coventry Ordnance Works cannon dating from 1918. Later, in 1934, the Blackburn Perth three-engined flying-boat, then the RAF's biggest and heaviest aircraft, went into service with one of these guns in the bows, in addition to three Lewis guns on the usual Scarff rings at bows, amidships and stern. The 1½ lb shells could have been dangerous to surfaced submarines, but there is no record that they were regarded as useful defence weapons.

Brief trials were also conducted in the USA, France and the Soviet Union with 20-mm and 37-mm guns on large aircraft, but with inconclusive results.

A far more important trend was the realization that, as aircraft speeds were rising steadily from the 100 mph maximum of the typical bomber of the mid-1920s to at least twice that speed, some form of shelter would be needed by the gunners. Indeed, there was evidence that the aerodynamic drag of the guns, when firing to either side, would become so great as to make manual aiming impossible. The answer appeared to be some form of power-driven turret, such as had long been used on warships; the main difficulties were weight and the provisions of drive power.

Windshields to turrets

The first companies to produce workable turrets were Martin in the USA, with a nose turret for the Type 130 B-10 bomber mounting a 0·30-in Browning gun, and Boulton Paul in Britain with a pneumatic-motor traversed nose turret for the Overstrand, fitted with a Lewis. Turrets were also produced in France by 1934, but these were at first manually operated and served merely as windshields. The Amiot 143 for instance used un-powered turrets for the Lewis gun in the nose and for two similar guns in the ventral position amidships; together with another gun in the rear cabin section under the wing, the Amiot 143 could defend itself against attack from any direction, fore-shadowing the B-17 Flying Fortress. Later, the French MAC 1934 rifle-calibre gun supplemented and then replaced the Lewis.

Crude turrets also appeared on small numbers of Italian and Russian heavy bombers and on such flying-boats as the Short Sunderland, Consolidated PB2Y Coronado, Martin PBM Mariner, Blohm und Voss 138, Kawanishi H6K and H8K, and several Russian Beriev designs. There were many instances in the Second World War of

flying-boats fending off repeated attacks by fighters. A Sunderland, attacked by six Ju 88s, shot down one and crippled a second; another Sunderland shot down three Ju 88s out of eight – simply because of fire-power. Large aircraft were no longer defended merely by three Lewis guns on Scarff rings but by multiple belt-fed guns accurately trained by power-driven turrets.

By 1935, it was widely accepted that to have any hope of survival in enemy airspace, a large bomber would have to have power-driven gun-turrets. The turret was no longer a mere windshield but a precision aiming device, complete with a sighting system and operator controls so that the gunner could train his guns effortlessly and accurately, even with a 200-knot slipstream or when being pulled in a tight turn. By the start of the Second World War, there were almost twenty companies making power-driven bomber defence turrets. Every large bomber in production in either Britain or the USA had at least one turret.

But in most other countries, the power-driven turret was ignored, or accorded low priority. Germany clung to the belief that bombers could be adequately defended by two or four hand-held machine-guns, and similar thinking persisted in Italy, Japan and the Soviet Union. In France, however, every conceivable kind of bomber defence was tried – including catapults lobbing aerial mines timed to explode close to attacking fighters. Several French bombers had powered turrets, in some cases mounting 20-mm cannon, such as the extremely graceful twin-engined LeO 451, an excellent aircraft but which appeared too late to be of value to the French during the Second World War; a number were later used as transports by the *Luftwaffe*. The earlier Farman 223, first produced in 1937, had

20-mm guns in electrically-powered dorsal and ventral turrets which, in a hectic month of combat in June 1940, proved to be very effective even at long ranges, although handicapped by the fact that the gunners had only lately seen the equipment for the first time.

A typical example of how the turret evolved during the period before the war was the case of the Vickers Wellington. The prototype B 9/32, flown in June 1936, had transparent domes in the nose and tail which in production aircraft were expected to carry a single Lewis gun fired by hand through a slot, sealed on each side of the gun by a sliding wind-shield. By 1937, the Mark I production machine had power-driven turrets of a rudimentary kind. Each mounted twin belt-fed Browning guns which were elevated and traversed hydraulically by a Frazer-Nash system, while firing through an aperture in a broad flexible belt, arranged to slide freely in runners between the fixed upper (transparent) and lower parts of the installation. By 1939 the Mark 1A had gone into production with powered turrets of modern design, each with twin Brownings, and the Mark III of 1941 mounted the four-gun rear turret introduced to the RAF with the Whitley Mark IV and the production Sunderland of 1938.

This rapid advance in bomber armament had been made despite the fact that in the mid-1930s, the RAF had no modern gun of any kind, nor any under development. The position had been rectified in July 1935 by the conclusion of a licence agreement with the Colt Automatic Weapon Corporation for the conversion of their Browning machine-gun to take British 0·303-in rimmed ammunition and for the manufacture of the resulting gun in Britain. Later, in 1939, a licence was obtained for the 20-mm (0·787-in) Hispano cannon which went into large-scale production at the British MARC factory at Grantham and the BSA plant at Sparkbrook, though the first deliveries of this much bigger gun, in July 1940, were all for fighters.

With very few exceptions, such as the French bombers, the only defence of large combat aircraft in 1939 comprised rifle-calibre guns fired either by hand and trained manually or, in the case of British heavy bombers, aimed by a power-driven turret. It was to be a matter of profound importance that the *Luftwaffe*, misled by the ease with which the He 111 and Do 17 operated over Spain in 1937–39, standardised bomber-defence armament with three or four hand-held MG-15 machine-guns. Although this 7·92-mm gun was a good modern design, it was fed by hand-loaded magazines and in any case lacked the punch needed to deter the fighters the German bombers were soon to meet over England.

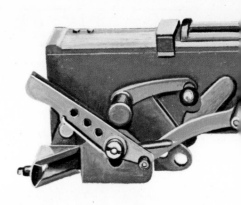

JAPANESE 7·7-mm TYPE 89

AIRCRAFT GUN (above)

Calibre: 7·7-mm **Magazine:** belt feed **Muzzle velocity:** 2,070 fps **Rate of fire:** 550 rpm

MAUSER MG 81 (below)

Weight: 13 lb 14 oz **Length:** 35 in **Calibre:** 7·92-mm **Operation:** Gas recoil **Muzzle velocity:** 2,800 fps **Rate of fire:** 1,300 rpm

ITALIAN 7·7-mm BREDA (bottom)

The most widely used aircraft defence weapon in the Italian air force until the cannon. In North Africa many were taken from crashed aircraft by Allied troops and fitted to trucks and light A.F.V.s

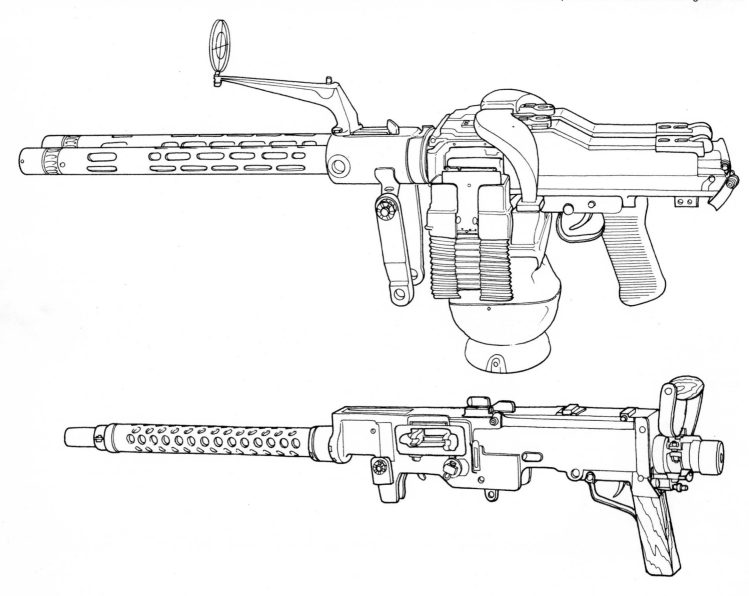

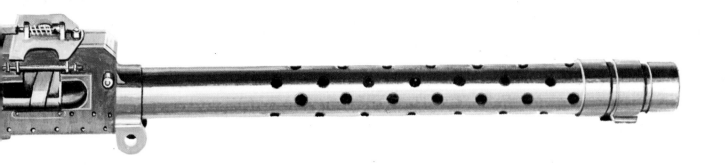

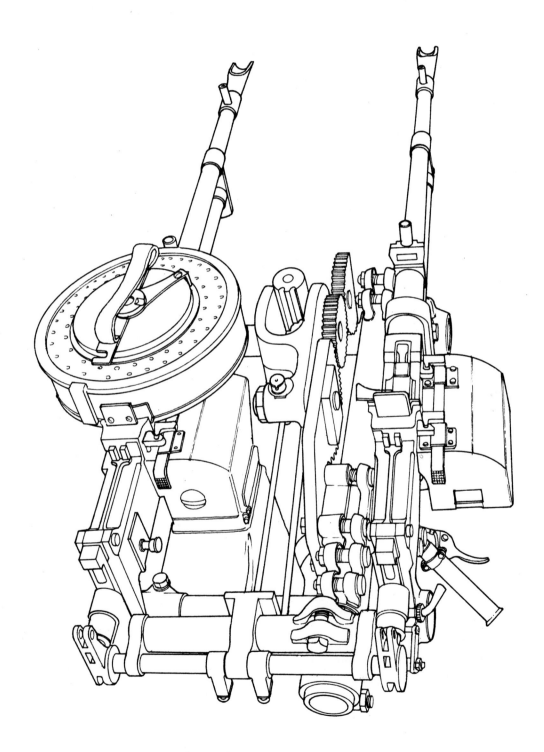

TWIN ·303 LEWIS A.A. MOUNTING

A typical British A.A. mount used against low flying aircraft.
This pair of Lewis machine-guns could send up a total firepower of 1,150 rpm

B-17D 'FLYING FORTRESS'

Gross weight: 50,000 lb **Span:** 103 ft 9 in **Length:** 67 ft 11 in
Engine: 4×Wright Cyclone R-1820 **Armament:** 6×·50; 1×·30
machine-guns **Crew:** 9 **Speed:** 323 mph at 25,000 ft **Ceiling:**
37,000 ft **Range:** 2,100 miles **Bomb load:** 10,500 lb

Spearhead of the USAAF's daylight raids on Occupied Europe. The
D model carried less armament than later versions, one of which – the
B-40 fighter – carried up to 30 machine-guns and cannon in an
unsuccessful attempt to provide an escort for B-17 formations

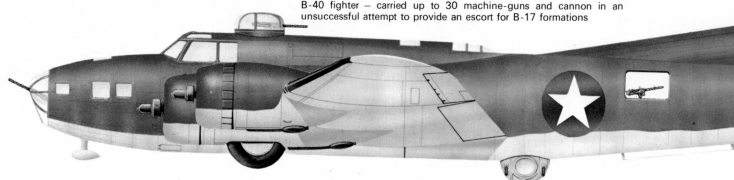

B-17E 'FLYING FORTRESS'

Gross weight: 53,000 lb **Span:** 103 ft 9 in **Length:** 73 ft 10 in
Engine: 4×Wright R-1920-65 **Armament:** 15 machine-guns **Crew:**
9 **Speed:** 317 mph at 25,000 ft **Ceiling:** 36,600 ft **Range:** 3,300
miles **Bomb load:** 4,000 lb

This version of the famous B-17 was the first to live up to the name
'Flying Fortress', with the addition of tail, ventral and front upper gun
turrets, the last power-operated

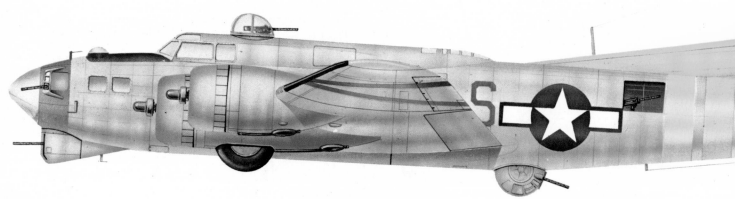

B-17G 'FLYING FORTRESS'

Gross weight: 55,500 lb **Span:** 103 ft 9 in **Length:** 74 ft 4 in
Engine: 4×Wright Cyclone R-1820 **Armament-** 11 machine-guns
Crew: 10 **Speed:** 287 mph at 25,000 ft **Ceiling:** 35,600 ft **Range:**
2,000 miles **Bomb load:** 6,000 lb

Among other modifications, the G model of the B-17 introduced a
two-gun 'chin' turret to help repel attacking fighters

BENDIX UPPER GUN TURRET
TYPE A9B

Elevation and operation power: $\frac{1}{2}$ hp electric motor **Rotation power:** $\frac{1}{2}$ hp motor **Guns:** 2 × Browning M2 ·50 – in **Radius:** 360° **Max. rotation:** 33° per second **Elevation:** horizontal – 92° **Foot charging:** left and right

A profile cam stops guns firing when any part of the aircraft comes in line of fire – to prevent the gunner shooting off his own tail, for example

Except for the special case of the de Havilland Mosquito, which was able to rely on its remarkable flight performance, British bombers of the Second World War relied for their defence mainly on power-driven turrets equipped with rifle-calibre Browning guns. Operational experience resulted in a gradual shift of the main weight of firepower towards the rear. For example, the Handley Page Halifax began life in November 1940 with a two-gun nose turret, two-gun dorsal turret and four-gun tail turret, but from 1943 onwards the standard armament was merely a single hand-operated gun in the nose and four-gun dorsal and tail turrets.

Extended fire
Together with the Lancaster, the Halifax formed the backbone of RAF Bomber Command's night attacks on Occupied Europe between 1941 and 1945, and in both aircraft the turrets could fire for extended periods. In 1939, the typical ammunition capacity of a turret was 500 rounds per gun, but for the last two years of the war British heavy bombers frequently carried 8,000 rounds, weighing almost 800 lb, stored in long boxes in the rear fuselage. There was no powered feed system, each Browning merely pulling its long belt by tension from the gun itself. The gunner, seated in the turret behind local small areas of armour-plate, had a reflector sight and either a joystick or handlebar-type controls for elevation and traverse. Flash eliminators

prevented the gunner from losing his night-adapted vision when he fired at attacking fighters.

Although the penalty in weight and drag of these turrets was considerable, there was never any doubt they were effective even though the gunner often had to fire just as the aircraft entered a violent evasive manoeuvre. In sharp contrast, the policy of the day-bombers of the US Army Air Force (which became the US Air Force in 1946) was to maintain straight and level flight in formation and to defend themselves against fighter attack by massed firepower. By 1941, American bombers had abandoned most rifle-calibre guns in favour of the Browning 0·5-in (12·7-mm), used in both hand-held and turret mountings. By 1943 the heavies of the US 8th Air Force, which daily penetrated German airspace, were in greater need of defensive armament than bombers had ever been. Though each aircraft mounted ten or eleven 0·5-in guns, eight of them in four powered turrets, the opposition was so intense that losses were very severe. Increasingly, the enemy fighters devised methods of attack that reduced their exposure to the bombers' fire, eventually standing-off and firing at long range with 30-mm cannon, rockets and, ultimately, guided missiles. Though the American bombers carried more than 2,000 lb of armour, and the crews wore new flak jackets which protected the torso by over-lapping squares of manganese steel, the slow day-bomber was sorely pressed.

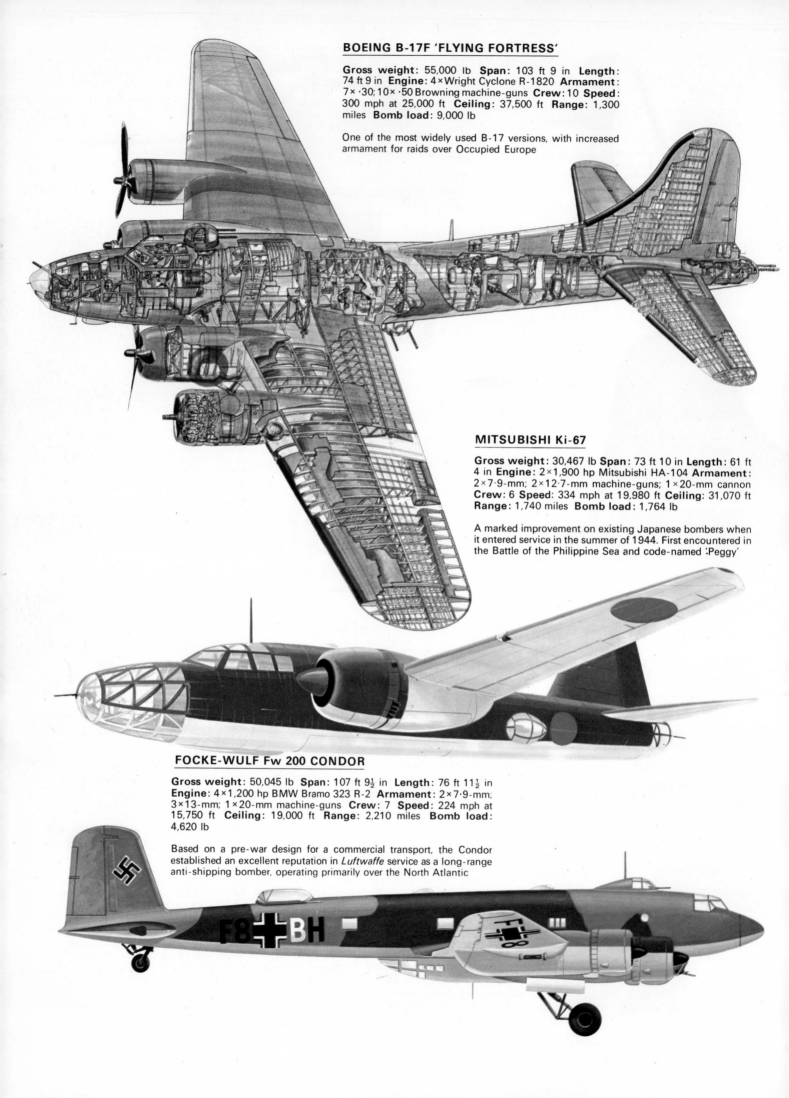

BOEING B-17F 'FLYING FORTRESS'

Gross weight: 55,000 lb **Span:** 103 ft 9 in **Length:** 74 ft 9 in **Engine:** 4×Wright Cyclone R-1820 **Armament:** 7× ·30; 10× ·50 Browning machine-guns **Crew:** 10 **Speed:** 300 mph at 25,000 ft **Ceiling:** 37,500 ft **Range:** 1,300 miles **Bomb load:** 9,000 lb

One of the most widely used B-17 versions, with increased armament for raids over Occupied Europe

MITSUBISHI Ki-67

Gross weight: 30,467 lb **Span:** 73 ft 10 in **Length:** 61 ft 4 in **Engine:** 2×1,900 hp Mitsubishi HA-104 **Armament:** 2×7·9-mm; 2×12·7-mm machine-guns; 1×20-mm cannon **Crew:** 6 **Speed:** 334 mph at 19,980 ft **Ceiling:** 31,070 ft **Range:** 1,740 miles **Bomb load:** 1,764 lb

A marked improvement on existing Japanese bombers when it entered service in the summer of 1944. First encountered in the Battle of the Philippine Sea and code-named 'Peggy'

FOCKE-WULF Fw 200 CONDOR

Gross weight: 50,045 lb **Span:** 107 ft 9½ in **Length:** 76 ft 11½ in **Engine:** 4×1,200 hp BMW Bramo 323 R-2 **Armament:** 2×7·9-mm; 3×13-mm; 1×20-mm machine-guns **Crew:** 7 **Speed:** 224 mph at 15,750 ft **Ceiling:** 19,000 ft **Range:** 2,210 miles **Bomb load:** 4,620 lb

Based on a pre-war design for a commercial transport, the Condor established an excellent reputation in *Luftwaffe* service as a long-range anti-shipping bomber, operating primarily over the North Atlantic

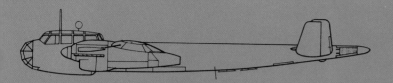

DORNIER Do 217 VI

The Do 217 was a development of the basic Do 17 design, following the Do 215. The VI, the first prototype, flew in August 1938. It was stressed for bigger loads and had increased wing span (62 ft 4 in) and length (60 ft 10 in). A new air-brake in the form of a ribbed umbrella which opened out from the tail extension was also incorporated

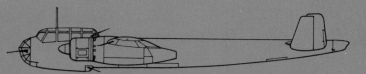

DORNIER Do 217 V7

The air-brake fitted to the VI prototype proved troublesome and was rarely used operationally. It was abandoned on the V7 prototype, which was the first to be fitted with radial engines – two 1,550 hp BMW 139s

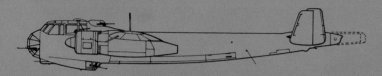

DORNIER Do 217 E-2

The E-series were the first production models of the Do 217. The E-2, initially intended as a dive-bomber, was fitted with the umbrella air-brake, though this was soon removed. It carried a 2,200-lb bomb load, and was armed with one 13-mm MG 131 in a power-operated dorsal turret and another in the ventral position

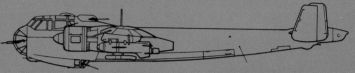

DORNIER Do 217 E-5

The final production model of the E-series, the E-5 was designed to carry the Henschel Hs 293 rocket-propelled radio-controlled glider bomb on carriers outboard of the engine nacelles

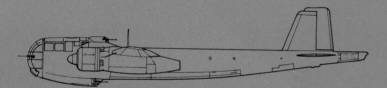

DORNIER Do 217K VI

The K-series of which the K VI was a prototype, was developed from the E-series, with a redesigned, more rounded nose, and powered by two BMW 801D radials

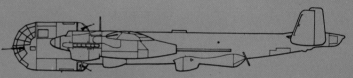

DORNIER Do 217P-O

A high-altitude reconnaissance-bomber developed in 1942. The P-series had increased wing-span (80 ft 4½ in) and were powered by two DB 603A engines, with a DB 605T in the fuselage driving a two-stage compressor. 2,200 lb of bombs and six MG 81 machine-guns were carried, while speed (388 mph) and ceiling (53,000 ft) were both increased

German bombers even earlier had shown themselves to be anything but invincible, particularly during the Battle of Britain. Their design was such that all that could be done, short of an extensive redesign for which the German aircraft industry was not equipped, was a succession of modifications. During the Battle of Britain, the Ju 88 was urgently modified until, in its A-4 version, the original three MG-15 machine-guns had been augmented by two to three additional MG-15s, a 13-mm MG-131 cannon and usually one or two fixed MG-81 machine-guns. In many aircraft the upper rear gunner had to manage four separate hand-held MG-15s projecting at different angles on ball-and-socket mountings. Turrets were rare, although MG-131 guns in electrically-powered turrets were fitted to the Do 217 E-2 and many other Do 217 sub-types, and various Fw 200 C Condors had turrets with either the MG-131 or the far more powerful MG-151/15, a high-velocity 15-mm weapon.

But German armament was at best a botch-up born of urgent necessity. Late models of the Do 217 had four fixed rearward-firing MG-81s in the extreme tail and some had a pair of these fixed in the rear of each

engine nacelle, all eight guns being 'sighted' and fired by the pilot – using nothing more accurate than a rear-view periscopic sight.

The one area in which the Germans did considerable pioneering work was in remotely controlled 'barbettes' (unmanned gun positions). These were lighter than the conventional form of turret and offered less drag. Moreover, in theory at any rate, it was possible for a gunner at a single sighting station to control several barbettes and bring many heavy-calibre guns to bear on a single target. The first aircraft to be equipped with this type of armament was the Messerschmitt Me 210 two-seater night fighter, with a 13-mm MG-131 on each side of the rear fuselage, aimed by the navigator in the rear cockpit. A refined version of the same scheme was used on the much more numerous Me 410. The He 177 heavy bomber usually had a 13-mm MG-131 barbette on the upper forward fuselage and all the candidates for the new Bomber-B specification – the Do 317, Fw 191 and Ju 288 – would have had three to five remotely controlled cannon barbettes offering very great firepower and low drag. But the war ended before these could be put into production.

The armament of Italian, Japanese and Russian bombers was less advanced and chiefly consisted of 7·7-mm, 12·7-mm or 20-mm guns in individual hand-held mountings. However, the Japanese did use a crude form of electrically-driven 20-mm turret on the Mitsubishi Ki-67 and G4M2 bombers, produced respectively for the Army Air Force and Navy Air Force, while the Soviet Union adopted a manned unpowered turret in the rear of both inner engine nacelles on the big four-engined Petlyakov Pe-8.

The greatest and most advanced form of firepower was used in the American heavy bombers. The Douglas A-26 Invader of 1944 was fitted with remotely-controlled upper and lower twin 0·5-in turrets and usually had very heavy fixed nose armament fired by the pilot, who could also use the upper turret when it was locked facing forward. But the biggest advance of the whole war was seen in the Boeing B-29 Superfortress strategic bomber which, though fully pressurised, had five sighting stations and five powered turrets (four of them remotely controlled) with ten or twelve 0·5-in and one 20-mm guns, giving it a remarkable concentration of firepower.

ENGINE DEVELOPMENT

Significant improvements to aircraft engines were made in both America and Britain in the years just preceding the war, but the most radical developments of the war years came from Germany, leading to the production of the V-1 'Doodlebug' guided missile

Most of the engines used in the bombers of 1939 were sound and reliable and capable of considerable further refinement. There was no need to increase the number of engines merely to provide against failure of one engine. For example one of the longest-ranged bombers of the 1930s, the Vickers Wellesley – which for many years held the world absolute distance record at 7,162 miles – had only a single Pegasus engine. The slightly later Vickers bomber, the Wellington, had two Pegasus engines simply because it was bigger and heavier. But during the war there was soon abundant evidence that attacks against well-defended targets were best made by four-engined aircraft (excepting the unique Mosquito) which could make it home even with one or two engines knocked out by defensive fire.

Whereas the reliable engines of the late 1930s had made the twin-engined airliner as safe as one with four engines, there seemed a good case for fitting a bomber

with four engines or even more. It is strange that the British Air Ministry, among those of other nations, should have resisted this trend. In 1936 it grudgingly allowed four engines for the Short Stirling, yet planned the proposed new heavy bombers from Handley Page and A.V. Roe around two very powerful engines of a totally untried type. Fortunately for the Halifax these untried engines, the Rolls-Royce Vulture, were expected at first to be in short supply so its design was changed to specify four Merlins. The rival Avro Manchester stayed with the Vulture, with the result that it was plagued by engine failures and was taken out of service in 1942.

Ignoring the obvious
In the *Luftwaffe* the position was even worse. The He 177, and later the Ju 288, Do 317 and Fw 191, were all planned to use two engines of new design. The result was that the He 177 was notorious for engine failure, while the others never

completed their development. All the time it was glaringly obvious that with four DB 605, Jumo 213 or BMW 801 engines distributed conventionally across the wing span, the Germans could have fielded a bomber of excellent range and striking power.

It is paradoxical that, apart from the rather unsuccessful Stirling, the only four-engined bombers planned in the 1930s to make their mark during the war were the US Army's B-17 and B-24. Other four-engined heavy bombers were put into limited service by the Soviet Union, Italy and Japan, but played only a minor role.

At the outbreak of the Second World War, the Bristol air-cooled radial engines provided 52 per cent of the horsepower of the RAF – and for bombers the percentage was even higher. The pinnacles of development of the poppet-valve engine family were the 1,520 cu in Mercury, with nine 6½-in-stroke cylinders, and the 1,753 cu in Pegasus with a one inch longer stroke.

HANDLEY PAGE HALIFAX Mk II
(opposite above)

Gross weight: 60,000 lb **Span:** 98 ft 10 in **Length:** 71 ft 7 in **Engine** 4×1,390 hp Rolls Royce Merlin XX **Armament:** 8×·303 Browning machine-guns **Crew:** 7 **Speed:** 285 mph at 17,500 ft **Ceiling:** 23,000 ft **Range:** 1,860 miles **Bomb load:** 13,000 lb

The performance of the Mk II Halifax was improved by higher powered engines. The nose gun turret of the Mk I, which experience had shown was seldom used, was replaced with a streamlined fairing

HALIFAX Mk II SERIES I (opposite below)

This sub-variant of the Mk II Halifax mounted a two-gun Boulton Paul dorsal turret amidships but dispensed with the manually-operated beam guns, giving it a total of 6×·303 machine-guns

SHORT STIRLING Mk III (below)

Gross weight: 70,000 lb **Span:** 99 ft 1 in **Length:** 87 ft 3 in **Engine:** 4×1,650 hp Bristol Hercules XVI **Armament:** 8×·303 Browning machine-guns **Crew:** 8 **Speed:** 270 mph at 14,500 ft **Ceiling:** 17,000 ft **Range:** 2,300 miles **Bomb load:** 14,000 lb

First of the three British heavy strategic bombers to enter service, in August 1940, the improved Mk III was the standard version in 1943 and 1944

AVRO MANCHESTER (bottom)

Gross weight: 50,000 lb **Span:** 90 ft 1 in **Length:** 70 ft **Engine:** 2×1,760 hp Rolls Royce Vulture **Armament:** 8×·303 machine-guns **Crew:** 7 **Speed:** 264 mph at 17,000 ft **Ceiling:** 19,200 ft **Range:** 1,630 miles **Bomb load:** 10,350 lb

Developed just before the war as a medium bomber, but marred by the unorthodox Vulture engine which led to its withdrawal in 1942, less than two years after it entered service

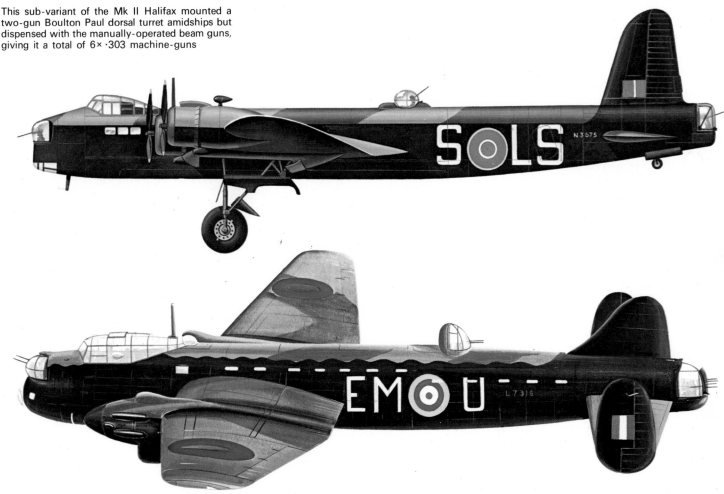

1 W/T visual indicator
2 Fuel jettison valve controls
3 Undercarriage hydraulic instruments
4 Fuel instruments
5 Bomb doors and bomb release lights
6 RPM indicator instruments
7 Throttles
8 Airscrew pitch controls
9 Mixture controls
10 Way to nose turret and bomb aimer's position
11 Compass
12 Pilot's seat
13 Control column
14 Trim controls
15 Ground steering controls
16 Oxygen connection
17 Bomb sight steering indicator
18 Blind landing indicator
19 Radio compass
20 Flap indicator
21 Main electrics switches
22 Undercarriage indicator lights
23 Boost instruments
24 Turn and bank indicator
25 Compass repeater
26 Altimeter
27 Air speed indicator
28 Artificial horizon
29 Climb and descent indicator

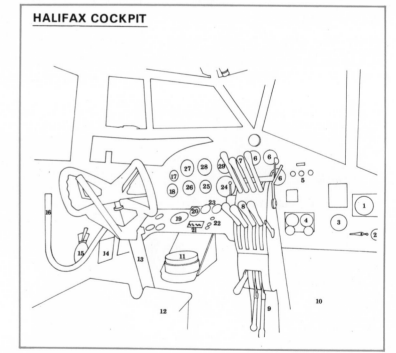

HALIFAX COCKPIT

Both were exceedingly refined engines, with geared drive, single or two-speed supercharger, automatic boost control and provision for a variable-pitch or constant-speed propeller. Both gave over 900 hp, well over twice the power of the original 1,753 cu in Jupiter. In the second half of the 1930s both were put into enormous volume production by a scheme of 'shadow factories' set up by Bristol, the Air Ministry and several car firms. These provided engines for such aircraft as the Harrow,

Bombay, Hampden, Blenheim, Sunderland, Swordfish, Wellesley, Wellington and the Gladiator fighter. The Pegasus, in particular, was also widely built in other countries.

By 1937 Roy Fedden's design team at Bristol had finally solved the problem of how to mass-produce standardized and interchangeable sleeves, and the first of the sleeve-valve engines, the 905 hp Perseus, was coming into production. The first unit to use them was an RAF squadron of

Vildebeeste torpedo-bombers, which found justification for the claim that the new kind of engine offered smoother running, greater efficiency (with lower consumption of both fuel and oil) and much better potential for future growth in power. These factors, combined with lower cost, faster manufacture and greater reliability, all stemmed from a dramatic reduction in the number of parts. The new engines were cleared for production just in time to play a major role in the Second World War.

The Perseus was soon followed by the 1,050/1,200 hp Taurus, a two-row engine only 46 inches in diameter, used in the Beaufort and Albacore torpedo-bombers, and then by the bigger two-row Hercules. This began life in 1939 at 1,375 hp and by the end of the war was rated at up to 1,800 hp. The Hercules was vital to the RAF programme of large aircraft, though in 1939 it was flying only in test and experimental aircraft. Bristol planned an even bigger engine, the Centaurus, planned for a power range from 2,000 to 3,500 hp, but this was still on the bench when war was declared.

Armstrong Siddeley Motors had never been able to rival the success of Bristol, but their 350 hp Cheetah radial was made in very large numbers and before the war was in service with the Avro Anson coastal reconnaissance bomber. The much bigger two-row Tiger, of 795/910 hp, powered the Blackburn Shark torpedo-bomber and the first models of the Armstrong Whitworth Whitley, but all the later Whitleys used Merlins.

The Rolls-Royce Kestrel, used in the Heyford and Hendon heavies of the RAF in 1933–39, hardly figured at all during the war although many hundreds of these 460/745 hp engines had been fitted into Hawker Hart and Hind day-bombers only a few years previously.

Around 1936, it looked as if future heavy bombers were going to use large and very complicated engines such as the Rolls-Royce Vulture, the Rolls-Royce Exe, the Fairey P24 Prince, and the Armstrong Siddeley Deerhound. In fact none of these was ever to see operational service apart from the short and unhappy period with the Vulture already mentioned.

In Germany there were three main classes of engine. The most conventional were the BMW 132 (derived from the American Pratt & Whitney Hornet) and Bramo Fafnir air-cooled radials, the former giving about 850 hp and the latter about 900/1,000 hp – but at the cost of higher weight and fuel consumption. The second German category consisted of the vee petrol engines. The BMW VI had its output raised from 620/660 hp to 725/750 hp by increasing the compression ratio, but in 1934, Daimler Benz and Junkers had been developing much more powerful inverted-vee engines which, by 1937, had been cleared for service. These were the DB 600 and the Jumo 210, both giving over 700 hp – the former soon reaching 900 hp.

Fuel injection

By 1937 development was fast proceeding on two later engines, the DB 601 and Jumo 211, both in the 1,000 hp class. These were destined to play an all-important role in the coming conflict, and were unusual in several respects. One was their inverted arrangement, which was used to advantage by bomber manufacturers to achieve a clean installation, with the engine hung from two large, forged, light-alloy beams. A second was that their superchargers were mounted on one side at the rear, the impeller shaft running transversely. But the most important new feature was that by 1938 both engines used direct fuel injection. Instead of having a carburettor, they had a system for measuring the engine's fuel requirement and arranging for a 12-plunger metering pump to deliver a precise amount of petrol to each cylinder in turn. This system could not ice up, gave rapid starting in all climates and continued to function perfectly even with the aircraft inverted or in any other manoeuvre. Its only possible drawback was that it was complex, though this only affected production man-hours, not reliability.

The third German category comprised the Jumo two-stroke diesels. The first of these unusually thin, flat engines was flown in 1929, and by 1934 the Jumo 205 was in production at about 570 hp for the Ju 86, the *Luftwaffe's* first really effective bomber. The heavy-oil diesels were more efficient than petrol engines (so that even allowing for the greater weight of the engine, the weight of engines and fuel for a long bombing mission was less), while their less-volatile fuel reduced the risk of catching fire after suffering battle damage. Yet the Jumo diesels faded from the scene and played only a small role in a most unexpected type of mission, bombing from the stratosphere.

While the French and the Italians rather inefficiently produced a wide range of different families of engines of every conceivable type, the USA had by 1939 abandoned practically everything in favour of the excellent and highly refined air-cooled radials from Pratt & Whitney and Wright. The main P & W engines were the R-1830 Twin Wasp, which had reached the 1,200 hp level, and the much bigger R-2800 Double Wasp which in 1939 was running on the test-bed.

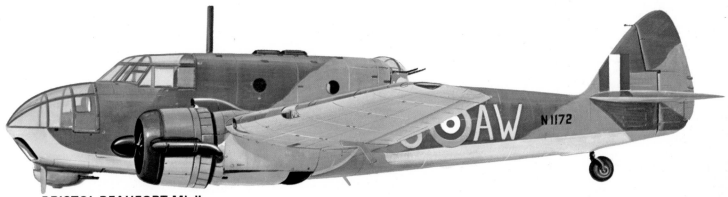

BRISTOL BEAUFORT Mk II

Gross weight: 21,050 lb **Span:** 57 ft 10 in **Length:** 44 ft 7 in **Engine:** 2×1,200 hp Twin Wasp **Armament:** 4×·303 machine-guns **Crew:** 4 **Speed:** 268 mph **Ceiling:** 25,000 ft **Range:** 1,054 miles **Bomb load:** 1×1,605 lb torpedo or 1,500 lb bomb load

RAF Coastal Command's standard torpedo-bomber from 1940 to 1943, when it saw service in the North Sea, English Channel, the Atlantic, Mediterranean and North Africa

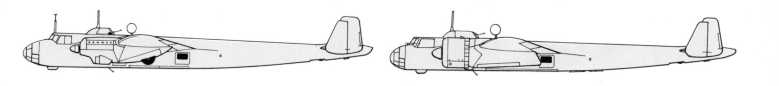

DORNIER Do 17 E-1

The first production model of the Do 17, the E-1, produced in 1936, had two 750 hp BMW V1-7·3 engines, giving it a top speed of 220 mph, ceiling of 18,000 ft and 990 miles range with a 1,760-lb bomb load

DORNIER Do 17 M-1

Powered by the Bramo 323A engine, the M-1 entered production in 1938, and had a downward firing MG 15 fitted as standard

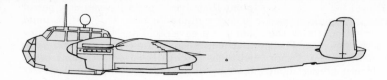
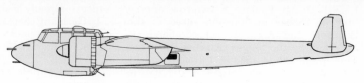

DORNIER Do 17 S

Similar to the M-series, but with the deepened forward fuselage and fully glazed nose which were to become characteristic of the type. Powered by DB 600A or G liquid-cooled engines, the Do 17 S was used primarily as a recon-naissance-bomber

DORNIER Do 17 Z-10

The last Do 17s before the designation was changed to Do 215, the Z-series reverted to the Bramo radials used on the M-series. A night fighter carrying an early form of Lichtenstein radar, the Z-10 had no less than four 20-mm cannon and four MG 17s in the nose

Wright's main engine was the R-1820 Cyclone, which in the Boeing B-17 had at last emerged with an operational turbo-supercharger which harnessed much of the otherwise wasted energy of the hot exhaust gases, and added 60 per cent to the power transmitted to the propellers above 25,000 ft altitude. In addition to this dramatic development, Wright had run the first R-2,600 (2,600 cu in) Double Cyclone in 1937. Rated at 1,500 hp, this was the most power-ful conventional engine available and it was destined to partner the Double Wasp in powering many Allied bombers, starting with the Martin Baltimore and B-25 Mitchell.

Behind all the fierce competition with piston engines, the dogged proponents of the gas turbine had at last begun to achieve success. In Britain Frank Whittle, on special duty while detached from the RAF, had run his first experimental jet-propulsion engine in April 1937. It ran well, causing a sudden astonished re-think among the vast majority of 'experts' who had previously refused to show any interest in his work. In Germany, Ernst Heinkel ran a somewhat similar experimental unit a month later, designed by one of his young engineers, Pabst von Ohain. While Whittle at last received an Air Ministry contract for a flight engine, and Gloster began to build the aircraft for it, Heinkel moved much faster. By the end of August 1939 his jet, the He 178, had already flown.

Although the emergence of the potent Focke Wulf Fw 190 fighter, with its air-cooled radial engine, gave the RAF an unpleasant shock in 1941, the official view continued to be that liquid-cooled engines made aircraft go faster. So, in spite of the fallacy of this statement – and the fact that such engines were complicated, costly and vulnerable in battle – the Rolls-Royce Merlin continued throughout the war as the main engine type of the Lancaster and Mosquito, the two bombers that did the biggest and best job of all for RAF Bomber Command.

In contrast, the excellent Bristol Hercules was used in only a few Lancasters, in the Halifax and in such indifferent machines as the Stirling and Albemarle, while the splendid new 2,500–3,000 hp Centaurus was fitted to the Buckingham – which was never used as a bomber at all. Altogether, British bomber engines made little progress during the war apart from a steady refinement of existing designs.

In Germany the situation was exactly

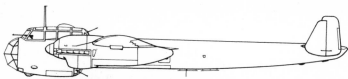

DORNIER Do 215 B-1

Gross weight: 19,600 lb **Span:** 59 ft ⅔ in **Length:** 51 ft 10 in **Engine:** 2×1,100 hp Daimler Benz DB 601Aa **Armament:** 6×7·92-mm ma-chine-guns **Crew:** 4 **Speed:** 292 mph at 16,400 ft **Ceiling:** 31,170 ft **Range:** 965 miles **Bomb load:** 2,200 lb

DORNIER Do 215 B-4

Similar to the B-1 except in the type of equipment carried

DORNIER Do 215 B-1

A reconnaissance-bomber which carried cameras as well as twenty 110-lb bombs

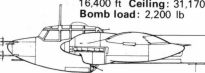

DORNIER Do 215 B-5

A night-fighter version, whose solid nose con-tained one 20-mm MG FF cannon and three 7·9-mm machine guns

the reverse. There were by 1942 so many radical new designs and concepts that there had to be a ruthless pruning of more than forty engines and projects. Work was concentrated on the three major German engine types. The DB 601 had yielded to the faster-running (3,200 rpm) Jumo 213, rated at 1,750 hp. The excellent new BMW 801, the 14-cylinder air-cooled radial fitted to the Fw 190, had been put into production in various forms for several important bombers, beginning with the Do 217 and Ju 88. By 1942, German engines were marching forward almost too boldly, and the interminable problems that were encountered delayed not only the 1939 Bomber-B specification so much that it never got into production, but also the He 177.

The He 177 was planned in 1938 as an outstanding long-range heavy bomber, using two large propellers each driven by a pair of coupled engines. On top of this radical arrangement it was planned to use evaporative steam cooling, such as the RAF had sought for fighters in 1930, but this was soon abandoned in favour of ordinary radiators. The first engine used for the He 177 was the Daimler Benz DB 606, comprising a pair of DB 601 engines geared to a single propeller shaft, which had an unfortunate habit of overheating to the point of catching fire. By early 1943 the DB 606 had been replaced by the more

powerful DB 610, made up of a pair of DB 605s, but this behaved no better. Heinkel's later bombers, the He 274 and He 277, both used four individually mounted DB 603 engines, these being an enlarged and improved version of the 605 rated at 1,850 hp.

No gas-turbine engines were used in Allied bombers before the end of the war, but in Germany there was one true jet reconnaissance bomber and one unique jet-propelled pilotless bomber or guided missile. The former was the Arado 234, which went into service in September 1944 powered by two Jumo 004B turbojets. These engines had axial compressors and, bearing in mind the primitive state of the technology and the need to manufacture in vast quantities, they were outstanding pieces of engineering. Take-off thrust was 1,980 lb and reliability was good, though if the engine suffered a flame-out (extinction of combustion) it was essential to shut off the fuel before trying to relight.

The missile was, of course, the Fieseler Fi 103, commonly called the V-1 or Doodlebug. Its Argus pulse-jet was a simple assembly mainly welded from mild-steel sheet, giving a thrust of about 660/750 lb at low altitude. Although very noisy, inefficient and short-lived, it was ideal for its purpose, taking only about 50 man-hours to build and having remarkably high reliability in very arduous circumstances.

HEINKEL He 177 A-5/R2

Gross weight: 68,343 lb **Span:** 103 ft 1¾ in **Length:** 66 ft 11 in **Engine:** 2×2,950 hp Daimler-Benz DB 610A-1/B-1 **Armament:** 3×7·9-mm; 3×13-mm machine-guns; 1×20-mm cannon **Crew:** 5 **Speed:** 303 mph at 21,500 ft **Ceiling:** 26,250 ft **Range:** 3,400 miles **Bomb load:** 4,964 lb + 2 mines, torpedoes or missiles

This variant of the He 177 was used extensively on the Russian Front for bombing, transport and ground-attack duties, fitted for the latter role with 50-mm or 75-mm cannon

VERGELTUNGSWAFFE I FZG-76

Gross weight: 4,800 lb **Span:** 17 ft 6 in **Length:** 26 ft **Engine:** Pulse jet 600-lb thrust **Armament:** 1,870 lb warhead **Speed:** 390 mph **Range:** 150 miles

One of Hitler's secret weapons, the threat of the V1 was contained first by intercepting and bringing down the rockets and later by destroying their launching sites. Nevertheless, the V1 played an important part in the development of unguided and guided missiles

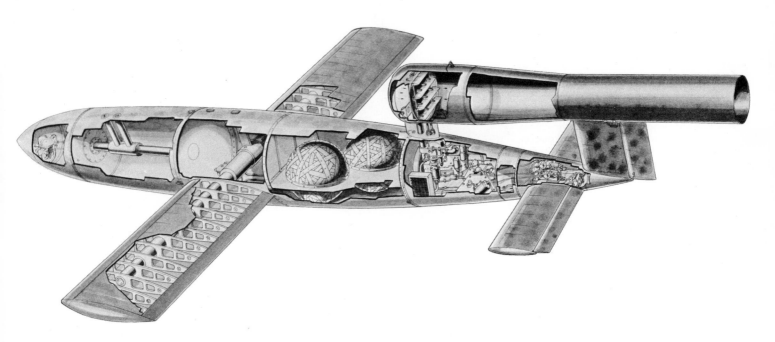

RADAR

Radio and radar were the weapons in the hard-fought secret war
between the technologists of the two sides. The Allied effort
concentrated initially on radar for defence, but in the later stages
of the war sophisticated radio methods were used to increase
bombing accuracy, forcing the Germans to defensive measures,
countered again by British anti-radar devices

Air power was the dominant factor in the Second World War. Although psychological strategic bombing did not always achieve the results promised by its proponents on both the Allied and Axis sides, the use of bombers – against military and industrial targets, in tactical support of ground forces, and for anti-shipping strikes at sea – was fundamental to the final victory. This was largely due to the tremendous advances in technology – greater even than those made during the First World War.

These, in many ways, were simply improvements on First World War performances. Bombing was carried out on a far greater scale but it was primarily for the same purposes and against the same kind of targets. There was little new in bomber tactics; in fact, many of the lessons of the First World War, such as the necessity for fighter escorts during daylight raids, had to be re-learned. The US Eighth Air Force bombers raiding Occupied Europe from 1942 onwards could be escorted by fighters, but when, in 1943, they began to attack targets deep in Germany, beyond the range of any Allied fighter of that time, the losses became so great that the offensive had to be called off. It was only renewed in 1944 with the arrival of the Mustang long-range fighter which could escort the B-17s on their missions over Germany.

The only really new development, apart from the manufacture of the atomic bomb at the end of the war, was in radio and radar techniques. These made it much easier for bombers to reach and locate their targets, especially at night or in bad weather. But they also enabled fighter defences to locate enemy bombers. Thus, throughout the war, a separate battle of technology was fought as each side strove to develop its own navigational aids and at the same time to deny the enemy use of his.

During the 1930s scientists both in Britain and Germany were working on the newly discovered electronic aids to navigation, but because of the different objectives of the two countries, the one defensive and the other offensive, development followed two opposite courses. Thus, while the Germans gave priority to the use of radio aids for bombing, the British concentrated on building up a defensive system of radar, a field in which they were more advanced thanks to the pioneering work of R. A. Watson-Watt of the National Physics Laboratory.

The two German systems which emerged were based on the 'Lorenz' beam. This was basically two slightly over-lapping radio beams, one transmitting Morse dots and the other Morse dashes. Where the signals interlocked, an aircraft received a steady note; any deviation either way resulted in a changed signal. Thus the pilot could follow a predetermined course.

The simpler of the two methods was the 'bent leg' (*Knickebein*) which employed two Lorenz beams, one to hold the bomber on course right up to the target, while the second crossed the first at the point where the bombs should be released. At ranges of about 180 miles from the beam transmitters, this system gave the crew a 50 per cent chance of placing bombs inside a one-mile diameter circle, and its accuracy was even less at greater ranges.

Another method, the X-device, was developed for more precise bombing. This employed four Lorenz beams, each on a different frequency. One held the bomber on course to the target while the other three crossed it at precise intervals. The first intersection gave warning of approach while at the second and third, the navigator started the two hands of a special clock which rotated independently. When the second hand caught up with the first, an electrical contact was made and the bombs were released automatically. The combination of the clock and the Lorenz beams gave the X-device great accuracy since it provided

data on the aircraft's speed, an essential requirement for precision bombing. A practised crew could place bombs within a 400-yard diameter circle at 180 miles from the transmitters. Because the X-device was so complicated to use however, it was confined to the specially trained crews of *Kampfgruppe* (wing) 100.

The disadvantage of the Lorenz beam was that it was vulnerable to radio counter-measures. By day of course, during the Battle of Britain, British fighters could be vectored on to incoming enemy bombers located by radar (reflected radio waves able to be picked up and seen on a cathode-ray tube). The chain of radar stations built along the southern and eastern coasts of England was a major contribution in defeating the *Luftwaffe's* attempt to bomb Britain into submission, providing a scientific means of interception which greatly increased the efficiency of the RAF's woefully low fighter strength. Friendly aircraft were distinguished by the transmission of a special radar pulse called IFF (Identification Friend or Foe). But it was during the German night raids which followed, once the Spitfires and Hurricanes of Fighter Command had overcome the threat by day, that the Lorenz systems came into use.

One counter-measure was to jam the beams, but a more successful method was

to deflect them so that the Germans unwittingly dropped their bombs at sea or in open country. For use against the bombers themselves, night-fighters were developed, carrying a new and – at that time – highly secret form of interception radar which enabled aircraft to be located in darkness. The first British aircraft to be equipped with AI (aircraft interception) was the Bristol Blenheim fast bomber but it was not really suited for the purpose. The Bristol Beaufighter and the American Douglas DB-7 Havoc, both conversions of light bombers, proved to be more effective night-fighters in late 1940. But although considerable success was achieved, it was not sufficient to provide a deterrent. The night-blitz on British towns was almost over before enough night-fighters became available in the summer of 1941.

Because efforts had necessarily concentrated on using radar for defensive operations, little was done in the early months of the war to provide electronic aids for bombers attacking targets in Germany and Occupied Europe. These had to rely on dead reckoning combined with visual fixes on known landmarks – an extremely unreliable method – and not until late 1941 did the RAF's first radar navigational aid became available.

Getting closer

The Gee system was based on three ground transmitters, about 100 miles apart, which transmitted a complex train of radar pulses across the continent of Europe. By means of a special radar receiver in the aircraft which enabled the time difference between the various signals to be measured, and referring these differences to a special Gee map, the navigator could determine his position to within six miles when 400 miles from the most distant transmitter. This was an improvement on the Lorenz system but it had the same vulnerability to jamming by the Germans and by the end of 1942 it had reached the end of its usefulness.

A much more successful radar device was the H2S system which could be carried in aircraft and could therefore operate beyond the range of beacons. This system gave a representation of the terrain below the aircraft on a cathode-ray tube, by means of a radar beam tilted downwards. Its only drawback was that it required a skilled crew to make the best use of the results. As the *Luftwaffe* had learned in 1940 and 1941, it was advisable to have the equipment used by picked crews to start marker fires at the target to direct the main bomber force – the only problem being that if the markers went wide, so would the majority of the bombs. The H2S device brought about a marked improvement in the accuracy of attacks when it was introduced in 1942, but still too many bombs were missing their targets during night raids. This was one of the main reasons why the US Eighth Air Force, starting its European operations in mid-1942, concentrated on daylight precision bombing in spite of the high casualty rate. An area-bombing night sortie was regarded as successful if the bombs were released within three miles of the aiming point.

In a concerted effort to improve bombing accuracy, RAF Bomber Command in 1942 created the Pathfinder Force, under the command of D. C. T. Bennett. This coincided with the introduction of the new 'Oboe' radar system which, while limited in range, provided a remarkably fine degree of accuracy. Two radar transmitters were set up at Dover and Cromer, sending out a stream of pulses which could be picked up and returned by an airborne transmitter in the aircraft. Ground operators could direct the pilot by means of radio instructions to fly along any determined path to the target and compute the bombing release point for him. Bombing accuracies of 200 yards or so were achieved by this method. The maximum range for an aircraft flying at 28,000 ft was 270 miles, which covered most of the Ruhr but not many other targets in Germany. However, after the Normandy invasion, beacons were set up in France and during the latter stages of the war, the Oboe system could be used to reach almost every target of importance in Germany.

Another limitation was that each pair of ground transmitters could control only one aircraft at a time on its bombing run of about ten minutes. Consequently, Oboe was used only in the high-altitude Mosquito bombers of the Pathfinder Force.

With the development by the British and American air forces in 1943 of a round-the-clock bombing offensive against Germany, the *Luftwaffe* found itself in the same position as RAF Fighter Command in 1940. Its fighters could cope with the American daylight raids, but there were no specialised night-fighters to combat the British night bombers. A number of twin-engined fighter-bombers and medium bombers were converted for night fighting duties, beginning with the Messerschmitt Bf-110G, but the most widely used was the G6 variant of the versatile Junkers Ju 88, some of which carried an upward-firing cannon mounted in the central fuselage. What gave these night-fighters such a devastating offensive power was the introduction of a German form of airborne interception radar, known as the Lichtenstein system.

This in turn led the British to devise counter-measures to confuse the German radar screens and radio signals, both in the air and on the ground. Lengths of tinfoil – 'Window' – corresponding to the wavelengths of German radar were dropped in large quantities to produce a vast number of echoes which obscured the echoes made by the aircraft. 'Mandrel' was a device carried by pairs of circling British aircraft which radiated signals to jam the German radar before it could detect incoming bombers. 'Piperack' was a rearward-facing device which shielded bombers in a cone behind the jamming aircraft. And 'Jostle' was a large radio transmitter carried by an aircraft to emit a raucous note on the same wavelength as the German fighter control so that instructions could not be heard. These counter-measures were used in many different combinations to keep the Germans guessing. They were the crude forerunners of today's sophisticated ECM (electronic counter-measure), the bomber's main defence against guided surface-to-air missiles.

BRISTOL BLENHEIM Mk IV

Gross weight: 12,500 lb **Span:** 56 ft 4 in **Length:** 42 ft 9 in **Engine:** 2×920 hp Mercury XV **Armament:** 5×·303 machine-guns **Crew:** 3 **Speed:** 266 mph at 11,800 ft **Ceiling:** 22,000 ft **Range:** 1,450 miles **Bomb load:** 1,320 lb

Primarily intended as a light bomber, the Blenheim served throughout the war in many roles for the RAF and was the first night-fighter to use airborne interception radar

BOMBS AND BOMB-SIGHTS

The technology of war-heads improved in the course of the war in two main areas: increasing accuracy and ability to penetrate targets previously impregnable; and increasing destructive force — culminating in the fire bombing of German cities and the atomic bombs dropped on Japan

British bombs changed very little between 1918 and 1937. Apart from the 20-lb Cooper used for practice, the standard high explosive bombs were 112-lb, 230 or 250-lb, and 520 or 550-lb. But in 1937 a completely new range of bombs was introduced with a better streamlined shape, improved ballistic properties (almost all were fitted with tail fins surrounded by an open cylindrical drum), and redesigned fuses and arming devices operated by a combination of pistol and a separate detonator. The pistol was merely a mechanical device, armed after the bomb's release, and containing a striker which was actuated on impact. The striker in turn fired an initiator cap in the detonator which, after a required period of delay by the burning of a pyrotechnic fuse, set off the main detonator and thus the explosive.

The new range included bombs of 2,000 lb nominal weight, one of which was specially designed for armour-piercing. In addition to the demolition bombs, used for the majority of bombing operations to produce either blast, fragmentation or mining effect (the explosive charge averaging some 50 per cent of the total weight), the RAF also introduced a comprehensive range of improved flares, flame-floats, smoke-floats and other pyrotechnic devices. A standard aerial mine was also produced, together with further versions of the long-lived 18-in torpedo weighing around 1,650 lb. By the outbreak of the Second World War, an incendiary bomb was also in production with a body of combustible magnesium – it had a hexagonal section so that clusters could be stacked in a minimum of space.

In 1939 the HE bombs produced in the greatest numbers were the 250 and 500-lb general purpose types, regarded as the most useful since they could be delivered by every RAF bomber then in service. Except for leaflets and, increasingly, incendiaries, they far outnumbered all other 'stores' dropped by the RAF during the first two years of the war. They were even the preferred weapons for attacks on the German Fleet which began soon after the outbreak of war, although it was obvious that they could cause little more than superficial damage to a capital ship. In fact, the results achieved were even less because a high proportion of the bombs in those early attacks failed to detonate. Not only was there a need for an improvement in navigation and in bombing tactics generally, there was also an urgent need for better bombs.

The range of bombs available to the *Luftwaffe* was slightly smaller, the standard HE weights being 50, 250 and 500 kg (110,

551 and 1,102 lb) and all having a straight-sided shape with braced tail fins. All were very simple to make, yet there is a well-authenticated story that in 1937 the *Luftwaffe* had not received a single modern bomb; to rectify the deficiency, Hitler himself suggested filling surplus gas cylinders with explosives. Only gradually did bomb production get into its stride, as the inevitability of a major war became recognised.

Electrical fuses

At first the Germans used methods similar to the British for fusing their bombs, but then they turned to a new and more reliable form of electrically-fired fuse. This contained a condenser which was charged from an electrical supply in the aircraft when the bomb was released. A second condenser was charged from the first by means of a resistor whose capabilities could be altered to provide the length of delay required before the ignitor was fired. In Germany in 1939, production began on a cylindrical magnesium incendiary bomb, and also a high explosive bomb of 1,000 kg (2,205 lb), both with annular fins. The Heinkel He 111 could carry two of the latter weapons on side-by-side external racks, but the standard weapon used against British cities from May 1940 onwards was the parachute mine.

The use of mines against 'soft' land targets, although unconventional at first, was actually only common sense. The mine was a large container of high explosive which, when detonated, released far more energy than a traditional GP-type bomb, even if bombs were available in such a size (2,200 and 3,300 lb). For marine use, special triggering and fuse systems were necessary. During 1940, both the British and Germans began to perfect mines of much greater sophistication than the old horn contact type. Ultimately, mines were provided with fuses sensitive to the various effects made by a passing ship, such as distortion of the Earth's magnetic field, sound wave vibrations, or slight reduction of the hydrostatic pressure. (These patterns were called magnetic, acoustic and influence.)

For use against cities, the ingenious marine fuses were merely replaced by impact fuses, sometimes triggered by a long pistol probe before the case struck the ground or a building. The need for a parachute was a hang-over from the original role when each mine had to be laid in a pre-designated area and yet protected against the shock of hitting the water.

Later in the war, a new form of radio

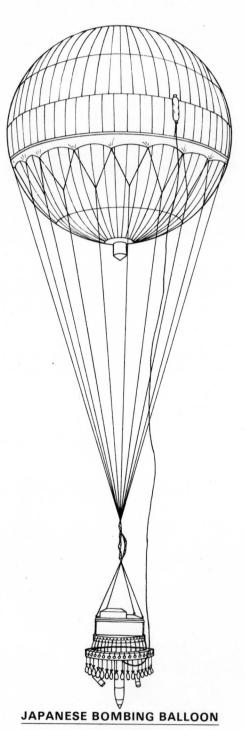

JAPANESE BOMBING BALLOON

Balloon volume: 19,000 cu ft **Envelope diameter:** 32·81 ft **Fuse:** 64 ft; approx. 1 hr 22 min burning time **Bombs:** 2 incendiary bombs; 1 × 15 kg anti-personnel bomb

One of the more bizarre bombing ideas of the war, these balloons were released by the Japanese and intended to be carried by the wind to the United States. Some of them travelled as far as Alaska

proximity fuse was developed, making it possible for a bomb to explode at a given height above the ground. This operated by means of a radio-frequency oscillator which received a reflection of its own waves from the ground as the bomb fell.

As a result of experience in the first year of the war, the RAF realised a very important fact. Previously, the bomb had been regarded as an aerial artillery shell, made in much the same way and given a streamlined form to minimise drag when carried in the slipstream and to prevent random tumbling after release. In fact, all that was needed in most cases was to deliver the maximum amount of chemical energy to the target. The bomber was seen in this new light as no more than a trucking system, with high explosive as the payload. The metal part of a bomb was merely a necessary evil, to be reduced in weight as much as possible. As all the payloads of the planned heavy bombers were carried inside an enclosed bomb-bay, there was no need for streamlining. The logical result was a completely new type of bomb called the Light Case (LC), in principle no more than a glorified oil drum.

The first LC bomb had a nominal weight of 4,000 lb. It was a welded drum of thin mild steel, painted dark olive and provided with three windmill-armed fuses on its bluff front face. Empty cases were filled by pouring in molten RDX (sometimes called Exogen), an explosive which combined ease of manufacture and high safety qualities with a very powerful blast effect.

It had been discovered by a German as far back as the end of the 19th century, but it was only during the Second World War that a means was found of producing it in quantity. In use, the 4,000-pounder was soon dubbed the 'blockbuster' and it was the ideal partner to the incendiary in the area-bombing attacks on cities which were the staple diet of Bomber Command for the rest of the war. All the four-engined heavies could carry the big bomb, as could the Wellington, and by 1944, even the Mosquito could take one as far as Berlin, in a specially enlarged bomb-bay.

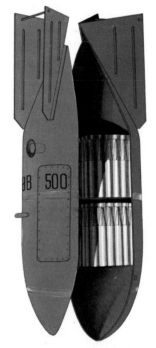

GERMAN INCENDIARY
CONTAINER BOMB

Weight: 500 kg **Length:** 5 ft 6 in **Diameter:** 18·5 in **Contents:** 120×1-kg incendiary bombs

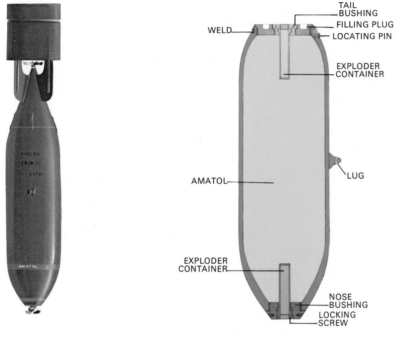

BRITISH MC 500-lb BOMB

Drawing and section of one of the most common types of bomb dropped by the RAF in the early years of the Second World War. The explosive used was Amatol

JAPANESE BOMBS

Clockwise from top:
Type 2 No 25 Mk 111
Weight: 250 kg **Length:** 69 in
Type 99 No 80
Weight: 750 kg **Length:** 92·1 in
Type 1 No 25
Weight: 262 kg **Length:** 71·75 in
Type 97 No 6
Weight: 59 kg **Length:** 40 in

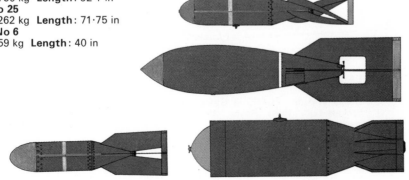

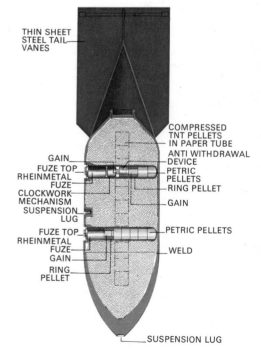

GERMAN 250-kg HE BOMB

Overall length: 64·5 in **Body length:** 42 in **Overall width:** 18 in **Body diameter:** 14·5 in **Charge/weight ratio:** 52·2%

But the supreme exponent of blockbusting was the Lancaster, whose 33 ft long bomb-bay was completely unobstructed by any longitudinal or transverse structure. By 1942 the Lancaster was carrying 8,000-lb bombs, essentially two 4,000-pounders bolted together, and for special targets it also carried a triple-unit 12,000-pounder, the Tallboy. The ballistic properties of the 4,000-lb bomb rested mainly on keeping the centre of aerodynamic pressure aft of the centre of gravity, but when three were joined end-to-end it was deemed advisable to put on a stabilising tail.

Although the RAF dropped many other weapons during the war, the two most outstanding were both designed by a team at Vickers led by Barnes Wallis, who had earlier been responsible for the Wellington. The first was the famous device used by 617 Squadron, the Dambusters. To deliver high-explosive to the face of a dam protected by torpedo netting, Wallis invented a bomb in the form of a huge drum, carried semi-externally by a modified Lancaster. The drum was hung on crutches at left and right with its axis arranged transversely, and shortly before the attack was rotated at high speed by a separate auxiliary engine in the bomber's fuselage. Released at a

height of sixty feet, the spinning bomb then skipped across the lake surface behind the dam, slowing when it had passed the final net and sinking down in contact with the face of the dam to be detonated by a hydrostatic fuse at the correct depth.

Wallis's other great contribution was a supreme form of conventional HE bomb, for use against the most hardened targets (notably U-boat pens, with reinforced-concrete roofs up to thirty-five feet thick). This was a free-falling (supersonic) bomb of beautiful streamline form, spun by four canted tail-fins, with a heavy-case body and pointed nose. Its weight was no less than 22,000 lb, and its name of 'Earthquake' was singularly appropriate. Dropped against large solid structures, such as the great railway viaduct at Bielefeld, an Earthquake detonated deep underground caused a tremor so severe that the structure was brought down by the shock waves.

An alternative weapon used against U-boat pens was the Disney bomb devised by Capt Terrell RN. This streamlined 4,500-lb hard-case bomb had a rocket in its tail ignited by a barometric fuse after a free fall from above 20,000 ft down to 5,000 ft. This boosted terminal velocity to about 2,400 feet a second, a speed greater than that of

any weapon of such a size other than the V-2 rocket. Owing to stowage difficulty, it was finally agreed to deliver Disney bombs in pairs carried externally by the Boeing B-17s of the US Eighth Air Force. Later, the B-29 successfully carried external pairs of 22,000-lb Earthquakes. Apart from this, the bombs of the US services were generally conventional, though it was chiefly American research that in 1944 led to the use of napalm, a jellied mixture of petroleum fuels (the name stemmed from naphtha and palm oil) carried in a simple container – often the drop tank of a fighter.

Mention should be made, however, of the awe-inspiring technique of filling a complete B-17 with high explosive and directing it at a major target under radio control. This campaign, Project Aphrodite, was aimed at first against the huge 'V-weapon' structures in the Pas de Calais, and war-weary Fortresses, redesignated BQ-7, were turned into huge guided missiles containing 20,000 lb of Torpex triggered by an impact fuse system. A courageous pilot took off manually, in an open cockpit, and then bailed out by parachute near the British coast after setting the fuses. A director aircraft took over the steering of the BQ-7 by radio.

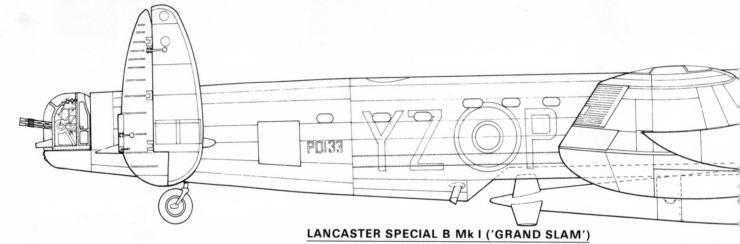

LANCASTER SPECIAL B Mk I ('GRAND SLAM')

Gross weight: 71,000 lb **Span:** 102 ft **Length:** 69 ft 6 in **Engine:** 4×1,280 hp Rolls Royce Merlin XX **Armament:** 6×303 Browning machine guns **Crew:** 7 **Speed:** 280 mph at 18,500 ft **Ceiling:** 23,500 ft **Range:** 2,700 miles **Bomb load:** 22,000 lb

A special modification of the Lancaster, with the dorsal turret removed, to enable it to carry the 22,000-lb 'Earthquake' or Grand Slam bomb

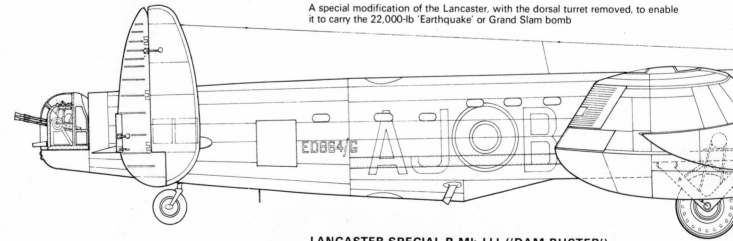

LANCASTER SPECIAL B Mk III ('DAM BUSTER')

Gross weight: 70,000 lb **Span:** 102 ft **Length:** 69 ft 6 in **Engine:** 4× Packare-built Rolls Royce Merlin 224 **Armament:** 8×303 Browning machine-guns **Crew:** 7 **Speed:** 287 mph at 11,500 ft **Ceiling:** 24,500 ft **Range:** 1,660 miles **Bomb load:** 14,000 lb

A Lancaster specially adapted to carry the spinning-drum bomb developed by Dr Barnes Wallis for the raid on the Mohne and Eder dams on 17 May 1943

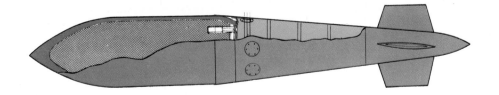

12,000-lb 'TALLBOY'

Total weight: 11,885 lb **Overall length**: 21 ft **Body length**: 10 ft 4 in **Body diameter**: 3 ft 2 in **Charge/weight ratio**: 45%

The Tallboy bomb was basically three 4,000-lb light-case bombs bolted together, with tail fins added for stability

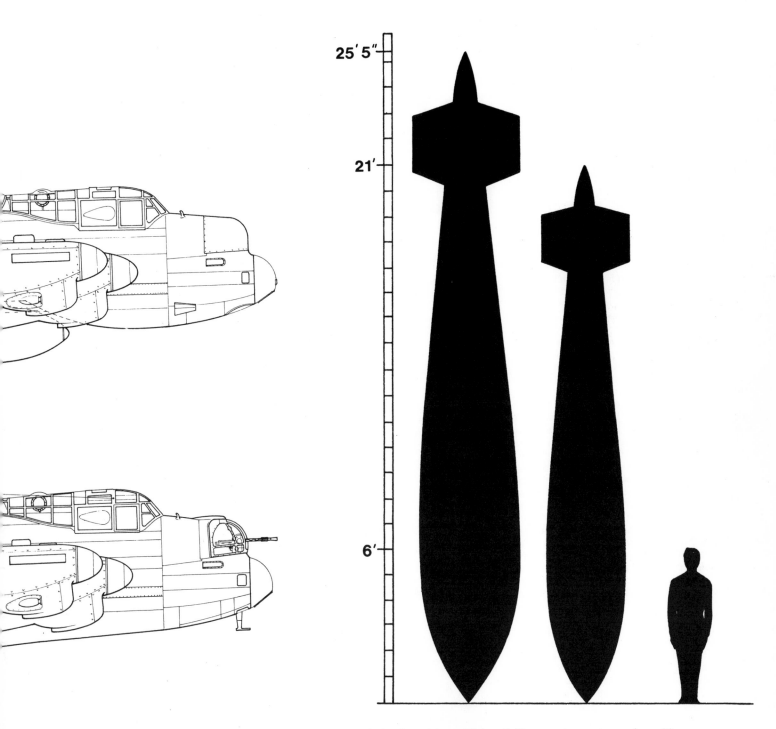

Left: Grandslam Right: Tallboy — drawn to scale, with a human figure added for comparison

Some indication of the explosive power of an Aphrodite attack is afforded by the fact that, when a converted US Navy Liberator commanded by Joseph P. Kennedy Jr (brother of the future US President) exploded prematurely with the crew on board at 15,000 ft over Blyth, Northumberland, severe blast damage on the ground extended over a radius of six miles.

These radio-controlled bombers were as far as the Allies got in creating the concept of the guided missile in the Second World War. The Germans, however, were more imaginative. Radio-controlled bombers existed in abundance under the Mistel programme, together with an even greater number which were merely set on course by a manned fighter carried on top of the bomber and then, after the fighter had uncoupled, left to fly to the target in a straight shallow dive on auto-pilot. The commonest Mistel missile was a rebuilt Ju 88 with a circular section front fuselage (warhead) triggered by a long nose probe.

Much more advanced in conception were the true guided missiles. Fritz X (FX) or 'PC 1400', an armour-piercing bomb with cruciform fixed wings, had a complicated tail fitted with guidance spoilers controlled by radio from the launch aircraft. The Hs 293 was a stand-off missile with less punch but longer range, and it took the form of a miniature aircraft, with rocket boost, steered by radio links similar to those of FX. Both weapons became operational in August 1943 with units of *Kampfgruppe* 100 equipped with special sub-types of Do 217, and the following month FX began sinking battleships with apparent ease (though HMS *Warspite* limped into Malta after being struck by three). There were many other *Luftwaffe* missiles, such as the Bv 246 which flew on wings of reinforced concrete and the L 10 equipment which converted a torpedo into an air-launched stand-off missile.

Perhaps the most unexpected development was the Japanese piloted missile, the Yokosuka MXY-7 Ohka (Cherry Blossom), flown in suicide attacks against US forces in the Pacific. Carried to within about fifty miles of its target by a conventional bomber (usually a G4M2 'Betty'), the Ohka was then released and flown by its pilot seated in a cramped cockpit between the stubby 5-metre (16 ft 5 in) wing and the twin-finned tail. Most of the distance to the target was covered in a fast glide, and though the device was incapable of much evasive action, it was small and difficult to intercept. Three miles from the target, the pilot ignited three solid-fuel rockets in the tail, arriving in a steep dive at something like 620 mph. The whole front half of the fuselage was a warhead containing 2,645 lb of tri-nitrol aminol. In its day, the Ohka was practically unstoppable once it had neared its target, but US fighters usually managed to destroy the mother-planes before the missiles were launched. Even so, many direct hits were scored in these suicide attacks, and they were taken more seriously than implied by the name given to them by the US Navy – *Baka*, the Japanese word for fool. Towards the end of the war, Japanese suicide attacks were carried out mostly by conventional aircraft filled with explosive.

The ultimate weapon of the Second World War was, of course, the atomic bomb, the outcome of combined work by British, American and French scientists. Based on the fission principle, the tremendous de- structive power of the two bombs dropped on Japan resulted from the release of energy which raised the air to a very high temperature and caused radiation on various wavelengths. The bombs were dropped from Boeing B-29s flying at about 30,000 ft, on Hiroshima on 6 August 1945 and on Nagasaki three days later. The first destroyed more than four square miles of the city and killed some 80,000 people, while the second destroyed one-and-a-half square miles, killing 40,000. In fact, the physical damage was not as great as that caused by the big incendiary raids on Germany when whole cities were set ablaze and swept by firestorms created by the upward rush of hot air.

But those first atomic bombs were only a foretaste of the much more powerful nuclear weapons which were to be developed later. So great is the energy released by an atomic bomb that it embraces all the known destructive principles, including blast and penetration, and some, resulting from radioactivity, whose delayed effect still cannot be measured precisely.

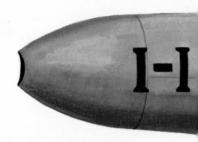

YOKOSUKA MXY-7 OHKA

Gross weight: 4,718 lb **Span**: 16 ft 5 in **Length**: 19 ft 10 in **Engine**: 3×solid propellant rockets, 1,764 lb total thrust **Crew**: 1 **Speed**: 403 mph; terminal velocity 576 mph **Ceiling**: NA **Range**: 20 miles **Bomb load**: 2,645 lb

Japanese piloted suicide bomb, air-launched from specially adapted G4M2 motherplane

HS 293 ROCKET BOOSTED GLIDE BOMB

Total weight: 1,730 lb **Span**: 10 ft 2·857 in **Length**: 10 ft 5·25 in **Fuse**: impact **Warhead**: 550 lb Trialen

A glide bomb designed to be released from a Dornier 217 bomber. It was radio controlled, and the rocket boost motor burned for 10 seconds after launch

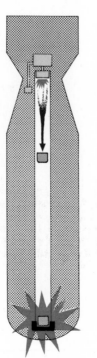
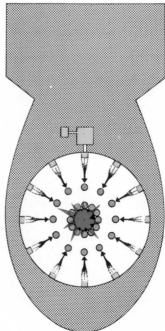

'LITTLE BOY' (left)

Weight: 9,000 lb **Diameter**: 28 in **Length**: 10 ft

The atom bomb dropped on Hiroshima, a 'gun-type' weapon in which one piece of Uranium 235 was fired into another, cup-shaped piece to produce the nuclear explosion

'FAT MAN' (right)

Weight: 10,000 lb **Length**: 10 ft 8 in

'Fat man', the bomb dropped on Nagasaki, used the implosion method, with a ring of 64 detonators shooting pieces of Plutonium together to create the explosion

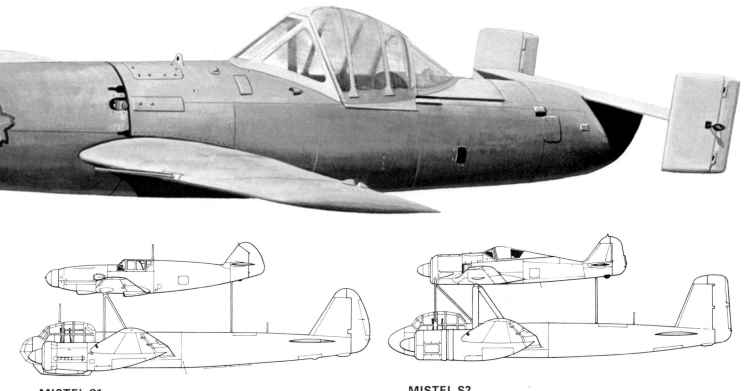

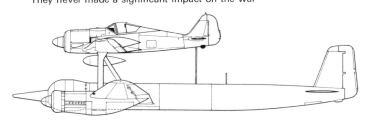

MISTEL S1

Bomber: Ju 88 A-4 **Fighter:** Messerschmitt Bf 109F

MISTEL S2

Bomber: Ju 88 G-1 **Fighter:** Fw 190A-8

Under the Mistel programme various types of plane, most commonly a rebuilt Ju 88, had their forward fuselage filled with explosives were guided by an attached fighter towards their target, then released and either radio-controlled or left to dive onto the target on auto-pilot. They never made a significant impact on the war

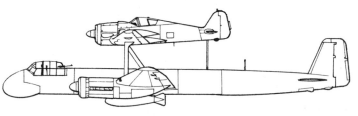

MISTEL 3C

Bomber: Ju 88 G-10 **Fighter:** Fw 190A-8

'FÜHRUNGSMACHINE'

Bomber: Ju 88 H-4 **Fighter:** Fw 190A-8

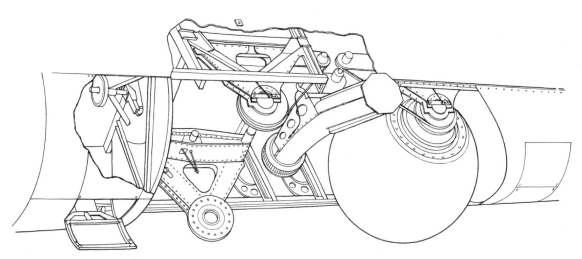

TWIN HIGHBALL

experimental installation in Mosquito B-IV

The Highball bomb was designed by Barnes Wallis after the success of the Dambusters raid. It was an experimental installation of two bombs for use against Japanese shipping in the Far East, to be delivered by Mosquito bombers

Bomb-sights

In 1939 the standard bomb-sights in use by all the major air forces were merely refined versions of the primitive sights used in the First World War. The sight was a purely mechanical device, usually fixed in the nose or belly of the bomber and operated by a bomb-aimer (bombardier in the USA) lying prone on his stomach. He would first set up the sight rather in the way that a rifleman of 1914 would set up his backsight, the difference being that instead of feeding in the range he would insert the height of the bomber and the true airspeed, and usually the wind velocity and direction as well. This would align a sighting scale with the apparent path of the target, seen moving towards the bomber far ahead and below. Almost always the bomb-aimer would have to aim by passing corrective instructions to the pilot, either by hand signals or intercom voice.

Markers or cross-hairs arranged transversely would indicate the correct moment for release, when the bomb-aimer would either press a button, pull a trigger, start a clockwork sequence release, or even, on some of the older types of aircraft, release the bombs by manual linkage. Most bombers offered alternatives for release in singles, spaced groups, clusters, or in a long stick covering perhaps a mile of ground.

A major drawback of these course-setting sights was that they were accurate only under ideal conditions, and were hopelessly upset if the bomber departed significantly from straight and level flight. The corrections to a bombing run had to be made quickly and deftly, often with flak bursting all around the bomber or while under attack from enemy fighters. Any evasive action by bank or sideslip might mean that either the bombing run had to be made again or that the bombs would fall wide of target. In fact, many of the early high-level attacks by both the *Luftwaffe* and the RAF were extremely inaccurate.

To rectify these shortcomings, improved types of sights were devised. In August 1942, the RAF Pathfinder Force introduced the Mk XIV sight in which the sighting head in the nose of the aircraft was supplemented by a computer unit further aft. The bomb-aimer sighted in the usual way, looking through an inclined optically-flat glass panel, with the sight set with true airspeed, ground speed, wind velocity and altitude; an electro-mechanical calculator box then kept the sight on target even while the bomber took evasive action. By 1943 the Mk XIV was in all Bomber Command heavies and, as the T-1, was also used by the USAAF.

The Norden sight

The Americans, however, had an even more advanced sight, the Norden. In 1928 Carl L. Norden had begun to develop a sight that could be linked with an autopilot in such a way that the bombardier would aim the aircraft directly, with corrective actions made automatically. The SBAE (Stabilised Bomb Approach Equipment) was a special autopilot comprising gyros, servo-motors and feedback follow-up systems to impart control-surface movements proportional to the deviation of the bomber from the desired flight path.

The sight was mounted in the nose behind a flat glass panel in the usual way, but instead of mere crossed wires, the sighting head consisted of an optical telescope which could be trained on the target by the bombardier and kept in alignment by a drive motor and two-axis linkage. The act of keeping the sight pointing at the target automatically commanded the aircraft to steer for an accurate bombing run, making correctly banked turns. When the target reached the correct angular direction the bombs were released automatically. The bombardier would then cut out the sight and restore control to the pilot. Though the widely publicised claim that with this sight a B-17 or B-24 at 25,000 ft could 'drop a bomb in a pickle barrel' was obviously an exaggeration, the Norden was the most advanced high-altitude sight used in the war.

Radar aids

German, Russian and Japanese sights were without exception conventional, apart from the special equipment used on the versions of the Do 217, Fw 200C and other aircraft equipped to launch FX or Hs293 guided bombs. As mentioned earlier, various radar and radio navigational aid systems were often used directly as an aid to bombing or accurate target-marking; indeed, the accuracy of Pathfinder Force, and consequently that of the entire might of Bomber Command, depended on Oboe. The British H2S radar, publicly revealed in 1944 by widespread stories in the American press, gave a picture of the terrain beneath on a PPI (plan-position indicator) cathode-ray tube face and was especially useful over regions of combined land (which looked bright) and water (which looked dark) so that river bridges and docks could be bombed with fair accuracy using this aid alone, even in conditions of total cloud cover.

At the other extreme of the technological scale was the sight used by 617 Squadron to breach the Mohne and Eder dams. The Lancasters were brought down to 60 ft above the water and held there by fixed spotlights at nose and tail, angled so that the spots coincided on the water when the planes were at exactly the right height. The bomb-aimer sighted on the twin towers of the dams, just 600 ft apart, by using a device like a boy's catapult with two upright prongs. According to Guy Gibson himself, the sight cost "a little less than the price of a postage stamp".

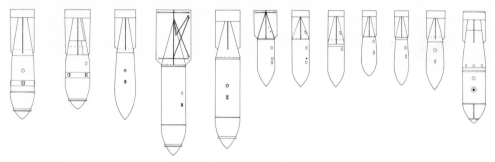

GERMAN BOMBS (to scale)

Left to right: SC 1,000 kg; SC 1,000 kg L; SD 1,400 kg (piercing); SC 1,800 kg; SC 2,000 kg; SC 500 kg; SC 500 kg; SD 500 kg A (splinter); SD 500 kg E (piercing); SD 500 kg II (piercing); SD 1,000 kg (piercing); BM 1,000 kg ('G' mine)

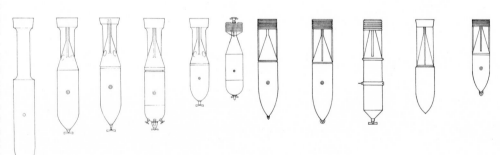

ITALIAN BOMBS (to scale)

Left to right: 800 kg; 500 kg; 500 kg C; 500 kg RO; 250 kg; 160 kg CS; 100 kg M; 100 kg T; 100 kg SP & SP1; 70 kg IP; 50 kg T

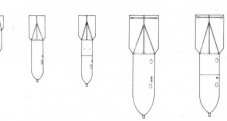

GERMAN BOMBS (to scale)

Left to right: SC 10 kg; SC 50 kg; SD 50 kg (splinter); SC 250 kg; SD 250 kg (splinter)

BOMBER OPERATIONS

Air power was the dominant force of the war, which was ultimately won by Allied superiority in quantity and quality of equipment based largely on the industrial might of the USA. The strategic air offensives of the last year of the war against Germany and Japan, in the bombing of cities and towns, brought not only physical but also psychological victory

BOEING B-29A SUPERFORTRESS

Gross weight: 141,100 lb **Span:** 141 ft 3 in **Length:** 99 ft **Engine:** 4×2,200 hp Wright Cyclone R-3350 **Armament:** 8×·50 machine-guns in remote-control turrets; 1×20-mm *or* 3×·50 machine-guns in tail **Crew:** 10 **Speed:** 358 mph at 25,000 ft **Ceiling:** 31,850 ft **Range:** 4,100 miles **Bomb load:** 20,000 lb

Designed to bomb Germany from bases in the USA should Britain have fallen, the B-29 came into service in 1944 and was used primarily against Japan. A B-29 carried the two atomic bombs dropped on Japan. After the war, it was the first bomber to equip the new USAF Strategic Air Command

The use of land-based bombers during the war was divided into distinct areas of operation – tactical co-operation with ground forces (including *Blitzkrieg* and airborne campaigns); strategic offensives against military, industrial and civilian targets in enemy homelands; and attacks at sea against shipping and submarines. In many instances these objectives overlapped, as in the bombing of U-boats at their coastal bases or assembly plants. And the bombers themselves were not confined to any single type of operation. The four-engined heavy strategic bombers sometimes took part in tactical missions, while such versatile aircraft as the de Havilland Mosquito and the Junkers Ju 88 played a part in all kinds of offensive, as well as serving in fighter roles. And while air power was the dominant factor of the war, it was most effective when used in combination with other forces.

This was well understood by the Germans in the early stages of the war. Their *Blitzkriegs* on Poland in September 1939, and on Norway, Holland, Belgium and France in May 1940, depended on the initial destruction of opposing air forces, particularly by the bombing of aircraft on the ground, so that the *Luftwaffe* could concentrate on supporting German ground forces. It was with such aims in mind that the Germans devoted so much effort in the pre-war period to the production of effective dive-bombers.

The first German mistake was the attempt to use air power to defeat the French and British armies trapped in Dunkirk. In order to give the *Luftwaffe* free reign, the German tanks which could have accomplished the task were halted on the outskirts of the city. There was good reason for the Germans to be confident of their air supremacy. They

had easily overcome the largely obsolete aircraft which the French and British had previously put into the air, except for the Hurricane fighter which was available only in very small quantities. The Fairey Battle light bomber, for instance, suffered a 70 per cent loss rate in daylight sorties during the Battle of France.

But at Dunkirk the *Luftwaffe* for the first time came up against British air superiority in the shape of Spitfires and Hurricanes which were within range of Dunkirk from bases in England. The air cover they provided was an important factor in the escape of a major proportion of the British army.

Fatal mistake

Had the Germans continued with their *Blitzkrieg* technique during the Battle of Britain, the later course of the war might have been very different. In spite of the effective combination of radar and well-organised fighter defences, the RAF was in a desperate situation by the end of August 1940 following German bomber attacks on airfields and the communications centres of Fighter Command. But at that point the Germans made another vital mistake – they changed from a tactical to a strategic offensive. After an RAF raid on Berlin on the night of 25 August, in retaliation for the bombing of London two nights previously, Hitler ordered the German air attacks to be concentrated against London.

Not only did this fail to shatter British morale, it also relieved the pressure on Fighter Command and gave time for the damaged airfields and radar bases to be repaired. Meanwhile, British bombers pounded the Channel ports where the German invasion forces had been gathered. By 13 October, it was clear that the plan to invade Britain was no longer possible. The

Luftwaffe had failed in its attempt to destroy the RAF, the necessary prelude to an invasion. Operation Sea Lion was 'postponed indefinitely', then cancelled altogether.

German bombers then switched from day to night operations, which the hastily improvised British night-fighters could do little to prevent at first. Indeed, if the Germans had continued their attacks on the docks of London and Liverpool in the spring of 1941, the disruption of supplies they caused might have forced Britain to surrender. But once again the opportunity was lost by a change of strategy – this time Hitler's decision to invade the Soviet Union. In June, most of the German bombers were transferred to the Eastern Front and the Battle of Britain petered out, won by the British fighter and radar defence system, lost by a curious failure of German intelligence to assess correctly the results of their air offensive, and to concentrate on the most vulnerable targets.

The German *Blitzkriegs* in the Balkans were a necessary preliminary to the invasion of Russia, firstly to secure and maintain the vital Rumanian oilfields, and secondly to protect the German flank from British bombers based on Crete (occupied by the British, following Italy's unsuccessful attempt to conquer Greece). Yugoslavia was attacked and overrun in April 1941, and by the end of that month Greece had also capitulated after a *Blitzkrieg* on the French pattern had destroyed key bridges and aircraft on the ground.

Two months later the British forces on Crete were overcome by a combination of landings by airborne troops and German air superiority. The German attack, though successful, was very costly. Many transport aircraft and a considerable proportion of the élite paratroop regiments were lost, and

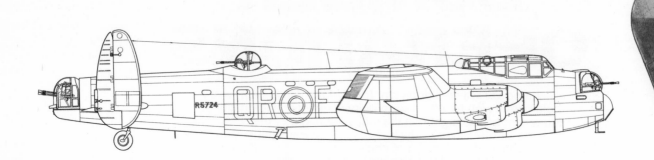

AVRO LANCASTER Mk I

Gross weight: 63,000 lb **Span:** 102 ft **Length:** 69 ft 6 in **Engine:** 4×1,280 hp Rolls Royce Merlin XX **Armament:** 10× ·303 Browning machine-guns **Crew:** 7 **Speed:** 280 mph at 18,500 ft **Ceiling:** 23,500 ft **Range:** 2,700 miles **Bomb load:** 14,000 lb

The most famous and successful heavy night bomber of the Second World War, the Lancaster first entered service with RAF Bomber Command in 1942

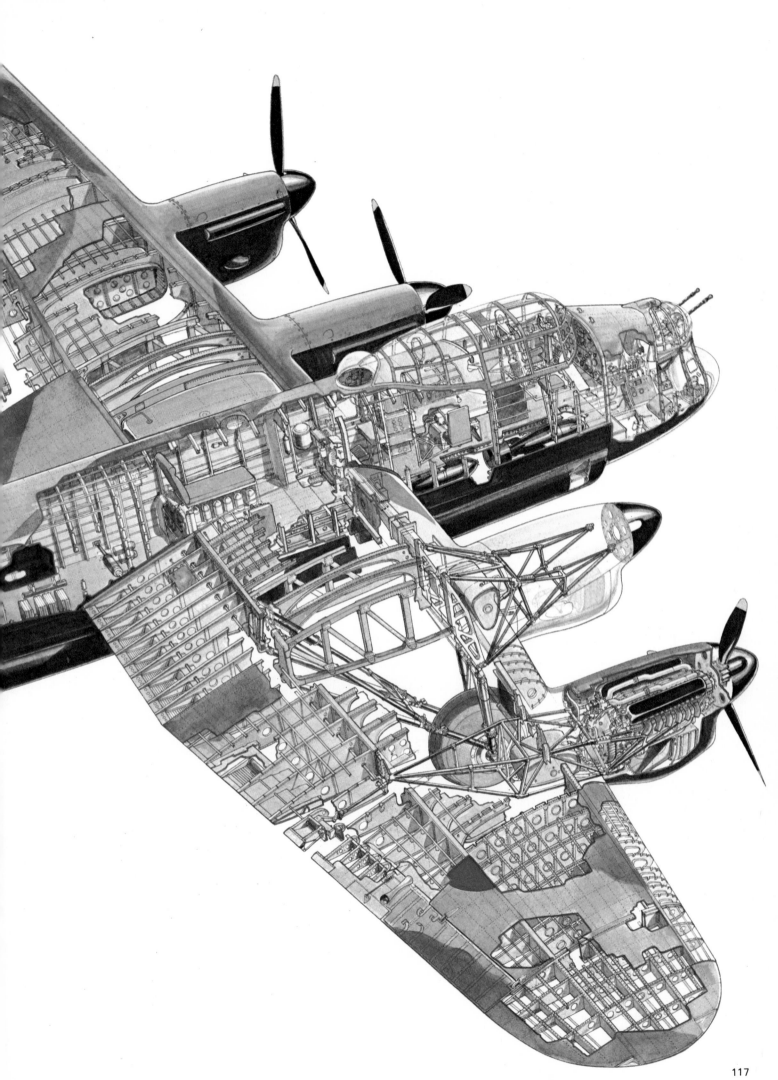

117

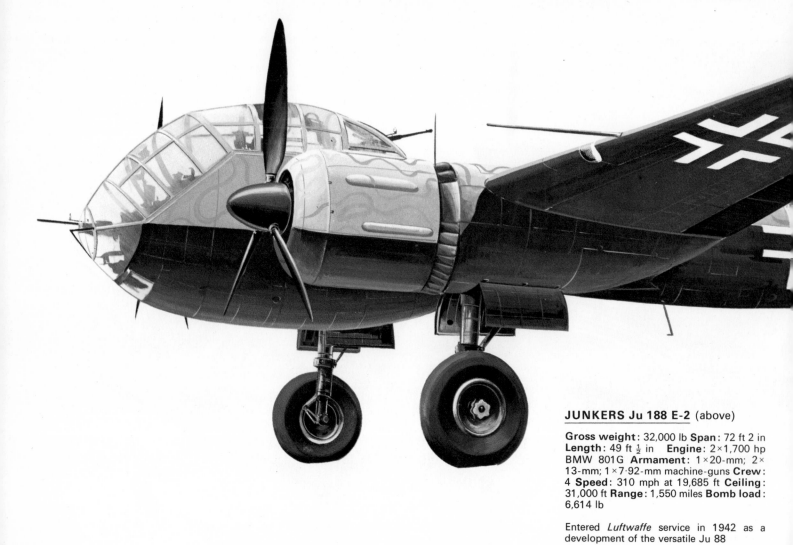

JUNKERS Ju 188 E-2 (above)

Gross weight: 32,000 lb **Span:** 72 ft 2 in
Length: 49 ft ½ in **Engine:** 2×1,700 hp
BMW 801G **Armament:** 1×20-mm; 2×
13-mm; 1×7·92-mm machine-guns **Crew:**
4 **Speed:** 310 mph at 19,685 ft **Ceiling:**
31,000 ft **Range:** 1,550 miles **Bomb load:**
6,614 lb

Entered *Luftwaffe* service in 1942 as a
development of the versatile Ju 88

the Germans never really recovered. Crete
was the last great German airborne campaign. Ironically, its success convinced the
Allies of the value of airborne operations
and they began to build up similar forces,
with disastrous consequences at Arnhem
in 1944.

After the Balkans, the Germans extended
their *Blitzkrieg* technique to the invasion
of Russia but this time, although initial
successes were achieved, the *Luftwaffe* was
unable to repeat its former brilliance. For
one thing, the attacks were made on a
broad front, instead of the short, sharp
thrusts of the previous campaigns. And as
the war continued, German bomber units
were called upon to operate on too many
widely-dispersed battlefronts, sapping their
ability to achieve further decisive victories.
From 1942 onwards, although it fought
grimly on until the end, the *Luftwaffe* was
increasingly fighting a defensive war for
which it had not planned, and for which it
lacked much of the necessary equipment.

The Japanese *Blitzkriegs* in the Pacific
and south-east Asia in December 1941 relied
even more heavily on the use of air power,
although in their case it was primarily
seaborne air power – a subject which needs
a book to itself. The attack on Pearl Harbour which destroyed most of the US Pacific
Fleet was carried out entirely by carrier-
based aircraft. But in the simultaneous

attacks on RAF bases in Malaya, as a
prelude to amphibious landings, land-based
Japanese bombers also played a part. The
most dramatic success of the light bombers
and torpedo-bombers operating from bases
in southern Indo-China was the sinking of
the British battleships *Prince of Wales* and
Repulse, the first time that capital ships at
sea had been destroyed by air attack.

Air strikes spearheaded all the Japanese
invasions during the following months as
their army and navy forces overran the
Philippines, the Dutch East Indies, south-
east Asia, and many of the islands of the
south-west Pacific. From their newly-
established bases in these areas, the Japanese could extend their bombing attacks
against the Allied forces, including some
bombing raids on Australia.

But the Allies were also learning the
value of tactical air operations, especially
with the arrival of suitable new aircraft.
This was first evident in the Middle East
where, in 1942, Baltimores and Mitchells
replaced the outdated Blenheims and Mary-
lands, and four-engined British and American bombers supplemented the faithful
Wellingtons in attacks on enemy supply
ports.

A mobile tactical air force was formed,
and provided continuous air cover in the
wide-ranging battlefields of the Western
Desert. The Allied invasions of enemy

YERMOLAYEV Yer-2

Gross weight: 32,730 lb **Span:** 75 ft
5½ in **Length:** 54 ft 1½ in **Engine:**
2×1,250 hp M-105 **Armament:** 1×20-
mm; 2×12·7-mm machine-guns **Crew:** 5
Speed: 311 mph at 19,000 ft **Ceiling:**
25,260 ft **Range:** 3,107 miles **Bomb
load:** 2,200 lb

This Russian long-range bomber was intended as a replacement for the Ilyushin
DB-3, and carried out raids on Germany
from 1941 onwards

KYUSHU Q1W TOKAI

Gross weight: 11,755 lb **Span:** 52 ft
6 in **Length:** 39 ft 8 in **Engine:** 2×610 hp
Hitachi Tempu 31 **Armament:** 1×20-mm
cannon; 1×7·7-mm machine-gun **Crew:**
3–4 **Speed:** 200 mph at 4,400 ft **Ceiling:**
14,730 ft **Range:** 814 miles **Bomb load:**
1,100 lb

A coastal patrol bomber introduced by the
Japanese Navy in the latter part of the
war in an effort to combat Allied submarines
off the Japanese mainland

COMMONWEALTH CA-11
WOOMERA (below)

Gross weight: 22,287 lb **Span**: 59 ft 2½ in **Length**: 39 ft 7 in **Engine**: 2×1,200 hp Pratt & Whitney Wasp **Armament**: 2×20-mm cannon: 5×·303 machine-guns **Crew**: 3 **Speed**: 282 mph **Ceiling**: 23,500 ft **Range**: 2,225 miles **Bomb load**: 3,000 lb

A dive/torpedo/attack bomber developed in Australia towards the end of the war, but not brought into service. Unusual for its remote control barbettes behind the engine nacelles

territory, beginning in North Africa and moving on to Sicily and finally Normandy in 1944, the greatest military assault in history, were spearheaded by air strikes which owed much to an appreciation of earlier German methods.

The turning point on the Eastern Front came in 1942 with the build-up of Russian tactical air forces to assist their ground troops. The Soviet aircraft industry had been moved back, behind the Urals, out of reach of German bombers – giving the Germans reason to regret the lack of a long-range strategic bomber. In Asia, tactical air power was a vital element in the Allied offensives from late 1943 onwards. The re-conquest of Burma was to a large extent made possible by the continuous operations of a tremendous Anglo/American air supply force, working under an air cover in which bombers assisted by bombing Japanese air bases.

Although it was not at first widely recognised, land-based bombers played a very important role in the war at sea: mines dropped by aircraft in European waters, for instance, sank more ships than those laid by surface vessels. From the beginning of the war the Germans, Italians and British all employed land-based bombers against enemy shipping with varying degrees of success, depending on the equipment available. Level bombing was generally found to be too inaccurate while the medium bombers used for that purpose were vulnerable to attacks by shore and ship-based fighters and to flak put up by convoys. Manoeuvrable fighter-bombers such as the Bristol Beaufighter and the Junkers Ju 88, adapted to carry torpedoes and attacking at low levels, were the most successful.

From the Allied point of view, however, U-boats posed the greatest threat to shipping. RAF Coastal Command suffered a serious lack of long-range patrol bombers during the first two years of the war, and large areas of the Atlantic were beyond their reach. But in 1942, long-range bombers began to become available, such as VLR (very long-range) Liberators, B-17s, and eventually de Havilland Mosquitos specially armed with a 57-mm cannon. These aircraft were able to cover the gap in the middle of the Atlantic and were assisted in their task of locating and attacking submarines by such aids as radar and Leigh lights; the latter was especially valuable in locating U-boats which had surfaced at night to re-charge their batteries or make a quicker passage.

The Germans had not developed the concept of air cover for their navy, nor did they have the long-range aircraft to provide it. Consequently the Allies won the Battle of the Atlantic, largely by superior air power. Whereas from 1939 to mid-1943, surface vessels sank 61 German and Italian submarines and assisted in 7 cases – while aircraft were responsible for only 9 – during the last two years of the war, surface vessels accounted for 224, land-based aircraft 239, ship-based aircraft 41, and a combination of surface and air forces 46. A further 64 U-boats were destroyed at their bases by bombing.

Ultimately, the war was won by Allied superiority in quantity and quality of equipment, based largely on the industrial might of the USA. Manpower played an important part of course, especially in the air where crews had to become increasingly skilled to use the ever more sophisticated instruments. Neither Germany nor Japan had the resources to match the Allied training programmes, under which, by late 1944, an RAF fighter pilot for instance had received nearly 300 hours of flying experience before being awarded his wings.

In terms of technology, however, the balance was more even. In some areas, such as jet aircraft and rocket-propelled bombs, the Germans were more advanced, and even made some progress towards the production of atomic weapons. Even the Japanese, at the end of 1944, were able to bring out a new bomber, the Mitsubishi Ki-67 Hiryu, which was such an advance on any of their previous aircraft that it came as an unpleasant shock to the Americans in the Pacific.

The build-up of Allied forces was a slow process, however: 83 per cent of the two million tons of bombs dropped on Germany throughout the war were dispatched in the last two years, when the RAF's early night raids were supplemented by daylight precision raids by the US Eighth Air Force. But the success of such raids was somewhat exaggerated by the Allied proponents of strategic bombing. Although nearly half of Cologne was devastated by the RAF's first thousand-bomber raid on the night of 30 May 1942, the city made a remarkable recovery.

The most damaging of the American daylight raids, on the ball-bearing works at Schweinfurt on 14 October 1943, caused only a temporary setback in production, while 60 of the 291 bombers involved were destroyed and 138 damaged, mainly by German fighters. The Americans were compelled to curtail their daylight bombing offensive until the introduction in the following spring of the long-range Mustang fighter which could provide an escort all the way to targets deep in Germany.

By 1944, the British and Americans had built up large bomber forces, and had the long-range fighters to protect them on the way to their targets. But having attacked most of the military targets available during and after the Normandy invasion, the Allies were reluctant to keep their bomber forces idle. In the last year of the war, therefore, they initiated vast strategic air offensives against Germany and Japan, aimed at bringing about a psychological victory by bombing cities and towns.

The moral validity of the raid on Dresden, the most destructive of the European war, is a matter of controversy to the present day. But there is evidence that such raids increased the determination of the German people to fight, no matter how hopeless the odds. Similarly, in spite of the terrible destruction of Japanese cities by the B-29 raids of the US Twentieth Air Force during the spring and summer of 1945, against practically no fighter opposition, when millions were made homeless and over 100 square miles of Tokyo and four other cities were destroyed, it was only with the dropping of the two atomic bombs on Hiroshima and Nagasaki that the Japanese felt compelled to surrender. Not only was the strategic value of these offensives questionable, they also compelled the defeated nations to concentrate their energies after the war on building up their destroyed cities and economies with aid provided by the United States. The resulting programme of reconstruction has become an increasing economic challenge to the victors in the post-war years.

TUPOLEV Tu-2

Gross weight: 24,232 lb **Span:** 62 ft **Length:** 43 ft 3⅔ in **Engine:** 2×1,400 hp AM 47 Mikulin **Armament:** 4×7·6-mm machine-guns; 2×20-mm cannon **Crew:** 4 **Speed:** 394 mph at 26,000 ft **Ceiling:** 34,775 ft **Range:** 880 miles **Bomb load:** 5,000 lb

Developed too late to see service during the Second World War but used widely afterwards by Russia and her satellite air forces

NORTH AMERICAN B-25J MITCHELL

Gross weight: 33,500 lb **Span:** 67 ft 7 in **Length:** 52 ft 11 in
Engine: 2×1,700 hp Wright R-2600 **Armament:** 6×·50 Browning
machine-guns **Crew:** 6 **Speed:** 272 mph at 13,000 ft **Ceiling:**
24,200 ft **Range:** 1,350 miles **Bomb load:** 3,000 lb

The J version of the B-25 Mitchell had a dorsal turret close behind
the cockpit and three 0·50-in guns in the nose; some in fact had no
less than eight guns in that position, adding to ten carried elsewhere

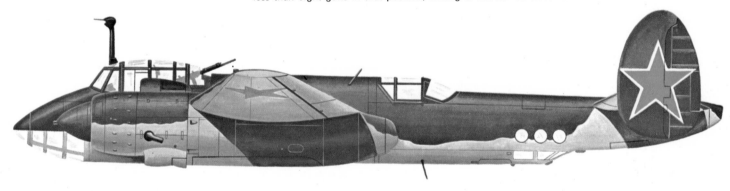

JUNKERS Ju 288 C-1

Gross weight: 47,120 lb **Span:** 74 ft 4 in **Length:** 59 ft 5¾ in
Engine: 2×2,950 hp Daimler Benz B 610 **Armament:** 6×13-mm;
1×15-mm machine-guns **Crew:** 4 **Speed:** 407 mph at 22,300 ft
Ceiling: 34,000 ft **Range:** 1,615 miles **Bomb load:** 6,614 lb

Developed to make use of an engine of new design, but abandoned
before development work had been completed

INDEX

JUNKERS Ju 87 B2 'STUKA'